Women in Africa

Women in Africa

Studies in Social and Economic Change

Edited by Nancy J. Hafkin and Edna G. Bay

Stanford University Press, Stanford, California

Stanford University Press
Stanford, California
© 1976 by the Board of Trustees of the
Leland Stanford Junior University
Printed in the United States of America
Cloth ISBN 0-8047-0906-8
Paper ISBN 0-8047-1011-2
Original printing 1976
Last figure below indicates year of this printing:
05   04   03   02

Preface

This collection of papers is the culmination of a project of the Women's Committee of the African Studies
Association. In response to the encouragement of the
Board of the Association, the Committee resolved in the
fall of 1973 to prepare a volume of articles on African
women. Our goal was to remedy two perceived problems
associated with women's issues—the relative paucity
of literature on African women, and the difficulty
encountered by female scholars in having their work
published.

We wish to express our appreciation to the African
Studies Association for its continued financial support
to the Women's Committee during the preparation of
this volume. And a special word goes to Raymond
Ganga and Berhanu Abebe for their critical and sup-
portive contributions to this endeavor, and for their
strong theoretical commitment to equality and
symmetry.

                                        N.J.H.   E.G.B.

Contents

Contributors   ix

Introduction   1
NANCY J. HAFKIN AND EDNA G. BAY

The *Signares* of Saint-Louis and Gorée: Women
Entrepreneurs in Eighteenth-Century Senegal   19
GEORGE E. BROOKS, JR.

The Dual-Sex Political System in Operation: Igbo Women
and Community Politics in Midwestern Nigeria   45
KAMENE OKONJO

'Aba Riots' or Igbo 'Women's War'? Ideology,
Stratification, and the Invisibility of Women   59
JUDITH VAN ALLEN

Luo Women and Economic Change During
the Colonial Period   87
MARGARET JEAN HAY

Ga Women and Socioeconomic Change in
Accra, Ghana   111
CLAIRE ROBERTSON

The Limitations of Group Action Among Entrepreneurs:
The Market Women of Abidjan, Ivory Coast   135
BARBARA C. LEWIS

Rebels or Status-Seekers? Women as Spirit Mediums
in East Africa   157
IRIS BERGER

From *Lelemama* to Lobbying: Women's Associations
in Mombasa, Kenya   183
MARGARET STROBEL

Protestant Women's Associations in Freetown,
Sierra Leone   213
FILOMINA CHIOMA STEADY

Women and Economic Change in Africa   239
LEITH MULLINGS

Less Than Second-Class: Women in Rural Settlement
Schemes in Tanzania   265
JAMES L. BRAIN

References Cited   285
Index   299

Contributors

EDNA G. BAY is Assistant Professor of African Studies at the University of Illinois in Urbana-Champaign. She taught in a girls' school in Malawi, where she first became concerned with women's issues in an African perspective. A historian who received her Ph.D. from Boston University, she has carried out field research in West Africa on the social history of royal women in the kingdom of Dahomey.

IRIS BERGER received her Ph.D. from the University of Wisconsin in 1973. She has been an Instructor in History at the State University College of New York at Oneonta, and in 1975–76 was visiting Assistant Professor at Wellesley College. Her research interests include the impact of African and other Third World revolutionary movements on women.

JAMES L. BRAIN worked for twelve years as a Community Development Officer in Tanzania and Uganda. He studied anthropology at the London School of Economics and later at Syracuse University, where he received his Ph.D. after carrying out research on village settlements in Tanzania. He is presently Professor in the Department of Anthropology at the State University College, New Paltz, New York.

GEORGE E. BROOKS, JR., is a historian whose major research interest is the Upper Guinea Coast of West Africa. He has published widely on the activities of European and American traders along the West African coast. Brooks received his Ph.D. from Boston University, and is Professor of History at Indiana University, where he teaches African and world history.

NANCY J. HAFKIN is Assistant Professor of History and Afro-American Studies at Boston State College. She studied history at Brandeis University and at Boston University, where she was associated with the African Studies Center. She did research in Portugal and Mozambique in 1970–71 on the history of nineteenth-century coastal Mozambique, and received her Ph.D. from Boston University in 1973. With Edna G. Bay, she is co-chairperson of the African Studies Association's Committee on Women.

MARGARET JEAN HAY received her Ph.D. in 1972 from the University of Wisconsin. She did fieldwork among the Luo of Kenya, and has published works on the changes in trade and agriculture brought about by the colonial regime and on the relationship between economic interaction and ethnic identity in the precolonial era. She is Assistant Professor of History at Wellesley College.

BARBARA C. LEWIS received her Ph.D. in political science from Northwestern University in 1969, and teaches at Livingston College, Rutgers University. She did dissertation research on the Transporters' Association of the Ivory Coast. Most recently, she has conducted a survey under the auspices of the Ivoirian Ministry of Planning on fertility, employment, and status among urban women.

LEITH MULLINGS is Assistant Professor of Anthropology at Columbia University. She received her Ph.D. in anthropology from the University of Chicago in 1975. Mullings has done research in both Africa and the urban U.S., and includes among her research interests social and economic change, urbanization, and medical anthropology.

KAMENE OKONJO is a Research Fellow at the Institute of African Studies, University of Nigeria, Nsukka. She studied economics at the University of Erlangen-Nürnberg, Germany, and is currently completing her doctoral work in sociology at Boston University. In 1971–72 she did fieldwork among Igbo women of Nigeria west of the Niger River.

CLAIRE ROBERTSON received her Ph.D. in African history from the University of Wisconsin in 1974. Her dissertation, on twentieth-century Ga women in Ghana, dealt with the relationship between changes in economic organization and marriage patterns in Central Accra. She is Assistant Professor of History at Bucknell University.

FILOMINA CHIOMA STEADY received her D.Phil. in social anthropology in 1973 from Oxford University. Born in Sierra Leone, she has conducted field research in Freetown, has taught at Yale University and at the University of Sierra Leone, and is currently Assistant Professor at Boston University.

MARGARET STROBEL studies women in the context of ethnicity, stratification, and social change in Swahili society on the East African coast. Strobel received her Ph.D. in history from the University of California, Los Angeles, in 1975, and was appointed interim director of the Women's Studies Program there.

JUDITH VAN ALLEN teaches courses on colonialism in Africa and on the historical formation of gender roles at Strawberry Creek College, an interdisciplinary program of the University of California, Berkeley. She is currently completing her doctoral dissertation in the Department of Political Science at Berkeley.

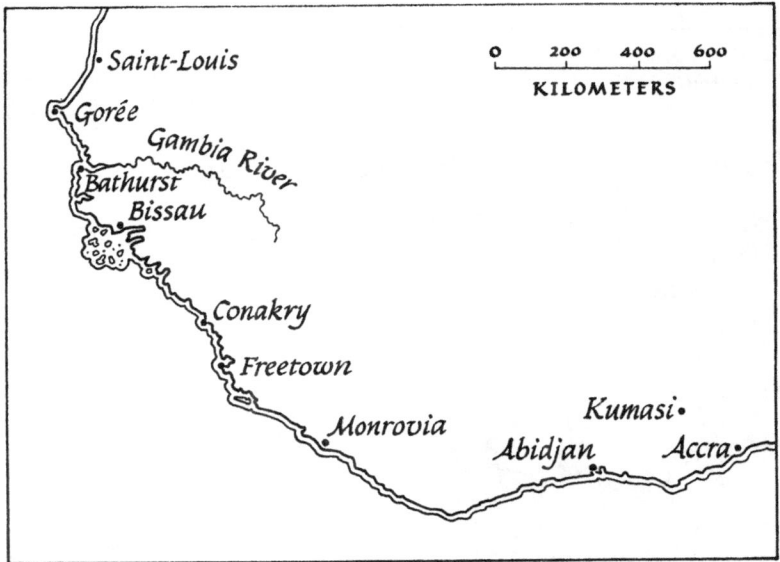

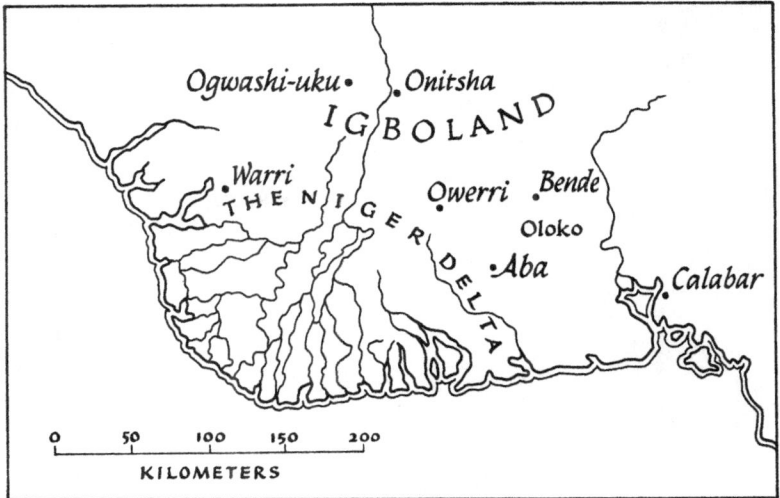

West Africa and the Niger Delta

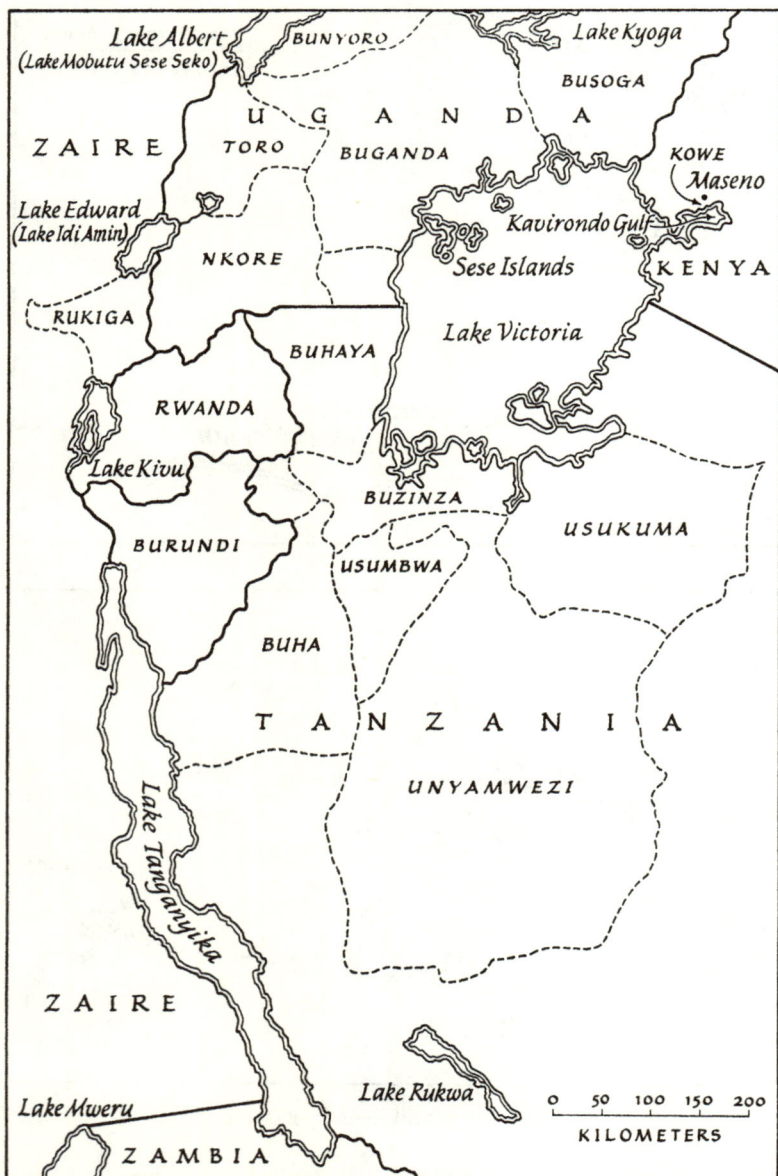

The Interlacustrine and Nyamwezi Regions of East Africa

Women in Africa

Introduction

NANCY J. HAFKIN AND EDNA G. BAY

THE PAPERS in this volume represent the results of recent field research in Africa south of the Sahara by scholars in various disciplines. The emphasis of the volume is on women and change in Africa—change in two senses. First, the articles discuss African women from a changed viewpoint; second, this new perspective in turn recognizes that women in Africa act as agents of change within their own societies.

The literature about African women has been written largely from a male perspective; that is, it has described women in terms of their relationships to men. Studies written by both male and female scholars have fixed women in orbits that revolve around men: typical is Remi Clignet's *Many Wives, Many Powers*, a monograph on polygyny that sees it as "a mechanism which facilitates the fulfillment of male aspirations" (Clignet 1970: 357). In part, the problem has been one of methodology. Men's activities in society have often been defined as those worth investigation, by African informants as well as by Western investigators. Thus women enter scholarly studies predominantly in the realm of marriage and the family. All too often, researchers have based accounts of women solely on data from male informants. An example of this is Evans-Pritchard's *Man and Woman Among the Azande*, which presents a picture of women based on oral data recorded by African male assistants from male informants, all compiled by a European male.

In dealing with the subject of women, a male researcher's attitudes may intrude with greater impact than might be the case if he were dealing with a less emotionally and culturally charged subject. The author of a recent work about Ugandan women was attracted to his topic by the physical appearance of the Hima (Elam 1973), and Clignet teases his reader with the sex appeal of his subject: "I must thank my wife, who is kind enough to believe that my interest in polygyny has remained solely intellectual" (Clignet 1970: xix). This concentration on African women as wives, lovers, and mothers has resulted in disproportionate attention to the sexual aspects of their lives. A reader can learn the most intimate details of African women's sex lives and at the same time remain ignorant of many other aspects of their social and economic lives. Many awaited the appearance of Kenneth Little's 1973 work *African Women in Towns: An Aspect of Africa's Social Revolution* in the expectation that it would point a new direction away from this concentration on sex roles. The work failed to live up to its promise, however; Beverly Brown, reviewing it for the *ASA Review of Books* (1975, no. 1: 14–15), notes that "Little does not even pretend to explore the totality of women's urban experience. . . . The charged and changing male-female relationships of African urbanites receive ample attention. Mistresses, concubines, prostitutes, outside wives, and disgruntled spouses dominate the pages."

Studies of African women have been plagued by more than the methodological and ideological questions of male perspectives, however. At times they have reflected the changing attitudes in European society toward women's issues. In effect, African women have sometimes become a field upon which the Western world has played out some of its concerns about women in general. For example, in the decades that followed the success of the women's suffrage movement in the West, European observers turned their attention to what they conceived as the plight of the African woman. Typical was the French administrator who declared that "the greater number of indigenous societies [in Africa] reserve for women a place which is clearly inferior, approaching that of a domestic animal" (Hardy 1939: 7). Colonialism, in the view of many, would foster the emancipation of non-Western women by raising living and educational standards. At the same time, women would be freed from the drudgery of farm labor and the oppression of their own social customs—evils that were said to include early betrothal, a lack of choice in marriage partners, and few or no divorce rights. Writers dealt with the problems of women's education and supported reforms designed to abolish bridewealth and polygyny and to improve women's inheritance rights.*

The 1940's war effort in Europe and America brought hundreds of thousands of women into the work force. But at war's end, European women were admonished to seek fulfillment in domestic activities and to abandon ambitions outside the home. By the late 1950's, this attitude was appearing in some scholars' visions of African women, whose virtues became their willingness to accept an inferior status vis-à-vis men. Evans-Pritchard, for example, commented that "from the outside and from our point of view, we may say that she [non-Western woman] has an inferior position, and she herself may feel this to be the case, but she is not resentful on account of it. She sees herself as different from man and as having a social status different from him; but . . . it is for her less a matter of level, than of difference, of status. Primitive women do not see themselves as an underprivileged class as against a class of men with whom they seek to gain social equality. They have never heard of social equality" (Evans-Pritchard 1965: 52).†

The 1960 publication of *Femmes d'Afrique noire*, which appeared in English three years later as *Women of Tropical Africa*, a collection of articles by female anthropologists, set the stage for a new phase in the study of African women. Researchers, particularly female ones, began to carry out an increasing number of studies of

* See, for example, B. Dobson, "Women's Place in East Africa," *Corona*, 6, no. 12 (1954), pp. 454–57; J. Durtal, "Où en est la femme noire?," *Hommes et Mondes*, 28, no. 3 (1955), pp. 366–76; M. Hunter, "The Effects of Contact with Europeans on Pondo Women," *Africa*, vol. 6 (1933), pp. 259–76; Hardy 1939; Léopold Senghor, "L'Evolution de la situation de la femme en A.O.F.," *Marchés Coloniaux*, vol. 226 (1950), pp. 541–42; and M. I. Shannon, "Women's Place in Kikuyu Society. Impact of modern ideas on tribal life. A long-term plan for female education," *African World* (Sept. 1954), pp. 7–10. Unfortunately, the colonial mentality has not altogether died away. A recently published work, Iris Andreski's *Old Wives Tales* (New York, 1970), revives and repeats these ethnocentric stereotypes.

† The title essay of Evans-Pritchard 1965 comes from the Fawcett Lecture he delivered on October 25, 1955, at the University of London.

women's activities in Africa. Gradually, more and more African
women scholars joined in the effort. The expansion of African-
area and Black-studies programs in the 1960's, coupled with the
development of a heightened feminist awareness on the part of
Western scholars, undoubtedly stimulated this interest. Unfortunately, early in this period some of the literature that emerged
was romantic or historically inaccurate. In a search for great glories
to counteract a past that had ignored and distorted the history of
women and of Africa, writers described great queens, amazons,
and matriarchy. Nzinga, a sixteenth-century monarch in Angola,
was described as an "Amazon Queen" who led an "army of fierce
women warriors" (Rogers 1972: 247). West Africa appeared as the
heartland of matriarchy, and the continent as a whole was portrayed as overrun by Amazon armies (Diner 1963: 183).* Other
writers gloried in the astonishing independence of West African
women and romanticized polygyny because it freed women from
having to cook for their husbands every night. However, with the
encouragement of field research and the accumulation of additional data, more balanced interpretations of women's activities
appeared that put less stress on individual rulers and more on the
mass of women. It is from this new material that the papers in this
volume have been drawn: they stress such themes as women's economic independence, the impact of women's associations, and the
political activities of women in traditional African societies.† In
addition to changing the picture of African women in the social,
economic, and political setting of their own societies, recent scholarship has suggested that the colonial impact, far from liberating
African women, actually diminished the prerogatives and rights
they formerly enjoyed.

* One queen does not a matriarchy make. The question of the existence of
matriarchies in Africa and elsewhere has been discussed by Joan Bamberger in
"The Myth of Matriarchy: Why Men Rule in Primitive Society," in M. Z.
Rosaldo and Louise Lamphere, eds., Woman, Culture, and Society (Stanford,
Calif., 1974). On Nzinga, see Joseph C. Miller, "Nzinga of Matamba in a New
Perspective," Journal of African History, 16, no. 2. E. G. Bay discusses one of
the few documented cases of women soldiers in precolonial Africa in her forth-
coming dissertation on Dahomey (Boston University).

† See also special issues of the Canadian Journal of African Studies (6, no. 2
[1972]) and of the African Studies Review (18, no. 3 [Dec. 1975]).

The papers in this collection attempt to analyze women not as objects but as actors. In documenting the wide variety of activities in which African women have participated, the authors go beyond descriptions of roles and statuses. Here, women interact with their societies and alter their environments; they become visible and thus part of history. At the same time, the authors recognize that women cannot be wholly in control of all the social and economic forces which affect their lives. Obviously, women's and men's existences and activities are closely interrelated; changes in the sphere of one must necessarily affect the other, even in societies where labor or social relations are strictly divided along sex lines. Margaret Jean Hay, for example, clarifies her analysis of the twentieth-century economic innovations among Luo women in western Kenya by tracing corresponding fluctuations in the economic activities of men. And George Brooks describes the growth of a commercial society based on the interactions of African women and European coastal traders in Senegal.

All the articles are concerned with women's participation in activities beyond the closed circle of child care or household maintenance. Following the distinction between "domestic" and "public" realms proposed by Rosaldo (1974: 23), we thus will view African women outside the "domestic" institutions and activities typically associated with women and "organized around one or more mothers and their children." Such "public" affairs are broad and various: economic efforts directed toward benefits for self or kin; the seeking of status through membership in associations; participation in political life (including community decision-making); or initiation and participation in religious or cult life. Patrilocal marriage, by which women move from their natal homes to their husbands' villages, may provide an important impetus toward "public" activities. In her discussion of Igbo women, Judith Van Allen notes that the women's organization most influential in policy making and community affairs was the *mikiri*, the association of *wives* of a village. Similarly Hay notes that exchanges and visits by Luo kinswomen separated by patrilocal marriage resulted in the diffusion of information on farming techniques and the distribution of new seeds—vital factors in the development of increased agricultural production and capital investment during the early twentieth century.

African women have varying degrees of economic independence, often despite social orders that place them under the authority of husbands or fathers. Wives and husbands in Africa usually have separate incomes, with clearly defined financial obligations to their children, their spouse, and their spouse's lineage. Married women generally have the right to own and acquire property that is separate from that of their husbands, and in many areas men and women are guaranteed equal rights to land use. Business transactions and earnings beyond marital obligations are considered a spouse's private affair. Claire Robertson and Leith Mullings, who have studied Ga society in coastal Ghana, describe here the financial expectations and occasional mutual suspicions between spouses regarding knowledge of business dealings. Women are said to lend money to husbands at rates only slightly less usurious than those offered to others.

Women typically develop economic skills well before marriage, though a husband may provide trade capital or fees for schooling to a new wife or fiancée. The few women who have gained access to Western education have been channeled by and large into the "feminine" professions—teaching, clerical work, nursing, and midwifery. Outside the so-called modern sector, women engage in a variety of occupations: they prepare farm products or cooked foods for market; raise surplus crops for sale; produce craftwork; and trade farm produce, prepared foods, or manufactured goods.

Retail trade appears to be the most widespread of women's occupations. In West Africa in particular, women may engage in trade as a major activity or in addition to other occupations or professions. Robertson, Mullings, and Barbara Lewis all discuss the problems of contemporary West African trading women. In the context of colonial economic pressures, Hay describes the development of trade as a major occupation among primarily agriculturalist Luo women. But records of women's entrepreneurial activities go far back into the precolonial past. Brooks draws on writers' accounts spanning three centuries to reconstruct the society of the *signares*, women traders in the Senegambia region. In collaboration with European merchants, *signares* became women of wealth and prestige, intermediaries providing access to African commercial networks. Over time, the African and Eurafrican *signares* evolved a new culture, a unique blend of their African and European backgrounds.

The independence of trading women, coupled with their marketplace outspokenness, has led many Western observers, past and present, to assume egalitarian sentiments in African societies. To the contrary, most African women live in societies with strong biases toward male superiority. In historical Dahomey, the formidable women soldiers boasted of their victories by singing "We marched against Attahpahms as against men. We came and found them women" (Forbes 1966: II, 108). Van Allen and Mullings note attitudes of male superiority in Igbo society, though they attribute sexism to different causes; and Robertson comments on the strong male bias among the Ga. Market women's groups have occasionally applied their leverage to the betterment of economic or political opportunities. More often, though, women have found it difficult to define and seek common goals, as Lewis found in her study of Abidjan women. The internalization of antifemale attitudes may be a factor in women's lack of a sense of economic power or political potential. In Africa, the economic independence of women is less a mark of privilege than a matter of necessity; women take responsibility for their economic well-being because they must, in the same sense that Western men traditionally accept "natural" economic responsibilities for themselves and their families. We should not be surprised, then, to see admirably strong and independent Ga trading women emulating Western-style nuclear-family marriage and financial dependence on a husband.

In many African societies, women's and men's spheres traditionally have been separate. However, the perimeters of the respective spheres do not remain constant, but vary according to ethnic group, geographical setting, social class, and historical era. Women frequently act collectively within their sphere, either through voluntary associations or through institutions paralleling those of men.

But this apparent structural complementarity does not necessarily imply equality between the sexes. As some of the following articles note, the male sphere was often accorded particular advantages, even in the precolonial period. Though women had a substantial measure of economic independence and a voice in political affairs in many parts of the continent, they were not dominant, as some have said, and they were not equal.

Even in the case of the traditional dual-sex political system documented by Kamene Okonjo for the Igbo, which appears closest to "separate but equal," the basic framework is one of patriarchy; Okonjo notes that "as elsewhere, men rule and dominate." The process of acquisition of status operated the same way for women as for men. In striking contrast to American society, where the most important roles for women are ascribed from their relationships to men (e.g., "The First Lady"), Igbo women's public status was achieved not from their husbands but from their own acquisition of titles. Though men and women both attained public status in the same way (through title-taking), men's greater access to the resources necessary for gaining titles and status gave them an advantage over women. Thus Igbo society had a democratic ideology, but not an egalitarian one. Van Allen cites the Igbo proverb "a child who washes his hands clean deserves to eat with his elders," which was meant to apply to both sexes. But as Van Allen says, the proverb does not add that "at birth some children are given water and some are not."

In addition to unequal access to resources, there were other ways in which African societies restricted women from attaining equal status with men. Numerous societies had cultural restrictions that kept women subordinate. James Brain describes a society in Tanzania where women were outspoken, chose the subclan political leaders, had much economic independence, and held secure rights to land and offspring. He attributes their lack of dominance in the face of such favorable conditions to cultural factors—in particular a long puberty rite for women that kept them in seclusion from the time of their first menstruation to their marriage (as long as six years in some cases).

Given the relative prominence of women in precolonial Africa (compare the position of women on the Arabian peninsula or in China), it is interesting that numerous African societies possessed culturally legitimated ways to ensure the subordination of women. For example, in many parts of West Africa women kneel in front of their husbands. These cultural patterns may represent a historical reaction by men against an earlier era when women's status was higher. A number of African societies have traditions that women once held power and were overthrown by men. One such story appears in James Ngugi's novel *A Grain of Wheat* (1967: 4). "Many years ago women ruled the land of the Agikuyu. Men had no property, they were only there to serve the whims and needs of women. Those were hard years. So they waited for women to go to war, [and] they plotted a revolt, taking an oath of secrecy to keep them bound each to each in common pursuit of freedom. They would sleep with all the women at once, for didn't they know the heroes would return hungry for love and relaxation? Fate did the rest; women were pregnant; the takeover met with little resistance." Clearly, this is not factual, for we know there were no matriarchies; but it may have a historical basis in an earlier period when the society in question was horticultural and matrilineal. In such a period women would have had greater status than they had after the shift to plow agriculture and patrilineality; and the folk memory may have come to link the decline in women's status and the growth in male stature to an imaginary political overthrow of the sort Ngugi describes.

Structural constraints to limit women's potential may have developed as societies moved toward greater male dominance. We can cite examples of such constraints from all over the continent. Many societies had menstrual taboos, keeping women apart in menstrual huts. Some secret societies were open only to postmenopausal women, and other male societies were designed to ensure women's submission. Rattray maintained that Ashanti would have been a matriarchy if women could have gone to war, but menstrual taboos kept them from doing so (1923: 81). Other rites of passage can be seen as culturally legitimated ways of suppressing women.

One of these is the clitoridectomy, which has been the subject of much debate. Though missionaries tried to eradicate it as a barbaric and heathen practice, anthropologists (including Jomo Kenyatta in his book *Facing Mount Kenya*) defended it as an integral part of many cultures, the destruction of which would entail the destruction of the whole culture: "Clitoridectomy, like Jewish circumcision, is a mere bodily mutilation which, however, is regarded as the *conditio sine qua non* of the whole teaching of tribal law, religion and morality" (Kenyatta 1938: 128). Though this may have been the case, and though both sexes went through a circumcision process, there is a real difference between circumcision of the male, which does not affect sexual pleasure, and circumcision of the female, which does. It can be argued that the use of clitoridectomy was a way of rendering women sexually subordinate.

Several authors indirectly face the question posed by Leith Mullings in her contribution: Does equality of access to the means of production necessarily correlate with social equality between the sexes? Mullings distinguishes between "equality," which she uses in the economic sense of equal access to the means of production, and "symmetry," which she defines as equality of access to political roles and statuses. Her analysis indicates that a number of precolonial African societies were characterized by "equality" but also by "asymmetry." Women could have equal access to the means of production and equal rights to the products of their labor, but they wound up subordinate because societies were asymmetrical in the valuation of their roles and in access to political office. Her conclusions from a study of the liberation movement in contemporary Mozambique, however, suggest that in at least one case a new African government is attempting to establish both "equality" and "symmetry" in the relations between men and women.

Several articles consider women's relationships to religion, in particular Islam, Christianity, and indigenous spirit-medium cults. In each case, the nature of women's religious activity and its social impact are shown to be complex issues not easily described by standard stereotypes. Christianity, for example, is associated with social conservatism among the Igbo of Nigeria and the Creoles of Sierra Leone, but in different ways. Missions discouraged Igbo women's participation in the politically important female association, and limited their education to Bible study and the learning of European domestic skills. In Sierra Leone, Creole women practice a Christianity as old as the formation of their unique ethnic community some 150 years ago. According to Filomina Steady, their self-defined Christian ideals help maintain a double standard of morality and limit women's leadership in the church. Among the Luo women of Kowe in Kenya, however, Christianity has acted as a progressive force in agricultural innovation. Early converts experimented with new crops and farm implements.

Islam is popularly associated with female repression. Margaret Strobel, however, finds that in the context of Muslim Mombasa society, Islam serves as a backdrop for the liberalizing activities of coastal Kenya women's associations. Similar Muslim women's associations in Freetown, Sierra Leone, have provided the impetus for change for women, particularly through their support of schooling for Muslim girls.

Iris Berger considers a phenomenon widespread in Africa— women's prominence in spirit-possession and spirit-medium cults. Her study of the East African interlacustrine region outlines several possible explanations for female participation: cult activities may serve as avenues of protest against male domination; they may offer women temporary authority in ritual situations; or they may allow individual women to attain positions of wide political prominence.

Many of the papers focus on women acting within women's associations or institutions. Women in Africa have joined together for centuries in organizations whose goals range from the narrowly economic to the broadly social or political. Probably most common are those associations surrounding commerce. Rotating credit associations, where members regularly contribute a specific sum of money, provide each member in turn with the proceeds, a large quantity of cash for personal use. Other economic associations provide assistance to members at moments of social or personal crisis.

Some groups, such as the Igbo *mikiri* described by Van Allen, are explicitly political, making policy for the whole community in areas defined as the women's sphere of interest. Following Berger's analysis, we may see spirit possession cults in part as associations of protest for women and lower-status men.

Outsiders have sometimes seen women's associations as "proof" of female power in African societies, or as evidence of strong feminist consciousness. Yet several articles suggest, to borrow a phrase from Margaret Strobel, that there has been a kind of sisterhood without solidarity. Women act together, but usually for personal goals only incidentally related to the fact that they are female. The potential for effective economic or social group action in the interests of women as a whole is seldom realized. The *form* of women's actions seems further determined by the socioeconomic background of the women within a particular society.

Strobel traces the history of two related forms of association among Muslim women of Mombasa, Kenya. The earlier *lelemama* dance groups, which arose out of Afro-Arab society, provided entertainment on festival occasions as well as status enhancement and mutual aid for members. Within the various associations there was some mixing of socioeconomic classes, and in particular a blurring of the distinction between people descended from slaves and people of free ancestry. Under the impact of reform in the Arab world and Westernization brought by colonialism, a new form of association developed. Membership patterns and an interest in prestige linked the new social-welfare organizations to the dance groups. However, a higher proportion of the members of the newer groups derived from the Western-educated elite. Strobel notes the lack of feminist orientation in both forms of association; in Mombasa, women's organizations are *of* but not *for* women. Creole women in Sierra Leone also appear to rank prestige and enhanced status high among the benefits of membership in their Western-style church associations.

Marketplace competition may prevent women from developing associational goals that would advance the general economic interests of women. Barbara Lewis's case study of market women in

Abidjan, Ivory Coast, compares associational patterns among ethnic groups. She finds that women's motivation to succeed in individual business enterprise does not extend to the successful pursuit of collective action. Ethnic-group exclusiveness and economic competition have prevented the associations from gaining strength; instead they have come to serve individual economic needs. The result of the failure of these rotating credit associations has been the emergence of an ambulatory banking system at increased cost and reduced financial security to its clients.

In Western societies the standard dictum is that politics is a male sphere. Annie Lebeuf (1963) took the lead in pointing out that in many African societies this was not the case: "By habit of thought deeply rooted in the Western mind, women are relegated to the sphere of domestic tasks and private life, and men alone are considered equal to the task of shouldering the burden of public affairs. This anti-feminist attitude ... should not allow us to prejudge the manner in which activities are shared between men and women in other cultures, more particularly ... in those of Africa" (Lebeuf 1963: 93). Two papers in this volume (Van Allen, Okonjo) explore women's political activities among the Igbo of Nigeria, where politics was traditionally the sphere of women as well as men.

Kamene Okonjo describes the system that operated among the Igbo living west of the Niger River as a "dual-sex system" in which political interest groups were defined and represented by sex. Each sex generally managed its own affairs and had its own kinship institutions, age grades, and secret and title societies. This system recognized that the activities assigned to women in the sexual division of labor were explicitly political. Women's realm included control of markets; from this sector emerged the *omu*, the Igbo woman monarch some Western observers called the "market queen," a term Okonjo discards because the *omu* was neither the wife nor the mother of a "king." Rather, the *omu* was regarded as the mother of all her citizens, and her role was complementary to that of the *obi*, the male monarch. The *omu* had her own cabinet, parallel to that of the *obi*. Her general sphere was the market and women's interests, but she had jurisdiction over men, too, in mar-

ket matters or when men brought cases involving their wives or
other women that were not settled amicably at the local level.
Mullings tells us that the Ga of southern Ghana also had a complementary dual-sex system with the *mantse* (father of the town) sharing power with the *manyei* (mother).

Judith Van Allen deals with those Igbo who lived not in mon-
archies but in "democratic village republics" (Afigbo 1972). In
these relatively decentralized societies, women's political roles grew
out of the lineage structure. Here not an *omu* but the *inyemedi*
(wives of the lineage) and the *umuada* (daughters of the lineage)
assumed major political functions for women. From the *inyemedi*
emerged the forum that functioned as an institution of daily self-
rule among women. It also made market rules that applied to men
as well as to women.

Societies where women held political roles have been documented in all parts of Africa, but there has been tremendous variation from society to society. In some, women held the highest positions—e.g., as paramount chiefs among the Mende in Sierra Leone
(see Hoffer 1974)—whereas in others their political roles were more
limited. Sometimes the public roles of women were quasi-political
and disguised. Whereas Igbo women took on political roles that
emerged directly from their roles as women, in other societies
women were regarded as men when they acted in the public realm.
For example, among the Lovedu of the Transvaal, women were
the sole monarchs in the nineteenth century, but the Lovedu rain
queens took "wives" sent to them by foreign and local chiefs. The
queen could not have an official husband, and it was from the
daughters of her "wives" (for whom she kept a "harem" of men)
that claimants to her throne emerged (Krige and Krige 1943).

In the interlacustrine kingdoms of East Africa that Iris Berger
describes, women were ordinarily expected to know nothing about
politics. Yet institutions existed by which women could rise above
the subordinate status assigned to them. The main vehicles for this
were spirit mediumship cults. Though these cults operated in the
religious sphere, there were no hard and fast lines separating religion and politics. There can be no question that women mediums

acted in quasi-political roles: when a woman became a spirit medium she gained political prerogatives normally reserved for men, sat on a stool, judged in trials, and accepted greetings as a chief. A few mediums attained such prominence that they presided with the king in ceremonies of spiritual renewal for the entire kingdom. Berger describes women in Nyabingi who even took on the attributes of kings, gathering large entourages, collecting tribute, being carried on litters, and consolidating their positions in the manner of male monarchs.

Western observers, frequently unaware of the prerogatives of women in many African societies, saw the advent of European colonialism as a positive event for African women. The light of Western Christianity and education would lift them from the toil of agricultural labor, the burden of polygyny and forced marriages, and the pain of clitoridectomy to a richer and more fulfilling life. But on the contrary, colonialism actually had a retarding effect on African women; they experienced a substantial loss in their economic and political status. One of the first to recognize this was Ester Boserup in her book *Woman's Role in Economic Development* (1970). She described how Europeans decided that men's cultivation was superior to women's and set out to replace them, even in areas where women had introduced cash-cropping: "Virtually all Europeans shared the opinion that men are superior to women in the art of farming; and it seemed to follow that for the development of agriculture male farming ought to be promoted to replace female farming. Many Europeans did all they could to achieve this" (Boserup 1970: 54).

Robertson and Mullings describe how the economic changes that accompanied colonialism brought setbacks to the coastal Ga women. When women turned enthusiastically to petty trading with the introduction of a money economy, several researchers regarded their position as enviable. But petty trading was precarious, and most women managed only a marginal subsistence from it. Women remained in this sector while men alone were gaining access to new job opportunities in the modern sector.

African women lost political as well as economic status under colonialism. When they introduced their systems of colonial rule, Europeans failed to see that African women had political roles and institutions in their societies. This myopia was particularly striking in the case of the British system of "indirect rule," under which women's institutions somehow disappeared. The dual-sex systems in Nigeria and Ghana gave way to single-sex ones in which men appropriated all power. The traditional principles of dispersed and shared political authority had no place in the colonial system.

African women did not accept their loss of status passively. The most dramatic example of their response came in the 1929 Women's War, which Van Allen describes. She calls it a "collective response to the abrogation of rights." Stimulated by what they perceived to be a move to tax their property, Igbo women organized through their *mikiri* network, attacked the Warrant Chief they suspected of carrying out the taxation scheme, and massed in protest at the colonial District Office. The British administration met the women's protest with police and soldiers, followed by retaliatory punitive expeditions.

In Kowe in western Kenya, Hay found that women used different tactics to respond to the devastating economic changes that accompanied colonialism. When men went off as contract labor to the White Highlands, women were forced not only to support themselves, their children, and frequently the men (whose migrant-labor wages were below subsistence) but also to meet colonial demands for sustained and sometimes increased agricultural production. The women responded with agricultural innovation and experimentation: they assumed more of the burden of agricultural labor; introduced labor-saving crops such as maize, cassava, and groundnuts; adopted new implements; and made trade and marketing a regular part of their lives. Hay concludes that the women of Kowe were agents of change during the colonial period, and that they thus "managed to meet the economic demands of the colonial economy and in a broader sense to stay even."

In most newly independent African countries, the process of deterioration of status that beset women under colonialism has continued. For Ga women the deterioration has accelerated. As the male-dominated modern commercial sector has grown, Robertson shows that increased importation of manufactured products has reduced cooperation among women and between spouses. Trade capital has been increasingly difficult to amass, and the result of Western education has been a reduction in the scale of business among traders. The deteriorating economic situation of small traders has left Accra women fighting to hold onto their economic independence.*

The decline in women's status has continued even in some of the most progressive African countries. James L. Brain found women in the *Ujamaa* villages that were to form the nucleus of socialist development in Tanzania sometimes worse off than they had been in traditional society. On rural development projects, women were expected to put in the same amount of time doing farm labor that men were; but women were also expected to continue with their domestic labor, and thus had a double burden. Brain faults government bureaucrats and their expatriate advisers for their insensitivity to women's needs in development, and notes that independence alone has not resulted in the restoration or safeguarding of women's rights.

In the liberation movements that developed in the 1960's in Portuguese-controlled areas of Africa, however, women made important contributions. And the newly independent regimes in Mozambique and Guinea-Bissau have been cited by many observers as models to be emulated in their treatment of women. As Mullings points out for Mozambique, male dominance and female subordination are seen as inequities that arose from colonialism and its resulting class stratification. The Mozambique government's commitment to the reconstruction of society makes equality for women a necessary part of social and economic change. Although it is too early to make final judgments on the position

* For a further discussion of the continuing decline in the status of women in Ghana, see Christine Oppong, Christine Okali, and Beverley Houghton; "Woman Power: Retrograde Steps in Ghana," *African Studies Review*, 18, no. 3 (Dec. 1975).

of women in Mozambique and Guinea-Bissau, many women in Africa and elsewhere look to them as models for the future.

From a wide range of viewpoints, this collection of articles presents a picture of women who have sought to control their lives, and who have understood and dealt with the forces that affect them. But these studies, in the questions they raise, also suggest the directions that research on women and attitudes toward their potential are increasingly likely to take. African women will continue to be seen as actors—participants in the political and economic processes that affect their lives and livelihood, and respondents to the forces of colonialism and modern economic development. But the limitations of their possibilities for effecting change, in the past and present, are now being assessed. To what extent is women's potential for exercising political power limited to the sphere of women? In the cases of instances of leadership by individual women, do they act in the interests of women, or as "classificatory males," beings who are socially or ritually recognized as having overcome the normal constraints on women? Are separate women's institutions in a society necessarily equal in economic or political power? Is there a positive correlation between the type and amount of work performed by women and their political influence in a society? With the understanding that colonialism was a restrictive force toward women's potential has come the recognition that postindependence development plans may be similarly detrimental. Does development policy "modernize" women into dependency roles unknown in traditional life? In sum, although the specific economic and social skills and rights of women in African societies have been increasingly acknowledged, the constraints on their ability to act to change or even to control their own lives have become more apparent.

The *Signares* of Saint-Louis and Gorée: Women Entrepreneurs in Eighteenth-Century Senegal

GEORGE E. BROOKS, JR.

FROM THE FIFTEENTH century on, Europeans traded along the coast of West Africa—the westernmost perimeter of a vast African commercial complex of whose extent even the most astute Europeans were only vaguely aware.* The earliest mariners along the coast were the Portuguese, who initially carried on a shipboard commerce. Soon, however, adventurers from Portugal and the Cape Verde Islands began to settle among coastal and riverine societies in order to benefit from increased proximity to the sources of this African commerce. Termed *lançados* because they "threw themselves" among Africans, these men established relationships with the most influential women who would accept them in order to obtain commercial privileges. In pursuit of their objectives, *lançados* adopted many of the customs and practices of the African societies; indeed, many shed so much of their Portuguese culture as to be characterized as *tangomaos*, "renegades." Descendants of their alliances with African women were called *filhos da terra*, "children of the soil," and, with their dual cultural background (and sometimes their mothers' social rank and prerogatives as well), were in an advantageous position to serve as brokers manipulating African and European trading networks.†

* I am indebted to the volume editors and to Jan Phillips Bianchi, Charles S. Bird, William B. Cohen, John Hargreaves, M. Jeanne Peterson, and Margaret Strobel for contributions and suggestions. Viviane Cochran and Ethel Richardson typed the penultimate draft.

† For background see Rodney 1970, chap. 3; António Carreira, *Cabo Verde; Formação e Extincão de uma Sociedade Escravocrata, 1460–1878* (Lisbon, 1972),

That African women in the Senegambia and Upper Guinea Coast regions did enjoy social rank and prerogatives seems clear. Malinke oral traditions relating to pre-European times make vague mention of Bainounka "queens" living along the upper Gambia River. There is more reliable evidence that women with outstanding qualities of leadership and with wealth acquired through trade ruled West African villages in traditional times (Galloway 1974, chap. 2). But further research is needed to fill the large gaps in our knowledge of the status and socioeconomic roles of women in West Africa before the arrival of the Europeans. What is certain is that African and Eurafrican women who were wealthy traders or possessed property and influence were treated with marked respect by Africans, Eurafricans, and Europeans alike. In the eighteenth and nineteenth centuries, such women were customarily addressed by the titles *nhara* (in Portuguese Guinea), *senora* (in the Gambia), or *signare* (in Senegal)—titles derived from the Portuguese *senhora*.* They often possessed numerous domestic slaves, trading craft, and houses, as well as quantities of gold and silver jewelry and splendid clothing. Indisputably they knew how to acquire wealth, how to employ it profitably, and how to enjoy it as well.

To date very little has been published on the *nharas* of Guinea-Bissau, and only slightly more on *senoras* in The Gambia. Though

chap. 2; and Jean Boulègue, *Les Luso-Africains de Sénégambie, XVI–XIX siècle* (Dakar, 1972), pp. 11–21.

* Women wielded considerable social and economic influence already in the seventeenth century in the Senegambia region and along the Upper Guinea Coast. Rufisque, on the Senegal coast, was one of the earliest Portuguese trading centers and had several women residents of note: a Senhora Philippa, described as a "dame Portugaise" by Boulègue (*Les Luso-Africains*, pp. 54–55), controlled European access to trade there in 1634; an unnamed "Portugaise" held the same power in 1669; and a Senhora Catti, the African widow of a Portuguese trader, served as commercial agent for the Damel (ruler) of the Wolof state of Cayor in 1685 (p. 71). A Eurafrican woman known as Marie Mar was renowned during this period for her aid to shipwrecked seamen (*Les Luso-Africains*, pp. 61–62, 72). But most famous of all was the formidable Bibiana Vaz, a Eurafrican who built up an extensive trading empire between the Gambia and Sierra Leone rivers in the 1670's and 1680's and who held captive the captain-major of Cacheu for fourteen months in 1684–85 and instigated a short-lived Eurafrican "republic" (Rodney 1970: 209–10).

both primary and secondary sources exist on the *signares* of Senegal, much of the literature is highly romanticized, biased, or distorted, based as it is on data collected by, or information available from, European men. In the course of this paper I attempt to point out many of the problems associated with these sources and to present a balanced assessment of the women traders of Senegal.

Senegal: Saint-Louis and Gorée

Although there were many influential trading women in the Senegambia and Upper Guinea Coast regions in the eighteenth and early nineteenth centuries, the largest number was concentrated in Senegal, and it was there that the greatest development and elaboration of what may be termed "signareship" occurred. This is not surprising, since during that period many more Europeans lived at Saint-Louis and Gorée than anywhere else in West Africa. Indeed, the number of Europeans at those two settlements at times probably exceeded the number at all the other forts, settlements, and factories in West Africa combined.

The island of N'Dar in the Senegal River—on which the French founded the settlement of Saint-Louis in 1659—is only a mile and a half long and an eighth of a mile wide. Gorée is an even smaller island—a half-mile long and a few hundred yards wide—cradled by the Cape Verde peninsula. A settlement there was established originally by the Portuguese, who were later ousted by the Dutch, who in turn were displaced by the French in 1677. The population of both islands increased steadily during the eighteenth century: Saint-Louis had an estimated population of some 3,000 by 1764, and more than 6,000 by 1785; Gorée had some 1,000 inhabitants in 1767, and some 1,800 by 1785.* European residents included the employees of successive French trading companies and the officers and troops of the garrisons. Some who sought their fortunes in

---

* See Dodwell 1916: 274; and Cariou n.d.: 35. I am grateful to Dr. Cariou for making his manuscript available to me in 1966; my interest in *signares* owes much to his scholarship. See also Silvain Meinrad Xavier Golberry, *Fragmens d'un voyage en Afrique, fait pendant les années 1785, 1786, 1787* (Paris, 1802), vol. 1, pp. 154–55; vol. 2, pp. 60–61.

Senegal were men with outstanding qualities, but many were of mediocre ability and character. Oftentimes the soldiers represented the dregs of European society—men with criminal records, debauched, and diseased—and were more likely to acquire "civilizing" influences from Africans than to impart them.

The role of African women (primarily of the Wolof and Lebou peoples) was a factor of great influence on the special developments that occurred in Senegal. These women had considerable independence of action in their own societies, and were strongly attracted by the economic opportunities that arose with the coming of the Europeans. And European men were no less attracted to them for their beauty and commercial enterprise. Given the circumstances, cohabitation and economic collaboration for mutual advantage were virtually inevitable.

Social and demographic data are sparse for the first half of the eighteenth century, but available evidence indicates that the principal characteristics of "signareship" must have evolved during the long period of uninterrupted French occupation of Saint-Louis and Gorée prior to 1758. Details recorded in André Delcourt's study of this period provide hints of the developments in progress. The regulations of the Senegal Company* forbade its employees to traffic with African women, but successive governors in Saint-Louis, confronted with local realities and needs, sought to obtain authorization for Company employees to marry local women. Governor Dubellay (1722–25) argued that such a policy would encourage long-term service and reduce the turnover of Company employees. But since there were only five young Eurafricans aged from twelve to fifteen in Saint-Louis suitable for marriage, Dubellay also suggested that the Company undertake to send out six to eight *parisiennes* aged fifteen to sixteen each year so that Company employees might marry them. The Company directors rejected both propositions, again expressly forbidding marriages between whites and women of color (Delcourt 1952: 95,123).

* The "Senegal Company" refers to La Compagnie Française des Indes et la Concession du Sénégal, which functioned until 1767.

A decade later, another governor, Devaulx (1733–34), together
with his advisory council, reopened the issue on the grounds that
Company regulations had not prevented sexual and commercial
arrangements and that sanctioning marriages might make clandestine commerce easier to control. They also invoked Christian pre-
cepts, adding that Eurafrican women and girls would be freed from
the necessity of living in sin, as was currently the case, since circumstances in Senegal made Eurafricans dependent on whites for
their existence. That Eurafricans were alleged to be dependent on
whites suggests that they—and their mothers—were held apart
from Wolof society. Their position was made marginal by the Company's practice of not permitting a woman's children to inherit
property acquired by a Company employee—a reprehensible policy productive of much injustice and ill-will. Delcourt (1952: 124ff.)
reports this policy in effect in the 1730's, but it seems to have been
abandoned a few years later. What happened is that Europeans
living in Senegal came to adopt Wolof and Lebou marriage and
inheritance practices, with the responsibilities and obligations they
entailed.

By mid-century, *signares* had attained considerable economic
consequence and had contributed to creating a Senegalese life-style
so attractive to Europeans that they refused to obey Company directives against cohabitation and commerce with African women.
Pruneau de Pommegorge's account (1789: 2–7), distilled from 22
years' experience in West Africa ending in 1765, would serve with
few modifications until well into the nineteenth century.*

The women on the island [Saint-Louis] are, in general, closely associated with white men, and care for them when they are sick in a manner
that could not be bettered. The majority live in considerable affluence,
and many African women own thirty to forty slaves which they hire to
the Company. Each year the domestic slaves make the voyage to Galam
engaged as sailors; they bring back to their mistresses fifteen, twenty, even
up to thirty weight of gold for the sale of two hogsheads of salt which

---

* For a more detailed description dating from a generation or so later, see
Lamiral 1789: 44–59. Among the minor changes that had occurred since Pruneau
de Pommegorge's time, *signares* were now shielded from the sun on their prom-
enades by parasols borne by young girls.

they are permitted to embark duty-free. The women have some of this gold made into jewelry, and the rest is used to purchase clothing, because they adore, as do women everywhere else, fashionable clothing. Their mode of dress, characteristically very elegant, suits them very well. They wear a very artistically arranged white handkerchief on the head, over which they affix a small narrow black ribbon, or a colored one, around their head. A shift *à la française*, ornamented; a bodice of taffeta or muslin; a skirt of the same and similar to the bodice; gold earrings; anklets of gold or silver, for they will wear no others; red morocco slippers on the feet; underneath their bodice a piece of two ells of muslin, the ends of which dangle beneath the left shoulder—thus appareled when they go out in public, they are followed by one or two young girls who serve as their chambermaids, likewise well dressed, but somewhat more lightly and a little less modestly than is our own custom. One becomes accustomed very quickly, however, to viewing these almost nude women without becoming embarrassed. Their customs are different from ours, and when one becomes accustomed to their nudity it ceases to make any more impression than if they were covered up.

The women being thus escorted when they go out, they frequently encounter a *griot* (a type of man who sings someone's praises in return for money); in such instances he does not lose the opportunity to precede them declaiming their praises with all the exaggerations he can think of, and some immodesties which they know, the women being so flattered that in the rapture excited by this adulation they often fling some of their garments to the singer when they have nothing left in their pockets to give him.

Next to finery, the greatest passion of these women is their dances, or *folgars*, which they sometimes hold until daybreak, and during which one drinks a great deal of palm wine, *pitot* (a type of beer), and also wines from France, when they are able to procure them. The usual way to praise those who have excelled in dancing is to fling a cloth or a handkerchief over them, which they return to the person who has thrown it, making a deep bow to thank him.

Some of these women are married in church, others *à la mode du pays*, which in general consists of the consent of both parties and the relatives. It is remarked that the latter marriages are always more successful than the former; the women are more faithful to their husbands than otherwise is the case. The ceremony which follows the latter form of marriage is not in fact as becoming as is the good behavior of the women.

The morning following the consummation of the marriage, the relatives of the bride come at daybreak and carry off the white cloth on which the couple have spent the night. Do they find the proof they search for? They affix the cloth at the end of a long pole, waving like a flag; they parade this all day long in the village, singing and praising the new bride and her chastity; but when the relatives have not in fact found such proof the morning after, they take care to substitute for it as quickly as possible.

Many aspects of Pruneau de Pommegorge's account continue to be relevant in modern-day Senegal. Senegalese women still possess an unrivaled flair for displaying clothing, jewelry, and other finery. *Or de Galam* (gold from Galam) is still the byword for quality and purity. The single white handkerchief headpiece described by Pruneau de Pommegorge soon evolved into the striking cone-shaped turban, artfully constructed with as many as nine colored handkerchiefs, that became the hallmark of *signares* in Senegal and The Gambia. *Folgar* is a Portuguese word that passed into West African languages to describe a carefree frolic or general rejoicing. The rites and reciprocities associated with marriage *à la mode du pays* are discussed in a later section.* *Griots* belong to a special endogamous social class, or "caste," associated with many societies living on the coast and in the interior of West Africa. They were (and are) professional entertainers, musicians, singers, and dancers (Gamble 1967: 45), and their role is analogous to that of the bards or troubadours of medieval Europe: they were attached to the leading families as praise-singers, keepers of family histories and genealogies, counselors to rulers, and educators of the young (see Bird 1971: 16–18). Traditionally, *griots* had the privilege of mocking people or using abusive language with impunity, with the result that they were generally well rewarded to ensure their favor. Female *griots* were often hairdressers, an occupation that gave them a matchless opportunity to learn and pass on gossip. They also had a reputation for lascivious dancing and for otherwise having an immoral influence on young women (Gamble 1967: 45).

In another section of his account, Pruneau de Pommegorge (1789: 28–29) testifies to the beauty, intelligence, and remarkable adaptability of Wolof women, which made them much sought after as slaves by French colonists in the West Indies. They were reputed to be so adept that within a few months of their arrival in the Antilles they knew how to sew, speak French, and perform

* For definitions of these and other terms, see R. Mauny, *Glossaire des expressions et termes locaux employés dans l'Ouest Africain* (Dakar, 1952), pp. 37, 48.

other duties as well as European servants, with the consequence
that they were especially sought after for service as chambermaids.
This Wolof "adaptability" is a theme discussed by numerous observers.

The Reverend John Lindsay, chaplain aboard one of the British
vessels that captured Gorée in December 1758, and a subsequent
visitor to Saint-Louis, also praised Senegalese women (1759: 77–78).

> As to their women, and in particular the ladies (for so I must call many
> of those in Senegal) they are in a surprising degree handsome, have very
> fine features, are wonderfully tractable, remarkably polite both in con-
> versation and manners; and in the point of keeping themselves neat and
> clean (of which we have generally strange ideas, formed to us by the
> beastly laziness of slaves), they far surpass the Europeans in every respect.
> They bathe twice a day, ... and in this particular have a hearty contempt
> for all white people, who they imagine must be disagreeable, our women
> especially. Nor can even their men, from this very notion, be brought to
> look upon the prettiest of our women, but with the coldest indifference,
> some of whom there are here, officers' ladies, who dress very showy, and
> who even in England would be thought handsome. You may, perhaps,
> smile at all this; but I assure you 'tis a truth. Negroes to me are no novelty;
> but the accounts I received of them, and in particular the appearance
> of the females on this occasion, were to me a novelty most pleasing. They
> were not only pretty, but in the dress in which they appeared, were even
> desirable. Nor can I give you any drapery more nearly resembling theirs,
> than the loose, light, easy robe, and sandal, in which we see the female
> Grecian statues attired; most of which were of exceeding white cotton,
> spun, wove into narrow slips of six or seven inches, and sewn together
> by themselves. Their hair, for it differs a little from wool, very neat and
> curiously plaited; and their persons otherways adorned, by earrings, neck-
> laces, and bracelets, of the purest gold.
> And indeed I cannot help thinking, that it was to the benefit of the
> African company in general, and the happiness of those they sent abroad
> in particular; that, with such promising inhabitants, the French suffered
> no white women to be sent thither.

There was, however, no easy fraternization, to the dismay of the
British seamen, and Reverend Lindsay was at pains to describe
(p. 79) the women's high reputation for chastity and respectable
behavior, a theme that will be discussed below.

Who the women described by Pruneau de Pommegorge and
Reverend Lindsay were, and what classes of society they belonged

to, are frustrating historical questions, since few sources mention either the names or the status of women discussed. And where the names of women are given, those of Eurafricans have no European surnames. The hierarchy of Wolof and Lebou social classes is as follows: freeborn (*jambor*); persons of slave descent (*jam*); blacksmiths and leatherworkers (*tega* and *ude*); persons descended from slaves of the above (*jam i tega* and *jam i ude*); griots (gewel); and persons descended from their slaves (*jam i gewel*). In traditional times, marriage across class lines was extremely rare. An exception was when a wealthy freeborn man, after marriage to several freeborn wives, married a *jam* woman (called a *tara*) for her beauty. In such cases, the *tara* and her children were accorded freeborn status (Ames 1956: 156–57). Sources suggest that many of the women associated with Europeans were *jam*. Probably a number, too, were from the *griot* class. Only one specific reference to a freeborn woman was found, that of a Walo [?] "princess" married to the French commandant of Gorée in 1758 (Lindsay 1759: 80, 89–90).

Also living at Saint-Louis, Gorée, and other West African commercial centers were numerous Africans known as *grumetes*, who were associated with European and Eurafrican trading activities. *Grumete* (Crioulo), *gourmet* (French), and *grumetta* (English) all derived from the word for ship's boy or cabin boy in various European languages, and *grumete* was the name given to Africans hired aboard European vessels as pilots and seamen from the fifteenth century on. *Grumetes* were recruited from West African seafaring peoples for a variety of tasks afloat and ashore: they served as boatbuilders, longshoremen, and guards for slave barracoons, but they were chiefly employed as sailors and their maritime skills made them invaluable to European and Eurafrican traders. They generally spoke *Crioulo*, "Black French," or "Black English," wore European-style clothing, and adopted some Christian practices. Almost no information has been recorded concerning *grumete* women; in some communities they seem to have belonged to the same African society as their men, in others they likely were local women taken to wife, and in still others they were perhaps a com-

bination of the two (Rodney 1970: 77, 79; Nardin 1966). Evidence
is lacking, but it is likely that the *grumete* communities at Saint-
Louis and Gorée together with the *jam* social grouping were the
principal sources of the women who associated with European
males.

Where Pruneau de Pommegorge and Reverend Lindsay dwelled
on the positive attributes of Senegalese women, the noted French
botanist Michel Adanson subjected them and the leading administrators in Senegal to a searching critique. Adanson, who had spent
the years from 1749 to 1753 in Senegal collecting and studying
specimens, prepared a *mémoire* for the Minister for Foreign Affairs
in 1763 on the occasion of the return of Gorée to French control
following the Seven Years War. (Both Gorée and Saint-Louis had
been captured by British forces in 1758; Gorée was returned to
France in 1763, but Saint-Louis remained under British control
until 1779.) He was highly critical of a number of corrupt practices
associated with *signares* that interfered with the proper administration of the Senegal Company and were grossly unfair to its lower-
ranked French employees. He charged that *signares* were accorded
double or triple rations—whatever they wanted—from the Company's stores, and that as a general practice their domestic slaves
were fed with meat and millet at the Company's expense. The
slaves of *signares* hired in the Company's service carried on trade
on behalf of their mistresses and those high-ranking Company
officials in collusion with them, with the result that the *signares*
obtained the choicest merchandise, including commodities not
available to the lower-ranked French employees. Adanson asserted
that these latter—Frenchmen who were workers, soldiers, sailors,
and even officers of the lower grades—went without, while the
"bloodsuckers" and their male associates banqueted upon provisions diverted from their use. He blamed such practices on the
Company's regulations forbidding its employees to marry and
bring out women from France; the consequences were that men
lavished upon African women housing and amenities that would
have befitted European women. He acknowledged that such behavior was not surprising, suggesting that in a hot climate men are

especially sensible to women's charms—not the least Frenchmen, who are always attracted to "a sex as dangerous as it is attractive."*

Adanson's *mémoire* is informative on other practices. Regarding the offspring of such unions, he states that boys were employed in the Company service as hired laborers and sailors (*grumetes*). They were not categorized as slaves, even in cases where the mother had been a slave. Girls were accorded the same privileges as their mothers, and made alliances with Company officials in furtherance of their own interests. The growing numbers of domestic slaves possessed by them, together with those owned by their mothers, were an increasing drain on the Company's resources.†

Whether as a result of Adanson's indictment of past administrative corruption or not, the French government introduced significant changes in West African commerce in 1763. Gorée was placed under royal administration with an appointed governor, and freedom of commerce was proclaimed. However, independent traders soon learned that free trade was little more than a declaration of principle insofar as West Africa was concerned. Collusion between commercial interests associated with the new Senegal Company (the Compagnie de Guyane) and royal officials made the measure a dead letter. The royal governors proved to be readily corruptible and preoccupied with lining their own pockets (Knight-Baylac 1970a: 58–60). *Signares* must have welcomed the advent of the royal administration, inasmuch as the new royal officials posted to Senegal, like the military officers, had little to occupy their time. Seemingly most followed the example of their superiors and associated with *signares* in illicit trading ventures.

The Abbé Demanet, who accompanied the French expedition

---

* Cited in Cariou n.d.: 18–19. Adanson is the earliest source located to date mentioning the title *signare*. According to him, the women so termed themselves. Poncet de la Rivière, the commandant of Gorée in 1764, related that women were called *signares* more for their "Portuguese appearance" than for their origins, since they were of French-African descent. De la Rivière's comment is cited in Madeleine Saulnier, "Une réception royale à l'île de Gorée en 1831," *Revue de l'Histoire des Colonies Françaises*, 6 (1918), p. 344, n. 1.

† Again I draw on Dr. Cariou's "Promenade à Gorée" (n.d.: 19). That children of a woman slave were accorded freeborn status following their mother's marriage to a freeborn man accords with traditional Wolof practice.

dispatched to reoccupy Gorée in 1763, criticized the lack of initiative European traders there and at other trading communities displayed while the women associated with them were becoming
wealthy in commerce (1767: 116–17): "Each and every one had become absorbed in his own diversions and was debilitated by indo-
lence. Simple clerks, ordinary employees with low-level appoint-
ments, reached expenses of 10,000 francs a year. One sees today on
Gorée, at Senegal, and in the Gambia some of their concubines who
have fortunes of 100,000 livres, even though prior to this business,
so pernicious in different respects, they owned nothing whatever."
Like other sources, Demanet is uninformative on the names of the
women or the means by which they carried on their commercial
affairs. Besides using their domestic slaves, *signares* presumably
employed relatives and took advantage of ties with African traders
and rulers on the mainland, but details on such matters are not
recorded in contemporary European accounts.

The revelations of Adanson and the Abbé Demanet concerning
conditions in Senegal are borne out by the research of Dr. Cariou
and Mme. Knight-Baylac on the history of Gorée. In 1749, ten of the
thirteen private properties on the island belonged to Eurafricans,
nine of whom were women. In 1767, the richest woman on Gorée,
Caty Louette, then associated with a Captain Aussenac, owned 25
male and 43 female domestic slaves. A plan of Gorée prepared in
1779 by Evrard Duparel shows that of eighteen compounds belonging to the French government, eleven were occupied by *signares* (Knight-Baylac 1970b: 402–3). Many of Adanson's and Demanet's charges are repeated in letters cited in a volume compiled
by J. Machat. *Signares* living on Gorée were castigated for spending
their days in idleness, for dressing in a manner calculated to arouse
violent passions, for inciting whites to debauchery, and for sowing
disunity and sickness among them. Royal administrators were
accused of collaborating with the *signares* in illicit commerce in
order to gain the wealth necessary to attract and support them and
indulge their taste for luxuries; in the meantime they prevented
other Frenchmen from doing the same (Machat 1906: 88–89).

The dearth of information concerning the British administra-

tion of Saint-Louis from 1758 to 1779 makes it impossible to compare events there with those on Gorée (held by Britain 1758–63 and
1779–83; French-ruled for the remainder of the century). John
Barnes, who arrived in Saint-Louis in December 1763 to take
charge of the post for the African Company described the fort as
a "dismal heap of ruins" and characterized the British garrison as
"a set of the most mutinous, drunken, abandoned fellows I ever
met with," which says as much about their officers. According to
Barnes, Saint-Louis had about 3,000 inhabitants, including a considerable number of nonindigenous Africans. Soldiers and sailors,
together with Africans, drank and brawled in the numerous taverns
on the island (Dodwell 1916: 274–75).

In contrast to France, which had allowed Saint-Louis to be ad-
ministered by monopolistic trading companies, Britain established
an ill-conceived "Province of Senegambia" (1765–83) that linked
Saint-Louis with James Fort in the Gambia River—the two separated, though, by French-ruled Gorée. Moreover, Parliament de-
creed free and open commerce for all British subjects and instituted
a governor's council composed of nine local inhabitants together
with four ex officio members (Martin 1927: 66–71). These and other
measures accorded Senegalese privileges and opportunities long
denied them under French rule. One important consequence was
that Eurafrican men asserted themselves as never before.

Economic and social developments at Saint-Louis are difficult to
trace for the period of British rule; unfortunately for historians,
Colonel Charles O'Hara, the governor of Senegambia from 1766
to 1775, was notorious for his negligence of official correspondence
and record-keeping. However, some idea of what went on during O'Hara's administration emerges from the complaints made
against him. The rise of Eurafrican men in the colony's affairs is
evident from a petition of grievances drawn up in 1776: it was
signed by fifteen inhabitants, all males, including one Eurafrican
who had become unofficially recognized as the "mayor" representing the population of Saint-Louis. O'Hara was accused of numerous arbitrary and despotic acts taken without consulting the
governor's council or following judicial process. The evidence col-

lected for an official inquiry reports other corrupt practices. Military officers were charged with openly engaging in commerce, contrary to regulations, with, one may safely assume, the collaboration of *signares*. One of the allegations against O'Hara himself was that materials allocated for the repair of the fort's walls and storehouses were used instead on the homes of his "concubines" (Martin 1927: 76, 88–90; Dodwell 1916: 296–98; Hargreaves 1969: 76–84). By the time France recaptured Saint-Louis in 1779, Eurafricans had acquired notable wealth and influence in the community, which French authorities were constrained to come to terms with in the years following.

War broke out between France and Britain in 1778. The following January a French squadron captured Saint-Louis to end more than two decades of British rule. Four months later, in May 1779, British forces captured Gorée, which they held until 1783, when by the terms of the peace treaty both Saint-Louis and Gorée were designated French possessions.

The decade between 1783 and the renewal of warfare between France and Britain in 1792 represents a period of considerable French commercial expansion in the Senegambia and along the Upper Guinea Coast. Profits from trade trickled down to all elements of society in Senegal. This, together with government disbursements on forts and public buildings and expenditures by the trading community on trading craft and a number of comfortable private residences, contributed to a period of unprecedented affluence for the inhabitants of Saint-Louis and Gorée. The period takes on a special romantic aura in popular literature and historical studies alike from its association with the name of the Chevalier de Boufflers, the last royal governor of Senegal. Boufflers forsook the sun-baked sands of Saint-Louis for the milder airs of Gorée, where he shared companionship and a commercial partnership with Anne Pépin, one of the island's beautiful *signares*.* The

---

* Evocative descriptions of this golden age of Goréen history can be found in Pierre Cariou, "La Rivale inconnue de Madame de Sabran dans l'Ile de Gorée," *Notes Africaines*, 45 (Jan. 1950), pp. 13–15; and *idem*, "Costumes d'autrefois à Gorée, *France Outre-Mer*, 270 (April 1952), pp. 38–41. The Chevalier de Boufflers was a *littérateur* of some note, in part owing to a correspondence ex-

Boufflers era is noteworthy, too, for the number of Frenchmen who published accounts of their experiences in West Africa prior to the French Revolution. Most of these accounts were written to promote schemes for French commercial expansion, but they include much descriptive material on West African peoples. Although they are very uneven in quality and insight, and marred in some instances by flagrant plagiarization, these sources contribute to the description and analysis of some of the most important features of "signareship" in Senegal.

Eurafrican Society in the 1780's

By the mid-1780's, Saint-Louis and Gorée had large populations of Eurafricans and free Africans who owned numerous domestic slaves. According to Golberry's estimates cited earlier (p. 21, fn.), Saint-Louis's population of more than 6,000 included some 2,400 Eurafricans and free blacks and about the same number of domestic slaves, besides 600 French soldiers, government officials, and members of the trading community, and about 60 permanent white residents. (There were, in addition, roughly 1,000 trade slaves held in the fort and in the cellars of houses on the island.) The population of Gorée was similar, but on a smaller scale: of an estimated total population of 1,840, there were 116 Eurafrican and free black property-holders and their families; 522 free blacks without property; 1,044 domestic slaves; 70 to 80 Europeans, including government administrators, officers, soldiers, and employees of the Senegal Company; and 200 or so trade slaves held for shipment.

It is impossible to estimate the number of *signares* among the Eurafrican and free black population cited above. Whatever their numbers, *signares* clearly were the chief element in creating a way of life on Saint-Louis and Gorée that combined features of Wolof and European society, and that was highly attractive and beneficial to European men who came to Senegal. That *signares* directed affairs for their own purposes is likewise evident.

---

changed with Mme. de Sabran, to whom he was secretly married. A poem from that wise and gifted Frenchwoman to the chevalier includes the memorable couplet "Sois constant tout au moins si tu ne m'es fidèle;/Penses à moi souvent dans les bras de ta belle."

Marriage "à la mode du pays"

One of the informative sources on *signares'* marriage patterns is Geoffroy de Villeneuve, who made two voyages to Senegal in 1785–88 and learned Wolof during the two years he lived at Saint-Louis and Gorée. He summarizes the prevailing practices (1814: 1, 68): "The women of color and the wealthy free black women take the Portuguese title *signare* or *nhara*: They freely contract a type of limited marriage with Europeans, regarding themselves as legitimate wives, remaining faithful, and giving the father's name to the children who result from the union. The departure of the white for Europe, with no expectation of returning, breaks the ties of matrimony, and she soon after enters a new contract. The ceremonies observed at the time of this union are the same as those of the Africans' marriages." Prélong, director of the hospital on Gorée from January 1787 to mid-May 1789, asserted that in most cases a woman's parents considered it a "great honor" for their daughter to marry a white man, and their consent constituted the only formality. The European arranged a large banquet to which all the woman's relatives were invited, and feasting and dancing continued for several days accompanied by the music of *griots.* The morning following the nuptials, the sheet stained with the evidence of the bride's virginity was paraded in triumph; this, Prélong noted, was the "sole dowry" that the woman brought the man. The practice was at the point of falling into disuse, he claimed, because Frenchmen found it repugnant, and because it was known often to be a hoax.

If the woman was a slave, the husband purchased her freedom as a wedding present. He also provided her with a place to live—depending on his means, a small house or an African-style dwelling. Following the marriage, the women were reputed to be very faithful, were assiduous in household duties, lavished tender care on their husbands, and contributed significantly to their careers by imparting their knowledge of the customs of the country. The husband purchased a slave for each child to provide for its support. Prélong reports that most of the children were baptized, but he offers convincing evidence that Catholicism was not firmly rooted among Gorée's inhabitants (Prélong 1793: 298–300; cf. Lamiral 1789: 53–54; and Labarthe 1802: 163–65).

The marriage arrangements described by Prélong and other French observers do not differ significantly from traditional Wolof marriage practices. According to Wolof custom (and Muslim law), the father had the right to arrange for his daughter's marriage without her consent. The prospective groom was expected to make generous presents to the bride and her parents whenever he visited them prior to the marriage, and he sealed the engagement with a special payment to the mother and father, *ndah i far*, "to drive off rivals." However, once the marriage payment was settled with the parents and the wedding took place, the husband could take his bride home immediately. This was a change from traditional practice, where consummation did not usually occur until a month or more following the wedding, which neither party might actually attend (Gamble 1967: 65–68; Ames 1956).

It is evident that the women considered themselves properly married, adhered to accepted norms of married behavior, and expected the same of their partners. The parade of the sheet attesting to the bride's virginity—so discomfiting to Europeans' sensibilities—was an integral part of the ceremonies, for virgins commanded higher bridewealth, and a girl's lapse from chastity prior to her marriage was an embarrassment to the family and grounds for immediate divorce. Following the marriage, a Wolof woman guarded her reputation by maintaining chaste behavior and by demanding the same of her husband as well. Whatever European men may have thought of their responsibilities and of restraints on their actions in contracting such marriages, it would seem that the women were quite successful in enforcing appropriate behavior. To be sure, Saint-Louis and Gorée were so small that it would have been virtually impossible to keep extramarital liaisons secret. But wives defended their rights with fearsome weapons: Reverend Landsay reported with shock that many women on Gorée kept sawfish blades in their houses ready to shred the flesh of rivals in any quarrel (1759: 80); and Prélong reported firsthand an instance of an African woman poisoning her former lover and the Eurafrican he left her for with a solanum (a plant of the nightshade family) that grew on Gorée (1793: 275–76). One may suppose that *signares* held no less potent a sanction over their husbands from their role in shared commercial enterprises.

When a European left Senegal, according to Labarthe (1802: 164–65), the custom on Gorée was for his wife to accompany him to the water's edge, where she scooped sand from his final footprint into a handkerchief, which she tied to the foot of her bed. She remained faithful to him unless she learned that he would not return, in which case she was released from the marriage and free to marry again. All the sources are curiously silent on the emotional aspects of the farewells. Probably some men found themselves too imbued with Senegalese ways ever to leave, and some of these must be counted among the permanent European residents recorded in the censuses.

When a woman remarried, she raised her new children along with those from her former marriage (or marriages), each child keeping its father's name. Information is lacking on a *signare*'s second and subsequent marriages, notably what role her parents had and whether they received bridewealth. At Gorée, a *signare*'s children inherited her wealth, following Lebou practice, which was for children to inherit from their mother without interference from their father. But practices may have differed at Saint-Louis, since the Wolof traditionally practiced double descent before the acceptance of Islam (Gamble 1967: 60–61, 94; Angrand 1946: 33).

There is every reason to suppose that *signares* or aspiring *signares*, rich or poor, were careful to ally themselves with worthy partners. Clearly the older, more experienced *signares* who had acquired households of domestic slaves and established commercial networks were a "catch" for European men. It is noteworthy, for example, that the impecunious Chevalier de Boufflers chose a woman nearly thirty years of age, one who had at least one child from one or more previous marriages, was already well-off from trade, and was the sister of Nicholas Pépin, the spokesman for

Gorée's inhabitants. Other high-ranking European officials must likewise have sought and negotiated partnerships with the wealthiest and most enterprising *signares* (Cariou 1950: 15).

Signares receive such disproportionate attention in European sources that it is difficult to assess what the circumstances may have been for women whose mothers were not *signares* and who were thus not provided with the contacts to attract a European administrator, Company official, or military officer. Such women, whether born at Saint-Louis or Gorée, African migrants from the adjoining mainland, or members of Eurafrican families located elsewhere on the Upper Guinea Coast, must have settled for the less eligible Europeans. They would be the persons mentioned as cohabiting with European soldiers, sailors, and lower-ranked Company employees, whose pay could not support the permanent relationships the *signares* demanded. Such liaisons doubtless ranged from casual affairs to relationships as long-term as those of the *signares*. Women likely took "calculated risks" with newly arrived Europeans, especially junior Company employees and young army officers, in hopes of eventually parlaying a liaison into a marriage. Some aspirant *signares* must have succeeded; at the least they acquired increased language ability and knowledge of European practices, and they probably augmented their store of wealth as well, thereby increasing the possibility that they might be more successful in the future.* Others, whether deficient in trading acumen or adaptability, may have returned to their societies or, in some cases, lapsed into casual prostitution. This would explain references to "excessive debauchery" and the spread of venereal disease.† Casual affairs

---

* Prélong 1793 contains a revealing anecdote about a young Eurafrican who, upon marrying a soldier, gave him her only valuable possessions—her gold jewelry—so he could enter trade (pp. 299–300). Launched by this "grubstake," the man succeeded to the enrichment of them both. It should be evident from the material in this paper, however, that *they* entered trade, and that her assistance was necessary for his success.

† On these matters see Knight-Baylac 1970b: 398–400; and Prélong 1793: 275. Prélong relates that marabouts living on the mainland opposite Gorée could cure venereal diseases with a treatment of sudorific herbs and milk in five to six weeks. African women requiring treatment crossed to the continent stating their intention to go "prendre le lait à la grande terre."

with whites outside marriage were not sanctioned by the Lebou
community on Cape Verde, for de Villeneuve reported that illegitimate babies fathered by whites or Eurafricans on the mainland opposite Gorée were killed, and that their mothers were enslaved
(1814: 4, 115–16).

Signares' Households

Signares who were successful in commerce and marriage presided
over large households and compounds inhabited by numerous domestic slaves. From the 1760's on, many of the houses in Saint-
Louis and Gorée were constructed of brick and stone by domestic
slaves who were trained to be expert masons and carpenters. Such
houses were surrounded by walls of the same material or by pali-
sades of reeds. The ground floors of the houses contained kitchens,
pantries, storerooms, and cells for securing trade slaves held for
sale. The *signare* and her family lived on the upper floor, which
had high-ceilinged, airy rooms with large windows opening onto
balconies. The windows were kept shuttered against sunlight during the day and were opened to sea breezes in the cool of the late
afternoon before sunset. Indicative of both the expansion of commerce and the increasing affluence of the inhabitants of Saint-Louis
and Gorée in the 1770's and 1780's are the growing number of such
dwellings: on Gorée, an increase from fewer than six in 1772 to
more than 50 by 1789, all constructed of slabs of basalt and lime
mortar made from seashells (Prélong 1793: 285).

An American shipmaster who traded at Saint-Louis in 1815 described the households and compounds and remarked on the many
economic activities that went on there (Bennett & Brooks 1965:
65–66).*

The houses are mostly built of stone and brick; they are large and convenient. The lower floor is appropriated to the servants, storerooms,
stables or any other purpose. The second floor is divided into a hall, a
sitting room, and several small bed apartments. One or more sides are

---

* For a description of the Eurafrican life-style on Gorée in 1815, see J. A.
Carnes, *Journal of a Voyage from Boston to the West Coast of Africa* (Boston,
1852), pp. 40–41, 47–48.

generally furnished with a piazza running the whole length, which affords a pleasant walk. The whole is surrounded by a high brick wall, the solitary gate to which is constantly guarded by one or two slaves who let no one or no thing out but with their master's order. These houses and walls are plastered and whitewashed and at a distance have a very elegant appearance. A closer view, however, so connects the idea of a Prison with thick walls, grated windows, and guarded gates as to destroy the lively interest excited in a stranger's mind on viewing them from shipboard. Each house may in fact be considered a fortress where the master on his sofa views and directs from the piazza his numerous slaves below. These all have their huts ranged round the wall within the yard, and it is not uncommon to see carpenters, coopers, blacksmiths, weavers, tailors, etc., all in operation at once at their respective works belonging to the same yard. For every man of any note makes it a point to have one or more families of his slaves brought up to each kind of work either of use or ornament.

Fortunate indeed was the European who could associate with a *signare* possessed of such a household and skilled labor force.

Domestic slaves were treated indulgently—indeed, almost like members of the family—by their owners. This was especially true in the cases of the women who were responsible for household work and child-rearing, and of their children, who were brought up together with those of the *signare*. Domestic slaves were never sold into the trade except in extraordinary circumstances—for threatening the life of a free person or exhibiting incorrigible antisocial behavior. Their value as sailors, boatbuilders, carpenters, blacksmiths, coopers, masons, and weavers was well appreciated by their owners, who recognized the shortsightedness of according them bad treatment (Lamiral 1789: 338–40; Pelletan 1800: 99–100). The increasing number of domestic slaves on Gorée is another measure of the growing commerce and wealth of the island's traders in the second half of the eighteenth century. Estimates of 131 in 1749, 710 in 1767, more than 1,200 in 1774–76, and 1,044 in 1785–86 generally represent between two-thirds and three-fourths of the entire population of the island at each date.*

Signares' residences were the centers of entertainment and recre-

* Knight-Baylac 1970b: 401–2. It appears that some of the domestic slaves had their own slaves (p. 405).

ation at Saint-Louis and Gorée, inasmuch as both communities
lacked cafés, theaters, opera houses, and other diversions popular
with Europeans of the time. The *folgars*, or "balls," featured European-style dancing by mixed couples and provided *signares* with
opportunities for displaying their beauty, richest costumes, jewelry,
dancing ability, and social graces. Though the principal purpose
of the *folgars* was social and recreational, it seems certain that they
had other functions as well. What better opportunity for an
unattached or newly arrived European to meet a potential partner,
perhaps through the introduction and manipulation of a *signare*
who was married to one of the most influential men in the government, Company, or military garrison, and who was also acting as
matchmaker, preceptor, and confidant for female relatives and
friends? To be sure, such matchmaking would be concerned with
important commercial opportunities, especially when the man had
privileged access to trade goods, shipping, or other resources largely
controlled by the Europeans in the community.

Folgars must likewise have served as occasions to acculturate
members of the community to elite social mores. If the *signares*
and Europeans held center stage, there were also *griot* musicians,
domestic slaves serving refreshments, and numerous onlookers
taking it all in. Girls and young women, especially, would have
observed the *signares* and European men closely, memorizing the
dance steps, listening to their conversations, and learning their
mannerisms. Slave or free, they would have watched in anticipa-
tion of opportunities to come.* The *folgars* and other recreations
arranged by the *signares* thus represented an admirable combina-
tion of pleasure and business, with a style and character far removed from the debaucheries associated with European recreations
in forts, factories, and settlements elsewhere on the coast—excesses
of all sorts precipitated by boredom, homesickness, poor health,
and depression, all of which contributed to a mean and short-lived
existence in West Africa. Marriage to *signares* provided Europeans

---

* For the heterogeneous assemblage attending a *folgar* at Saint-Louis in
1841, see the watercolor by Edward Auguste Nousveaux reproduced in Henri
Nicholas Frey, *Côte Occidentale d'Afrique* (Paris, 1890), pp. 12–13.

with a life-style, a regimen, that contributed much to their survival and well-being in tropical Africa.

Certain realities, sometimes forgotten, concerning Europeans living in eighteenth- and early-nineteenth-century West Africa need to be appreciated. Europeans generally suffered from chronic poor health as a result of infection by malaria, dysenteries, and other tropical ailments imperfectly diagnosed and treated. Prélong, who examined the hospital records on Gorée, reported that between one-sixth and one-fifth of the Europeans there died each year; for Saint-Louis, he asserted, the rate was three in ten. Nearly all the deaths occurred during the rainy season, from July to October.* Under the circumstances, a European living in a *signare*'s household enjoyed the best possible conditions: a companion who spoke his language and was familiar with European ways, a stable home life, regular and well-prepared meals, and sensible recreational outlets, all of which were conducive to good health, both physical and psychological. And during periods of illness, he could rely on nursing and attentive care from the *signare* and her female domestics.

Senegambia and the Upper Guinea Coast in Changing Times

The 1780's may well represent the high point of "signareship" in Senegal. The generation of European conflicts following the French Revolution caused considerable disruption of West African commerce. Gorée was captured by a British squadron in 1800, retaken by French forces in January 1804, and captured again by the British later the same year and held by them until the end of the Napoleonic wars. Following the French surrender of Saint-Louis in July 1809, the trade of the Senegambia stabilized somewhat; but the suppression of the slave trade contributed to years

---

* Prélong 1793: 264. Medical theories and treatments of the time are interestingly described in Philip D. Curtin, *The Image of Africa; British Ideas and Action, 1780–1850* (Madison, Wisc., 1964), pp. 71–87. Curtin calculates that "somewhere between 25 and 75 percent of any group of Europeans newly arrived on the Coast died within the first year. Thereafter, the death rate was much less, perhaps on the order of 10 percent per annum, but still substantial" (p. 71).

of commercial disorganization in the Senegambia and Upper Guinea Coast, until the commercialization of peanuts in the 1830's and 1840's provided a new economic base for the region.

The peace treaty ending the Napoleonic wars returned Saint-Louis and Gorée to France. As a consequence, many of the British traders who had settled in Senegal during the war years moved to the Gambia, where a detachment of British troops founded a new settlement, Bathurst, on Banjul Island at the mouth of the Gambia River in March 1816. The British traders often were accompanied by *signares,* who brought their families and domestic slaves. The latter, together with additional artisans engaged from Saint-Louis and Gorée, constructed residences and business establishments along the lines of those in Senegal. The number of Wolofs who settled in Bathurst was so considerable that "Jollof Town" became the settlement's most populous section. The business section was known as "Portuguese Town," since many Luso-Africans from along the Gambia River, Cacheu, Bissau, and the Cape Verde Islands moved to Bathurst. Thus the settlement of Bathurst owes much to "overlapping" Eurafrican traditions.*

The *signares* (termed *senoras* in the Gambia) lent a distinctive character to Bathurst in the early years of the settlement. The families that came from Senegal seem to have remained together, and there was considerable visiting back and forth with relatives in Saint-Louis and Gorée, which would have served to reinforce the social patterns derived from there. Yet for reasons that need to be elucidated, the institution of "signareship" did not take roots in the Gambia or continue beyond the first generation. Seemingly it was stifled by the influx of new arrivals from Britain, few of whom—whether traders, government officials, or military officers —deviated from "proper" British behavior to live openly with Eurafrican or African women, whatever they might do clandestinely. British authors are discreet about such matters, but it can

* For the early years of Bathurst and the contributions of the British traders and *signares* from Senegal, see J. M. Gray, *A History of the Gambia* (London, 1966), chap. 21; and F. Mahoney, "Notes on Mulattoes of the Gambia Before the Mid-Nineteenth Century," *Transactions of the Historical Society of Ghana,* 8 (1965), pp. 120–29.

be discerned that, in contrast to the family lives of the traders and their *signares,* there developed at Bathurst a rootless bachelor community of a type found elsewhere in British areas of West Africa. Open and unrepentant racism was one characteristic of this community; two others were reckless gambling and alcoholism.*

South of the Gambia, in the long-established Portuguese settlements at Cacheu and Bissau, circumstances were similar to those in Senegal. Some *nharas* wielded influence unmatched elsewhere in West Africa. The redoubtable Rosa de Carvalho Alvarenga was the dominant personality in the Cacheu area in the 1820's and 1830's: she was called upon to mediate differences between Portuguese authorities and local Africans as a court of last resort. Much of the authority exercised by her famous son, Honório Pereira Barreto, who became governor of Portuguese Guinea, derived from her preeminent influence in the area. Another illustrious *nhara* was Mae Aurelia Correia, whose influence with the Bijago people contributed to the fact that she and her husband, Caetano José Nozolini, dominated the commerce of the Geba and Grande rivers in the 1830's and 1840's. Along the Nunez, Pongo, and other rivers to the south where Eurafrican families operated as intermediaries, incoming European and Eurafrican traders who wanted to establish factories found it expedient to marry local Eurafrican women, some of whom were leading traders. A list of such notable women from the 1830's to the 1850's would include Eliza Proctor, Mary Faber, and Isabella Lightburn.†

* European debauchery is a neglected theme in West African history. British authors are generally very discreet, but for insightful accounts relating to The Gambia and Sierra Leone, see Thomas Eyre Poole, *Life, Scenery, and Customs in Sierra Leone and the Gambia* (London, 1850), vol. 1, pp. 159–61, 290–98; W. Winwood Reade, *Savage Africa* (New York, 1864), pp. 63–65, 323–24; and George Thompson, *The Palm Land or West Africa, Illustrated* (London, 1858; new ed., 1969), pp. 356–57.

† Little has been published concerning women traders in these areas. See the present author's "Enoch Richmond Ware, African Trader: 1839–1850, Years of Apprenticeship," *The American Neptune,* 30, no. 3 (July 1970), pp. 178–85, and no. 4 (Oct. 1970), pp. 232–33; Christopher Fyfe, *A History of Sierra Leone* (London, 1962), pp. 220, 226–27, 254–55; and Bruce L. Mouser, "History of Trade and Politics in the Guinea Rivers, 1790–1865" (unpublished Ph.D. dissertation, Indiana University, 1971), chaps. 5 and 6.

Perspectives on "Signareship"

If the development of signareship in Senegal has yet to be fully explored—especially with regard to the question of the social origins of the women concerned—the main lines of development seem clear. Signareship represented an economic nexus between European men pursuing personal gain (usually illegally) and African and Eurafrican women determined to acquire European merchandise. It was the women who provided access to African commercial networks, furnished households with skilled domestic slaves, and proved indispensable as interpreters of African languages and cultures: in short, *signares* skillfully manipulated two trading complexes and cultures to further their own ends. Yet signareship represented a social nexus, too, and *signares* helped create a way of life, an *ambiance*, that went far beyond the economic relationship. Once the process was well begun, it was so advantageous and attractive to all involved, at least in Senegal, that it became self-perpetuating. The two societies, Senegalese and French, partially blending, largely coexisting, created a complex cultural relationship that transcends facile explanation or analysis.

The Dual-Sex Political System in Operation: Igbo Women and Community Politics in Midwestern Nigeria

KAMENE OKONJO

A NUMBER of West African traditional societies have political systems in which the major interest groups are defined and represented by sex. We can label such systems of organization "dual-sex" systems, for within them each sex manages its own affairs, and women's interests are represented at all levels. Dual-sex organization contrasts with the "single-sex" system that obtains in most of the Western world, where political status-bearing roles are predominantly the preserve of men. In the single-sex system, women can achieve distinction and recognition only by taking on the roles of men in public life and performing them well. One of the most prominent examples of a dual-sex political system is found among those Igbo who live west of the Niger River in southeastern Nigeria. This paper will describe the operation of that system in precolonial times and will assess the effects of colonial rule and social change upon it.

The existence of dual-sex systems in West Africa is particularly interesting because most West African societies are patrilineal and patrilocal. As elsewhere, men rule and dominate. Seeing this outwardly patriarchal framework, many observers concluded that the position of women in these societies was totally subordinate; as a result of their misconceptions, they produced a distorted picture of the "oppressive" African man and the "deprived" African woman. This situation has been noted by Afigbo (1974), and it is now the task of other writers, particularly African writers, to help correct it.

Even before Afigbo's work, however, attempts to change these

impressions had been undertaken by some non-African authors.
Sylvia Leith-Ross wrote about the Igbo women of Owerri Province
in the 1930's; and the works of Margaret Green, G. T. Basden, and
W. Northcote Thomas also clearly brought out the important
roles that Igbo women played in traditional village life.* Denise
Paulme's collection *Women of Tropical Africa* was another laud-
able effort in the study of African women. And another paper
dealing exclusively with Nigerian women from a new perspective
(by Judith Van Allen) appears immediately after this one in the
present volume. My paper, like that of Van Allen, concentrates
on a specific ethnic group and seeks to show that Nigerian women
in traditional times were active political animals—this in support of Lebeuf's statement that "there are no valid historical
grounds for explaining the present lack of interest in political
matters so often found among African women as being a heritage
of the past" (1963: 96).

In Nigerian society in general, and Igbo society in particular,
women's lack of interest in political matters—or more accurately
their invisibility in present-day politics—is a legacy of the colonial
past. As Van Allen points out in her paper in this volume, the
British colonialists introduced sexist Victorian values into all
aspects of the life (religious, economic, and political) of the colonized Igbo. Such Victorian values extolled the ideology that "a
woman's place is in the home" and saw women's minds as not
strong enough for the masculine subjects of science, business, and
politics. The now famous 1929 Women's War (styled the "Aba
Riots" by the colonialists), in which over 60 Igbo women were shot
down, led to British inquiries but resulted in no greater recognition for Igbo women in village or local politics (see Okonjo
1974). So firmly entrenched were the British in their attitudes that
they were unable to see or understand the roles women played in
Nigerian political life.

* Sylvia Leith-Ross, *African Women: A Study of the Ibo of Nigeria* (1939;
2d edition 1965); Margaret Green, *Igbo Village Affairs* (1964); G. T. Basden,
Niger Ibos (1966); and Northcote Thomas, *Anthropological Report on the Ibo-
Speaking Peoples of Nigeria* (1914) are to all intents and purposes anthropologi-
cal narratives on the Igbo. The former two concentrate on the Igbo east of the
Niger, whereas the latter two also include material on the Igbo west of the
Niger. These four works constitute major sources for this paper.

Traditional Igbo Political Institutions

Though they share a common language and similar culture, the Igbo of Nigeria had no homogeneous political system. The 7,500,-000 Igbo who live east of the Niger River traditionally had what Afigbo calls a "democratic village republic" system of political organization, with authority widely dispersed in autonomous units (see Afigbo 1972; Green 1964: 5). The remaining 500,000 Igbo on the western side of the Niger and in the riverine towns of Onitsha and Ossomali, heavily influenced by the kingdom of Benin to the north, developed what Afigbo calls a "constitutional village monarchy" system.

In both types of systems the units were small, and political authority was widely dispersed along the following lines: between the sexes; among lineages and kinship institutions; by age grades; among secret and title societies; and among oracles, diviners, and other professional groups. There was no clear separation between judicial, executive, and legislative functions, and no distinction between the political and the religious in the governmental process. Both systems were what we characterized earlier as dual-sex systems: each sex generally managed its own affairs and had its own kinship institutions, age grades, and secret and title societies (see generally Afigbo 1972).

Among the Igbo who live on the western side of the Niger, the management of village affairs by sexes was more pronounced and more visible than it was on the eastern side, perhaps because of the influence of monarchy and the sharp delineation of roles and statuses. All the Igbo of each political unit to the west of the Niger were subject to two local monarchs, both of whom were crowned and acknowledged heads who lived in palaces and ruled from thrones. The two monarchs were the male *obi*, who in theory was the acknowledged head of the whole community but who in practice was concerned more with the male section of the community, and the female *omu*, who in theory was the acknowledged mother of the whole community but who in practice was charged with concern for the female section.

It is important to note that the *omu* was not a queen in the

Western sense. She was neither the wife of a king nor the reigning daughter of a king who died without a male heir. In fact, she did not derive her status in any way from an attachment or relationship to a king. The word *omu* itself means "mother," being derived from *nne omumu* or *omunwa*, "she who bears children." Even though some authors (notably Basden 1966) have taken the trouble to explain that "queen" was simply a courtesy title given to the *omu*, I feel that it is better not to employ that Western term for her at all.

The *obi* had his *onotu*, his council of dignitaries, to aid him and act as a restraining force against his arbitrary use of power. This council usually contained twelve elders who had taken the full titles of the community. As the female counterpart to the *obi*, the *omu* had her own cabinet (called the *ilogo*) made up of councillors with titular ranks and duties corresponding on a one-to-one basis to those of the *obi*'s councillors. The *omu*'s councillors were generally women who had taken the full women's titles of the community and women whose husbands had taken the full men's titles (Okonjo 1975; Basden 1966: 140).

The *ilogo* could challenge male authority in the community if necessary, for Igbo oral tradition tells of an *omu* who led a boycott by all the women of her community in which the women refused to cook for their husbands. Under the pressure of having to prepare their own meals, the men capitulated to the women's demands (Henderson 1972: 376, 525). But the dual nature of the system aimed at a harmonious and effective division of labor by which both sexes would receive adequate attention to their needs. And in fact there is no historical record of a conflict between an *obi* and an *omu*, or of any clash of functions. For the male and female cabinets, despite their similarities in structure, were meant to insure complementarity in their parallel functions. There was no duplication of roles, since duties were clearly described and delineated.

Duties of the omu and her cabinet. One of the major functions of the *omu* and her cabinet was to oversee the community market, which was held every four days. In traditional Igbo society marketing was the woman's domain. A woman prepared her family's daily meals and provided such essentials for the staple palm-nut soup as pepper, fish, palm oil, and salt through marketing her farm surplus. She also marketed her husband's agricultural surplus. The *omu*, in her capacity as head of the female side of the community, with her cabinet determined the rules and regulations under which the market—the domain of women—was to function. This included fixing prices for goods sold in the market and setting market prohibitions. The *omu* and her councillors presided over each market and acted as a court in judging cases and disciplining (largely through fines) any woman who broke the laws of the market. The *omu*'s cabinet included a policewoman (*awo*), who was responsible for seeing that the fixed prices and taboos in the market were observed; she arrested offenders and brought them before the *omu*'s court of justice. Among the market taboos I noted during my fieldwork in two towns were the following: (1) no one was to gather up sand from the market square when the market was in session; (2) widows in mourning were not to enter the market or engage in market transactions; (3) there was to be no fighting in the market; (4) there were to be no covered or upturned basins; (5) cocks were not to crow in the market; (6) women were not to carry things with both hands, i.e., one hand was to be left free; (7) palm nuts were not to be sold in bunches, but had to be separated first; and (8) peppers were to be boiled before being offered for sale.* These taboos were deeply rooted in traditional beliefs about medicine and magic. It was felt that violation of them could result in consistently poor market attendance, unfriendliness on the part of neighboring towns, epidemics, and death. To guard against such calamities, the *omu* performed "market medicines" and made occasional sacrifices to the supernatural powers—the community gods and ancestral spirits.

In an interview with the *omu* of Obamkpa, I asked "Our Mother, what part do you play in the running of this town?" She replied (in part) as follows.

* Much of the material on which this paper is based comes from data I collected during fieldwork in Obamkpa and Ogwashi-uku towns in Midwestern Nigeria in 1971 and 1972. In particular, I had the opportunity to interview the *omu* of Obamkpa.

My child, the *obi* is the head of the men, and I am the head of the women. I and my cabinet represent the women in any important town gatherings and deliberations. If decisions arrived at are such that the womenfolk are to be told about them, I get a woman [*onye oga*] to sound the gong [*ekwe*] to assemble the women. On less important occasions, my cabinet members pass the word around among the women by word of mouth.

If there is drought, we curse whoever caused it. If there is sickness and people are dying, my cabinet goes naked in the night with live brands to curse whoever brought it. If there is sickness in the next town, I do something with my cabinet to insure that sickness does not enter this town. There are medicines we make at the entrance to the town. These are just a few of my duties. I am the mother of the people, you know, and I have to insure in any way I can that they enjoy continued good health and happiness.

The *omu* added that market transactions could not begin unless she appeared to declare the market open or sent a cabinet member or messenger there with her medicinal chalk container.

Sitting on her throne in her house, the *omu* handled cases involving women that were brought to her from throughout the town. Men who had complaints against their wives that were beyond the competence of the family circle to deal with came to the *omu* to seek advice or redress. The *omu* gave advice to wives who sought it, and where she felt that she could not handle the situation herself, she and her cabinet sought the cooperation of the *obi* in council. Such cooperation in cases involving both sexes was the rule rather than the exception, especially in matters involving a man and his wife. Among the Igbo, arriving at a consensus on any major issue was vital. It was not enough for justice to be done; that such justice was done ought to be transparently clear to everybody.

In some towns, widows who had completed the stipulated mourning period went to the *omu* for the final rites of head-shaving and burning of the cloth used during the mourning period, and for the ceremonial cleansing bath. The *omu* had the prerogative of shortening the mourning period for a woman in cases of ill-health, pregnancy, lactation, or hardship.

The *omu* had direct responsibility for the institution of title-taking among women. Thus, if the *omu* had not acquired all the women's titles of the community at the time of her nomination by the town oracle, her relatives rallied to help her secure them, since she could only encourage and perpetuate an institution of which she was fully a part. One of the regulations that the *omu* of Obamkpa has passed to encourage title-taking states that no woman can be buried in a coffin unless she has taken the *inachi* title.

The duty of the *omu* was to represent all the women of her community, and consequently she had to be very responsive to her constituency. Though the women of the community did not form a corporate body, the *omu* sought their cooperation in and approval of any major decisions through the institution called the *ikporo ani*. The *ikporo ani* was a representative body of women chosen from each section or quarter of the village or town. Sometimes representation was on the basis of lineage, but selection was always based on achievement: the representatives were not necessarily titled women, but were those who had previously demonstrated qualities of logic and ability to "talk well"; as such they had come to enjoy the confidence of their areas or lineages and were regarded as "leaders of opinion." The women of the *ikporo ani* would meet at the summons of the *omu* and her councillors. They would report back to the other women, and again to the *omu*, until consensus was reached on any major issue. In this manner the entire *ikporo ani* felt part of the deliberations and bound by the final decisions.

In addition to the *omu*, her councillors, and the *ikporo ani*, who represented the entire women's constituency, there were other women's political institutions in the traditional Igbo system that functioned on a smaller base. Among these were the *umuada* and the *inyemedi*, which operated at the village or lineage level. Since Igbo society was exogamous and patrilocal, a woman had to leave her natal village when she married. To deal with the dislocations of this system and insure a simulated lineage structure for married women, a system of reciprocal ties was built up between a woman's two villages—the one in which she was born and the one into which she married. Women thus came to have two homes. In their natal village they were *umuada*, or daughters of the lineage and/or village; in the village of their marriage they were *inyemedi* (co-wives), i.e., co-wives of the village or lineage. In both they formed themselves into an *otu* (organization), thus giving rise to *otu umuada* and *otu inyemedi*.

The otu umuada. The *otu umuada* included all the married, unmarried, widowed, and divorced daughters of a lineage or village group. These women acted as political pressure groups in their natal villages in order to achieve desired objectives. They stopped quarrels and prevented wars. So powerful was their reputation that their natal villages had to reckon with them and their possible reaction to every major decision (Green 1964: 66).

As daughters of the lineage, their social position was significantly higher than that of the *inyemedi*. The former had the acknowledged prerogative of addressing the latter as "our wives," which in this patriarchal society indicated a lower status. The *otu umuada* could demand homage or duties from the *otu inyemedi*, and they would be obliged to comply. Apparently a spirit of goodwill and "sweet rivalry" surrounded such demands.

The higher status of the *umuada* was further indicated by their ability to perform certain rites and sacrifices. Their leader, the most senior *ada* of the lineage—the *ada-ebo*—had the duty of performing the final absolution rites for a new bride. The bride had to confess any clandestine affairs she had had since becoming affianced to her husband. If the *ada-ebo* was satisfied with the confession, she had the prerogative of granting absolution to the bride from the sins of her "previous life" through the performance of sacrifices. Moreover, the *ada-ebo* received confessions from adulterous lineage wives and performed purificatory rites for them; she also carried out purifying rituals in lineage houses and places regarded as polluted. These rites were vital if the gods and ancestral spirits were to continue to bless the lineage with good health, bounty, and offspring (Basden 1966: 225; Thomas 1914: 57).

The otu inyemedi. As is the case with women in other patrilocal societies, Igbo women had few rights in their marital villages. Though their children had full membership in the lineage, they themselves continued to be regarded as strangers. Consequently, they looked back to their natal villages as their only real homes when they needed shelter and succor.

Some villages would not allow a deceased daughter to be buried in her husband's village "among strangers, like one without a home to return to." She was regarded as having only temporarily left home to perform a duty (marriage and procreation); her death could not sever her from her own people. When a deceased daughter was borne back to her natal village, the cortege chanted *"Etete je afia olu uno"* ("The market basket always returns home"), and the chorus answered *"Ije inua o, Eiya a, ije inua o"* ("You went, you are back, *Eiya a*, you went, you are back"). Other villages would not allow deceased wives to be buried in their land unless such wives had borne sons.* In the light of the difficulties women faced in living away from their natal villages, we can see why institutions of wives emerged to safeguard their interests.

At the head of the *otu inyemedi* was the *anasi*, the most senior wife of the village or lineage in terms of length of marriage. And since the Igbo practiced polygyny, in individual households, too, the senior wife was accorded the status of *anasi*, which carried with it a number of rights and privileges. At the lineage level, though, the *anasi* ran the biggest "household" of all the lineage wives. She gathered her co-wives together, presided over meetings, advised or admonished women, and generally mothered everybody. At the meetings of the *otu inyemedi*, decisions were made on how to help fellow wives in times of illness or stress, and on how to keep lineage or village streams and markets clean. (These latter decisions were taken at the urging of the *omu*.) The women decided how to discipline recalcitrant, lazy, or adulterous husbands; they also handled cases of adultery and other breaches of marriage law, delivering swift and drastic punishments as deterrents to further delinquency. On the eastern side of the Niger, where women did most of the farming, they also made decisions about planting and harvesting

---

* Ogwashi-uku is an example of a town that will only allow deceased wives to be buried there if they have borne sons. Only sons can perpetuate a lineage, can minister to and become ancestral spirits. Not to have male children is regarded as the greatest calamity that can befall a couple.

and took joint action to destroy animals that had damaged their crops, even when such animals belonged to men of the community (Green 1964: 173–74).

Age-grade organizations. Though there was no direct female counterpart to the *otu ogbo* (age-grade organization, which originally embraced mainly men), girls of the same age group formed *otu umu agbogho* ("groups of eligible girls") as preparation for marriage. In these groups they practiced dancing and prepared for participation in a major dance that was to be a high point of their lives. Young men also participated in the dances by providing instrumental music to accompany the girls' chants. The dance groups provided training in social conduct for their members: for example, anyone violating dance-group rules by fighting or using obscene language was immediately expelled and became the object of derisive songs.

In the absence of other group activities for girls at that stage of their growth, dance-group membership provided a unique opportunity for girls to get to know one another better and to develop friendships that often lasted a lifetime. I recall hearing that my mother's best friend was her partner in the *egwu siliki* ("silken dance") some five decades ago.

Title societies. The attainment of titles was the only method by which women in traditional Igbo society could improve their social standing. Though the possession of titles did not in itself confer political power on the owner, a woman with titles enjoyed respect and could attain political power when she combined her acquisition of titles with a demonstration of leadership ability. Doubtless it was easier for titleholders to enter the decision-making bodies of their community than for those who had no titles to do so.

Titled women as a group never organized for political reasons, nor did they make decisions affecting the community as an association. At the community level, political decisions were the prerogative of the *omu* and her cabinet, although the *omu* often appointed her cabinet from titled women and informally sought their advice on baffling matters.

In ascending order of importance, the titles women in Obamkpa acquired were *inwene, ikenga, inachi,* and *ichi omaku.* As a mark of distinction titled women wore intricately threaded cowries and *aka* (red glass beads) around their wrists, with variations according to rank. There were also particular salutations appropriate for each title. Title-holding brought economic advantages to women: the acquisition of titles was a form of savings that insured them against destitution. Titleholders, including the *omu,* who held all titles and had the duty of encouraging other women to acquire them, shared the high title fees and other proceeds initiates paid.

Colonial Rule and the Decline of Dual-Sex Institutions

Colonial rule in Nigeria in the first decade of this century marked the beginning of the end of equality of the sexes in village as well as in national politics. As Basden noted earlier (1966: xiii), "what is not realised as it should be is that Native Law and Custom received its deathblow when the British Administration became operative in the Ibo country.... What now passes for native law and custom is but a travesty of what it was in the old days; it is but the shell; the kernel has been destroyed." The system of warrant chiefs that the British introduced in the guise of "traditional institutions" has been thoroughly discussed elsewhere (see Afigbo 1972). What is often overlooked is that under colonialism women in southeastern Nigeria suffered the greatest loss of power. Men could boast of some measure of participation because the British chose them to fill the newly created posts. In many ways the Women's War of 1929—the so-called "Aba Riots"—can be seen as Igbo women's demonstration for the right to be consulted on matters that affected them.

On the western side of the Niger, where monarchical organization made indirect rule relatively easy for the British to establish, the only monarch the British recognized was the male monarch, the *obi.* He alone received a monthly paycheck. His female counterpart, the *omu,* was relegated to the background, where her only role was to serve as intermediary between the *obi* and the women of the town. She could no longer make policy but had to take orders from the *obi.* When the British instituted local government

reforms in the 1930's, no mention was made of the institution of
the *omu* (Okonjo 1974: 19); throughout Nigeria women's political
roles were being eliminated (Egharevba 1960: 75–76; Biobaku
1960).

The *omu* lost her prestige and her clientele as her political and
religious functions were replaced by colonial rule and Christianity.
The introduction of clinics and foreign drugs replaced the sacrifices she and her *ilogo* had made in their role as guardians of the
health and welfare of the community. Cases that formerly had
come before her now went to the British-appointed colonial magis-
trate. The introduction of imported goods into the marketplace
ruined her system of price-fixing. New roads ended the practice
of making "market medicines" to induce customers to attend the
village market. The traditional title-taking that the *omu* had presided over was displaced as Christian converts acquired the new
title of *mississi* (Mrs.) that came with marriage in church and
brought higher status in the new social order. Other traditional
women's organizations lost some of their meaning as well: the
otu umuada and *otu inyemedi* no longer had intervillage disputes
to arbitrate; and schools replaced the social functions of the dance
societies.

The Resurgence of Traditional Values in Independent Nigeria

Since Nigeria achieved independence in 1960, the institution
of the *omu* has enjoyed a resurgence and has been largely "recon-
ditioned." After the long period of nonrecognition of the *omu*
during the colonial era, a renewed spirit of loyalty to her and support of her role is readily apparent in Igbo communities. A new
omu was installed in Ogwashi-uku in 1972 with much fanfare—it
was the first such event in the town since independence. Her cabinet retains its one-to-one correspondence with that of the *obi*, and
her duties have taken on new dimensions and directions. She and
her cabinet have embarked on self-help activities that include the
building of improved market stalls and the formation of weaving
cooperatives.

A Roman Catholic, the current *omu* of Ogwashi-uku has combined being a Christian with traditional service to her community. She seems to have evolved a harmonious working arrangement with the government, whereby she still fixes the prices of agricultural goods and handles minor cases in the market. Some market taboos are still in force, and violations of them now constitute many of the minor cases she deals with. Policemen come to her aid when cases cease to be minor—for instance, where fighting breaks out or bodily injury is involved. She and her cabinet are still committed to the improvement of the market and continue to make their "market medicine."

The new *omu* continues to occupy an elevated social position. She retains a uniformed policewoman and a "mouthpiece" (*onu omu*), who transmits messages and judgments in the marketplace on her behalf, as befits her quasi-spiritual position.

The institution of title-taking is also slowly staging a comeback. Now what actually prevents most women from acquiring titles is the choice of allocation of scarce economic resources if they have children to educate. The high charges involved in acquiring titles, and the fact that they cannot be inherited by one's children, deter some women from taking them. The new clientele for titles is coming from the ranks of salaried women, urbanites (particularly traders), and wives of wealthy men, who send sums to their home villages to cover all the expenses of title-taking.

The *otu inyemedi* and the *otu umuada* have also regained much of their precolonial vitality. They have lost their functions as arbiters of intervillage disputes to the courts, but they continue to carry out many of their other traditional functions—with certain modifications in order not to run afoul of the law.

Since independence, then, there has been a visible and deliberate move to resuscitate those roles that women traditionally played in public life. Both traditional women's organizations and new associations (such as contribution and prayer associations) have changed and developed to cater to new needs. Though women have been making progress on the village and community level in regaining much of the position they held in the precolonial dual-sex system, the national political level remains almost exclusively single-sex. There has been little if any appreciation of the complementary political roles men and women held in traditional society. Few women have been appointed to positions of importance by the military government in Nigeria. In theory, modern political roles are supposed to be "sex blind," in that office-holders are seen as representing a constituency of both sexes. Yet the absence of women from meaningful political representation in independent Nigeria can be viewed as showing the strength of the legacy of single-sex politics that the British colonial masters left behind.

'Aba Riots' or Igbo 'Women's War'? Ideology, Stratification, and the Invisibility of Women

JUDITH VAN ALLEN

THE EVENTS that occurred in Calabar and Owerri provinces in southeastern Nigeria in November and December of 1929, and that have come to be known in Western social-science literature as the "Aba Riots," are a natural focus for an investigation of the impact of colonialism on Igbo women.* In the development and results of that crisis can be found all the elements of the system that has weakened women's position in Igboland—and in much of the rest of Africa as well.† The "Aba Riots" are also a nice symbol of the "invisibility" of women: "Aba Riots" is the name adopted by the British; the Igbo called it *Ogu Umunwanyi*, the "Women's War" (Uchendu 1965: 5; Okonjo 1974: 25, n. 40). This is more than a word game. In politics, the control of language means the control of history. The dominant group and the subordinate group almost always give different names to their conflicts, and where the dominant group alone writes history, its choice of terminology will be perpetuated. Examples of this manipulation of language abound

* This paper is a revised version of papers presented at the 1971 African Studies Association meeting and at the 1974 UCLA African Studies Center Colloquium on "Women and Change in Africa: 1870–1970." I am grateful to Terence O. Ranger, who organized the UCLA colloquium, and to the other participants (particularly Agnes Aidoo, Jim Brain, Cynthia Brantley, Temma Kaplan, and Margaret Strobel) for their encouragement, useful criticisms, and suggestions.
† Today the Igbo, numbering about 8.7 million, live mainly in the East-Central State of Nigeria, with some half million in the neighboring Mid-Western State. The area in which they live corresponds approximately to Igboland at the time of the colonial conquest.

in American history, as any examination of standard textbooks will reveal.

Calabar and Owerri provinces covered roughly the southeast and southwest quarters of Igboland, the traditional home of the Igbo peoples. In November of 1929, thousands of Igbo women from these provinces converged on the Native Administration centers— settlements that generally included the headquarters and residence of the British colonial officer for the district, a Native Court building and a jail, and a bank or white trader's store (if such existed in the district).* The women chanted, danced, sang songs of ridicule, and demanded the caps of office (the official insignia) of the Warrant Chiefs, the Igbo chosen from each village by the British to sit as members of the Native Court. At a few locations the women broke into prisons and released prisoners. Sixteen Native Courts were attacked, and most of these were broken up or burned. The "disturbed area" covered about 6,000 square miles and contained about two million people. It is not known how many women were involved, but the figure was in the tens of thousands. On two occasions, British District Officers called in police and troops, who fired on the women and left a total of more than 50 dead and 50 wounded. No one on the other side was seriously injured.†

The British "won," and they have imposed their terminology on history; only a very few scholars have recorded that the Igbo called this the "Women's War." And in most histories of Nigeria today one looks in vain for any mention that women were even involved. "Riots," the term used by the British, conveys a picture of uncontrolled, irrational action, involving violence to property or persons, or both. It serves to justify the "necessary action to restore

* A number of Ibibio women from Calabar were also drawn into the rebellion, but the mass of the participants were Igbo.

† Perham 1937: 202–12. Afigbo 1972 and Gailey 1970 give more detailed accounts of the Women's War than does Perham; all three, however, base their descriptions on the reports of the two Commissions of Enquiry, issued as Sessional Papers of the Nigerian Legislative Council (Nos. 12 and 28 of 1930), on the Minutes of Evidence issued with No. 28, and on intelligence reports made in the early 1930's by political officers. Afigbo, an Igbo scholar, provides the most extensive and authoritative account of the three, and he is particularly good on traditional Igbo society.

order," and it accords with the British picture of the outpouring of Igbo from their villages as some sort of spontaneous frenzy, explained by the general "excitability" of these "least disciplined" of African peoples (Perham 1937: 219). "Aba Riots," in addition, neatly removes women from the picture. What we are left with is "some riots at Aba"—not by women, not involving complex organization, and not ranging over most of southeastern Nigeria.

To the British Commissions of Enquiry established to investigate the events, the Igbo as a whole were felt to be dissatisfied with the general system of administration. The women simply were seen as expressing this underlying general dissatisfaction. The British explanation for the fact that women rather than men "rioted" was twofold: the women were aroused by a rumor that they would be taxed at a time of declining profits from the palm products trade; and they believed themselves to be immune from danger because they thought British soldiers would not fire on women (Perham 1937: 213–17). The possibility that women might have acted because as women they were particularly distressed by the Native Administration system does not seem to have been taken any more seriously by the Commissions than women's demands in testimony that they be included in the Native Courts (Leith-Ross 1939: 165).

The term "Women's War," in contrast to "Aba Riots," retains both the presence and the significance of the women, for the word "war" in this context derived from the pidgin English expression "making war," an institutionalized form of punishment employed by Igbo women and also known as "sitting on a man." To "sit on" or "make war on" a man involved gathering at his compound at a previously agreed-upon time, dancing, singing scurrilous songs detailing the women's grievances against him (and often insulting him along the way by calling his manhood into question), banging on his hut with the pestles used for pounding yams, and, in extreme cases, tearing up his hut (which usually meant pulling the roof off). This might be done to a man who particularly mistreated his wife, who violated the women's market rules, or who persistently let his cows eat the women's crops. The women would stay at his hut all night and day, if necessary, until he repented and promised to mend his ways (Leith-Ross 1939: 109; Harris 1940: 146–48).*

"Women's War" thus conveys an action by women that is also an extension of their traditional method for settling grievances with men who had acted badly toward them. Understood from the Igbo perspective, this term confirms the existence of Igbo women's traditional institutions, for "making war" was the ultimate sanction available to women for enforcing their judgments. The use of the word "war" in this specifically Igbo sense directs attention to the existence of those female political and economic institutions that were never taken into account by the British, and that still have not been sufficiently recognized by contemporary social scientists writing about the development of nationalist movements.

Conventionally, Western influence has been seen as "emancipating" African women through (1) the weakening of kinship bonds; (2) the provision of "free choice" in Christian monogamous marriage; (3) the suppression of "barbarous" practices (female circumcision, ostracism of mothers of twins, slavery); (4) the opening of schools; and (5) the introduction of modern medicine, hygiene, and (sometimes) female suffrage. What has not been seen by Westerners is that for some African women—and Igbo women are a striking example—actual or potential autonomy, economic independence, and political power did not grow out of Western influences but existed already in traditional "tribal" life. To the extent that Igbo women have participated in any political action— whether anticolonial or nationalist struggles, local community development, or the Biafran war—it has been not so much because of the influence of Western values as despite that influence.

Traditional Igbo Political Institutions

In traditional Igbo society, women did not have a political role equal to that of men. But they did have a role—or more accurately, a series of roles—despite the patrilineal organization of Igbo society. Their possibilities of participating in traditional politics

* Similar tactics were also used against women for serious offenses (see Leith-Ross 1939: 97).

must be examined in terms of both structures and values. Also involved is a consideration of what it means to talk about "politics" and "political roles" in a society that has no differentiated, centralized governmental institutions.

Fallers (1963) suggests that for such societies, it is necessary to view "the polity or political system ... not as a concretely distinct part of the social system, but rather as a functional aspect of the whole social system: that aspect concerned with making and carrying out decisions regarding public policy, by whatever institutional means." Fallers's definition is preferable to several other functionalist definitions because it attempts to give some content to the category "political." Examples will make this clear. Let us take a society that has no set of differentiated political institutions to which we can ascribe Weber's "monopoly of the legitimate use of physical force within a given territory," and yet that holds together in reasonable order; we ask the question, What are the mechanisms of social control? To this may be added a second question, based on the notion that a basic governmental function is "authoritative allocation": What are the mechanisms that authoritatively allocate goods and services? A third common notion of politics is concerned with power relationships, and so we also ask, Who has power (or influence) over whom?

The problem with all of these approaches is that they are at the same time too broad and too narrow. If everything in a society that promotes order, resolves conflicts, allocates goods, or involves the power of one person over another is "political," then we have hardly succeeded in distinguishing the "political" as a special kind of activity or area or relationship. Igbo women certainly played a role in promoting order and resolving conflicts (Green 1947: 178–216; Leith-Ross 1939: 97, 106–9), but that does not make them political actors. In response to each of those broad definitions, we can still ask, Is this mechanism of social control or allocation, or this power relationship, a *political* mechanism or relationship? In answering that question, Fallers provides some help. It is their relationship to public policy that makes mechanisms, relationships, or activities "political."

There are many different concepts of "public" in Western thought. We will consider only two, chosen because we can possibly apply them to Igbo politics without producing a distorted picture. There seem to be actions taken, and distinctions made, in Igbo politics and language that make it not quite so ethnocentric to try to use these Western concepts. One notion of "public" relates it to issues that are of concern to the whole community; ends served by "political functions" are beneficial to the community as a whole. Although different individuals or groups may seek different resolutions of problems or disputes, the "political" can nevertheless be seen as encompassing all those human concerns and problems that are common to all the members of the community, or at least to large numbers of them. "Political" problems are shared problems that are appropriately dealt with through group action—their resolutions are collective, not individual. This separates them from "purely personal" problems. The second notion of "public" is that which is distinguished from "secret," that is, open to everyone's view, accessible to all members of the community. The settling of questions that concern the welfare of the community in a "public" way necessitates the sharing of "political knowledge"—the knowledge needed for participation in political discussion and decision. A system in which public policy is made publicly and the relevant knowledge is shared widely contrasts sharply with those systems in which a privileged few possess the relevant knowledge—whether priestly mysteries or bureaucratic expertise—and therefore control policy decisions.

Traditional Igbo society was predominantly patrilineal and segmental. People lived in "villages" composed of the scattered compounds of relatively close patrilineal kinsmen; and related villages formed what are usually referred to as "village groups," the largest functional political unit. Forde and Jones (1950: 9, 39) found between 4,000 and 5,000 village groups, ranging in population from several hundred to several thousand persons. Political power was diffuse, and leadership was fluid and informal. Community decisions were made and disputes settled through a variety of gatherings (villagewide assemblies; women's meetings; age grades; secret and title societies; contribution clubs; lineage groups; and congregations at funerals, markets, or annual rituals) as well as through appeals to oracles and diviners (Afigbo 1972: 13–36).* Decisions were made by discussion until mutual agreement was reached. Any adult present who had something to say on the matter under discussion was entitled to speak, so long as he or she said something that the others considered worth listening to; as the Igbo say, "A case forbids no one." Leaders were those who had "mouth"; age was respected, but did not confer leadership unless accompanied by wisdom and the ability to speak well. In village assemblies, after much discussion, a small group of elders retired for "consultation" and then offered a decision for the approval of the assembly (Uchendu 1965: 41–44; Green 1947: chaps. 7–11; Harris 1940: 142–43).

In some areas, the assemblies are said to have been of all adult males; in other areas, women reportedly participated in the assemblies, but were less likely to speak unless involved in the dispute and less likely to take part in "consultation." Women may have been among the "arbitrators" that disputants invited to settle particular cases; however, if one party to the dispute appealed to the village as a whole, male elders would have been more likely to offer the final settlement (Green 1947: 107, 112–13, 116–29, 169, 199). Age grades existed in most Igbo communities, but their functions varied; the predominant pattern seems to have been for young men's age grades to carry out decisions of the village assembly with regard to such matters as clearing paths, building

---

* Though there is variation among the Igbo, the general patterns described here apply fairly well to the southern Igbo, those involved in the Women's War. The chief exceptions to the above description occur among the western and riverain Igbo, who have what Afigbo terms a "constitutional village monarchy" system, and among the Afikpo of the Cross River, who have a double-descent system and low female participation in economic and political life (P. Ottenberg 1959 and 1965). The former are more hierarchically organized than other Igbo but are not stratified by sex, having a women's hierarchy parallel to that of the men (Nzirimo 1972); the latter are strongly stratified by sex, with the senior men's age grade dominating community decision-making. Afikpo women's age grades are weak; there is no *mikiri* or, because of the double-descent system,

bridges, or collecting fines (Uchendu 1965: 43). There was thus
no distinction among what we call executive, legislative, and judicial activities, and no political authority to issue commands. The
settling of a dispute could merge into a discussion of a new "rule,"
and acceptance by the disputants and the group hearing the dispute was necessary for the settlement of anything. Only within a
family compound could an individual demand obedience to orders; there the compound head offered guidance, aid, and protection to members of his family, and in return received respect,
obedience, and material tokens of good will. Neither was there
any distinction between the religious and the political: rituals and
"political" discussions were interwoven in patterns of action to
promote the good of the community; and rituals, too, were performed by various groups of women, men, and women and men
together (Afigbo 1972; Meek 1957: 98–99, 105; Uchendu 1965:
39–40).

Matters dealt with in the village assembly were those of common concern to all. They could be general problems for which
collective action was appropriate (for example, discussion might
center on how to make the village market bigger than those of
neighboring villages); or they could be conflicts that threatened the
unity of the village (for example, a dispute between members of
different families, or between the men and the women) (Harris
1940: 142–43; Uchendu 1965: 34, 42–43). It is clear, then, that the
assembly dealt with public policy publicly. The mode of discourse
made much use of proverbs, parables, and metaphors drawn from
the body of Igbo tradition and familiar to all Igbo from childhood.
Influential speech involved the creative and skillful use of this
tradition to provide counsel and justification—to assure others that
a certain course of action was both a wise thing to do and a right
thing to do. The accessibility (the "public" nature) of this knowledge is itself indicated by an Igbo proverb: "If you tell a proverb

---

ogbo (these terms are defined later in this paper, on pp. 68–69); Afikpo women
have not traditionally been active in trade; and female status among the Afikpo
is generally very low. Afikpo Igbo, unlike almost all other Igbo, have a men's
secret society that has "keeping women in their place" as a major purpose (P.
Ottenberg 1959 and 1965).

to a fool, he will ask you its meaning." Fools were excluded from the political community, but women were not.*

Women as well as men thus had access to political participation; for women as well as for men, public status was to a great extent achieved, not ascribed. A woman's status was determined more by her own achievements than by those of her husband. The resources available to men were greater, however; thus, although a woman might rank higher among women than her husband did among men, very few women could afford the fees and feasts involved in taking the highest titles, a major source of prestige (Meek 1957: 203). Men "owned" the most profitable crops and received the bulk of the money from bridewealth. Moreover, if they were compound heads, they received presents from compound members. Through the patrilineage, they controlled the land. After providing farms for their wives, they could lease excess land for a good profit. Men also did more of the long-distance trading, which had a higher rate of profit than did local and regional trading, which was almost entirely in women's hands (Green 1947: 32–42).

Women were entitled to sell the surplus of their own crops. They also received the palm kernels as their share of the palm produce (they processed the palm oil for the men to sell). They might also sell prepared foods, or the products of women's special skills (processed salt, pots, baskets). All the profits were theirs to keep (Leith-Ross 1939: 90–92, 138–39, 143). But these increments of profit were relatively low. Since the higher titles commonly needed to ensure respect for village leaders required increasingly higher fees and expenses, women's low profits restricted their access to villagewide leadership. Almost all of those who took the higher titles were men, and most of the leaders in villagewide discussions and decisions were men (Green 1947: 169; Uchendu 1965: 41). Women, therefore, came out as second-class citizens. Though status and the political influence it could bring were "achieved," and

* I rely here chiefly on Uchendu 1965 and personal conversations with an Igbo born in Umu-Domi village of Onicha clan, Afikpo division. Some of the ideas about leadership were suggested by Schaar 1970. His discussion of what "humanly meaningful authority" would look like is very suggestive for studies of leadership in "developing" societies.

though there were no formal limits to women's political power, men by their ascriptive status (membership in the patrilineage) acquired wealth that gave them a head start and a lifelong advantage over women. The Igbo say that "a child who washes his hands clean deserves to eat with his elders" (Uchendu 1965: 19). What they do not say is that at birth some children are given water and some are not.

Women's Political Institutions

Though women's associations are best described for the south—the area of the Women's War—their existence is reported for most other areas of Igboland, and Forde and Jones made the general observation that "women's associations express their disapproval and secure their demands by collective public demonstrations, including ridicule, satirical singing and dancing, and group strikes" (1950: 21).

Two sorts of women's associations are relevant politically: those of the *inyemedi* (wives of a lineage) and of the *umuada* (daughters of a lineage). Since traditional Igbo society was predominantly patrilocal and exogamous, almost all adult women in a village would be wives (there would also probably be some divorced or widowed "daughters" who had returned home to live). Women of the same natal village or village group (and therefore of the same lineage) might marry far and wide, but they would come together periodically in meetings often called *ogbo* (an Igbo word for "gathering"). The *umuada*'s most important ritual function was at funerals of lineage members, since no one could have a proper funeral without their voluntary ritual participation—a fact that gave women a significant measure of power. The *umuada* invoked this power in helping to settle intralineage disputes among their "brothers," as well as disputes between their natal and marital lineages. Since these gatherings were held in rotation among the villages into which members had married, they formed an important part of the communication network of Igbo women (Okonjo 1974: 25; Olisa 1971: 24–27; Green 1947: 217–29).

The companion grouping to the *umuada* was the *inyemedi*, the

wives of the lineage, who came together in villagewide gatherings
that during the colonial period came to be called *mikiri* or *mitiri*
(the Igbo version of the English "meeting"). *Mikiri* were thus
gatherings of women based on common residence rather than on
common birth, as in the case of *ogbo*. The *mikiri* appears to have
performed the major role in daily self-rule among women and to
have articulated women's interests as opposed to those of men.
Mikiri provided women with a forum in which to develop their
political talents and with a means for protecting their interests as
traders, farmers, wives, and mothers (Green 1947; Leith-Ross 1939;
Harris 1940; Okonjo 1974). In *mikiri*, women made rules about
markets, crops, and livestock that applied to men as well as women;
and they exerted pressure to maintain moral norms among women.
They heard complaints from wives about mistreatment by husbands, and discussed how to deal with problems they were having
with "the men" as a whole. They also made decisions about the
rituals addressed to the female aspect of the village's guardian
spirit, and about rituals for the protection of the fruitfulness of
women and of their farms. If fines for violations or if repeated
requests to husbands and elders were ignored, women might "sit
on" an offender or go on strike. The latter might involve refusing
to cook, to take care of small children, or to have sexual relations
with their husbands. Men regarded the *mikiri* as legitimate; and
the use of the more extreme sanctions—though rare—was well remembered.

Though both *ogbo* and *mikiri* served to articulate and protect
women's interests, it is probably more accurate to see these groups
as sharing in diffused political authority than to see them as acting
only as pressure groups for women's interests. Okonjo argues elsewhere in this volume that traditional Igbo society had a "dual-sex
political system"; that is, there was a dual system of male and female political-religious institutions, each sex having both its own
autonomous sphere of authority and an area of shared responsibilities. Thus, women settled disputes among women, but also
made decisions and rules affecting men. They had the right to enforce their decisions and rules by using forms of group ostracism

similar to those used by men. In a society of such diffuse political authority, it would be misleading to call only a village assembly of men a "public" gathering, as most Western observers unquestioningly do; among the Igbo, a gathering of adult women must also be accepted as a public gathering.

Colonial "Penetration"

Into this system of diffuse authority, fluid and informal leadership, shared rights of enforcement, and a more or less stable balance of male and female power, the British tried to introduce ideas of "native administration" derived from colonial experience with chiefs and emirs in northern Nigeria. Southern Nigeria was declared a protectorate in 1900, but ten years passed before the conquest was effective. As colonial power was established in what the British perceived as a situation of "ordered anarchy," Igboland was divided into Native Court Areas that violated the autonomy of villages by lumping together many unrelated villages. British District Officers were to preside over the courts, but they were not always present because there were more courts than officers. The Igbo membership was formed by choosing from each village a "representative" who was given a warrant of office. These Warrant Chiefs also constituted what was called the Native Authority. The Warrant Chiefs were required to see that the orders of the District Officers were executed in their own villages, and they were the only link between the colonial power and the people (Afigbo 1972: 13–36, 207–48).

In the first place, it was a violation of Igbo concepts to have one man represent the village; and it was even more of a violation that he should give orders to everyone else. The people obeyed the Warrant Chief when they had to, since British power backed him up. In some places Warrant Chiefs were lineage heads or wealthy men who were already leaders in the village. But in many places they were simply ambitious, opportunistic young men who put themselves forward as friends of the conquerors. Even where the Warrant Chief was not corrupt, he was still, more than anything else, an agent of the British. The people avoided using Native Courts when they could do so, but Warrant Chiefs could force cases into the Native Courts and fine people for infractions of rules. Because he had the ear of the British, the Warrant Chief himself could violate traditions and even British rules and get away with it (Anene 1967: 259; Meek 1957: 328–30).

Women suffered particularly under the arbitrary rule of Warrant Chiefs, who reportedly took women to marry without allowing them the customary right to refuse a particular suitor. They also helped themselves to the women's agricultural produce and domestic animals (Onwuteaka 1965: 274). Recommendations for reform of the system were made almost from its inception both by junior officers in the field and by senior officers sent out from headquarters to investigate. But no real improvements were made. An attempt by the British in 1918 to make the Native Courts more "native" by abolishing the District Officers' role as presiding court officials had little effect, and that mostly bad. Removing the District Officers from the courts simply left more power in the hands of corrupt Warrant Chiefs and the increasingly powerful Court Clerks. The latter, intended to be "servants of the court," were able in some cases to dominate the courts because of their monopoly of expertise—namely, literacy (Meek 1957: 329; Gailey 1970: 66–74).

The Women's War

In 1925, the British decided to introduce direct taxation in order to create the Native Treasury, which was supposed to pay for improvements in the Native Administration, in accordance with the British imperial philosophy that the colonized should pay the costs of colonization. Prices in the palm trade were high, and the tax—on adult males—was set accordingly. Taxes were collected without widespread trouble, although there were "tax riots" in Warri Province (west of the Niger) in 1927.

In 1929, a zealous Assistant District Officer in Bende division of Owerri Province, apparently acting on his own initiative, decided to "tighten up" the census registers by recounting households and property. He told the Chiefs that there was no plan to increase

taxes or to tax women. But the counting of women and their property raised fears that women were to be taxed, particularly because
the Bende District Officer had lied earlier when the men were
counted and had told the men that they were not going to be taxed.
The women, therefore, naturally did not believe these reassurances.
The taxation rumor spread quickly through the women's communication networks, and meetings of women took place in various
market squares, which were the common places for women to have
large meetings. In the Oloko Native Court Area—one of the areas
of deception about the men's tax—the women leaders, Ikonnia,
Nwannedie, and Nwugo, called a general meeting at Orie market.
Here it was decided that as long as only men were approached in
a compound and asked for information the women would do nothing. If any woman was approached, she was to raise the alarm; then
the women would meet again to decide what to do. But they wanted
clear evidence that women were to be taxed (Afigbo 1972; Gailey
1970: 107–8).

On November 23, an agent of the Oloko Warrant Chief, Okugo,
entered a compound and told one of the married women, Nwanyeruwa, to count her goats and sheep. She replied angrily, "Was
your mother counted?" at which "they closed, seizing each other
by the throat" (Perham 1937: 207). Nwanyeruwa's report to the
Oloko women convinced them that they were to be taxed. Mes-
sengers were sent to neighboring areas, and women streamed into
Oloko from all over Owerri Province. They "sat on" Okugo and
demanded his cap of office. They massed in protest at the District
Office and succeeded in getting written assurances that they were
not to be taxed. After several days of mass protest meetings, they
also succeeded in getting Okugo arrested, tried, and convicted of
"spreading news likely to cause alarm" and of physical assault on
the women. He was sentenced to two years' imprisonment (Gailey
1970: 108–13).

News of this victory spread rapidly through the market-*mikiri-
ogbo* network, and women in many areas then attempted to get rid
of their Warrant Chiefs and the Native Administration itself.
Nwanyeruwa became something of a heroine as reports of her

resistance spread. Money poured in from grateful women from villages scattered over a wide area but linked by kinship to Nwanyeruwa's marital village. Nwanyeruwa herself, however, was "content to allow" leadership in her area to be exercised by someone else. The money collected was used not for her but for delegates going to meetings of women throughout southern Igboland to coordinate the Women's War.

The British ended the rebellion only by using large numbers of police and soldiers—and, on one occasion, Boy Scouts. Although the shootings in mid-December and the growing numbers of police and soldiers in the area led the women to halt most of their activities, disturbances continued into 1930. The "disaffected areas"—all of Owerri and Calabar provinces—were occupied by government forces. Punitive expeditions burned or demolished compounds, took provisions from the villages to feed the troops, and confiscated property in payment of fines levied arbitrarily against villages in retribution for damages (Gailey 1970: 135–37).

During the investigations that followed the Women's War, the British discovered the communication network that had been used to spread the rumor of taxation. But that did not lead them to inquire further into how it came to pass that Igbo women had engaged in concerted action under grassroots leadership, had agreed on demands, and had materialized by the thousands at Native Administration centers dressed and adorned in the same unusual way—all wearing short loincloths, all carrying sticks wreathed with palm fronds, and all having their faces smeared with charcoal or ashes and their heads bound with young ferns. Unbeknown to the British, this was the dress and adornment signifying "war," the sticks being used to invoke the power of the female ancestors (Harris 1940: 143–45, 147–48; Perham 1937: 207ff; Meek 1957: ix).

The report of the Commission of Enquiry exonerating the soldiers who fired on the women cited the "savage passions" of the "mobs"; and one military officer told the Commission that "he had never seen crowds in such a state of frenzy." Yet these "frenzied mobs" injured no one seriously, which the British found "surprising"; but then the British did not understand that the women were engaged in a traditional practice with traditional rules and limitations, only carried out in this instance on a much larger scale than in precolonial times.*

Reforms—But Not for Women

The British failure to recognize the Women's War as a collective response to the abrogation of rights resulted in a failure to ask whether women might have had a role in the traditional political system that should be incorporated into the institutions of colonial government. Because the women—and the men—regarded the investigations as attempts to discover whom to punish, they volunteered no information about women's organizations. But would the British have understood those organizations if they had? The discovery of the market network had suggested no further lines of inquiry. The majority of District Officers thought that the men had organized the women's actions and were secretly directing them. The women's demands that the Native Courts no longer hear cases and that "all white men should go to their own country"—or at least that women should serve on the Native Courts and a woman be appointed a District Officer—were in line with the power of women in traditional Igbo society but were regarded by the British as irrational and ridiculous (Gailey 1970: 130ff; Leith-Ross 1939: 165; Perham 1937: 165ff).

The reforms instituted in 1933 therefore ignored the women's traditional political role, though they did make some adjustments to traditional Igbo male and male-dominated political forms. The number of Native Court Areas was greatly increased, and their boundaries were arranged to conform roughly to traditional di-

---

* A few older men criticized the women for "flinging sand at their chiefs," but Igbo men generally supported the women though they nonetheless considered it "their fight" against the British. It is also reported that both women and men shared the mistaken belief that the women would not be fired upon because they had observed certain rituals and were carrying the palm-wrapped sticks that invoked the power of the female ancestors. The men had no illusions of immunity for themselves, having vivid memories of the slaughter of Igbo men during the conquest (Perham 1937: 212ff; Anene 1967: 207–24; Esike 1965: 11; Meek 1957: x).

visions. Warrant Chiefs were replaced by "massed benches," which allowed large numbers of judges to sit at one time. In most cases it was left up to the villages to decide whom and how many to send. Though this benefited the women by eliminating the corruption of the Warrant Chiefs, and thus made their persons and property more secure, it provided no outlet for collective action, their real base of power (Perham 1937: 365ff).

In 1901 the British had declared all jural institutions except the Native Courts illegitimate, but it was only in the years following the 1933 reforms that Native Administration local government became effective enough to make that declaration at all meaningful. The British had also outlawed "self-help"—the use of force by anyone but the government to punish wrongdoers. And the increasingly effective enforcement of this ban eliminated the women's ultimate weapon: "sitting on a man." In attempting to create specialized political institutions on the Western model, with participation on the basis of individual achievement, the British created a system in which there was no place for group solidarity, no possibility of dispersed and shared political authority or power of enforcement, and thus very little place for women (Leith-Ross 1939: 109–10, 163, 214). As in the village assemblies, women could not compete with men for leadership in the reformed Native Administration because they lacked the requisite resources. This imbalance in resources was increased by other facets of British colonialism— economic "penetration" and missionary influence. All three—colonial government, foreign investment, and the church—contributed to the growth of a system of political and economic stratification that made community decision-making less "public" in both senses we have discussed and that led to the current concentration of national political power in the hands of a small, educated, wealthy, male elite. For though we are here focusing on the political results of colonialism, they must be seen as part of the whole system of imposed class and sex stratification.*

* Leith Mullings, in her paper "Women and Economic Change in Africa" elsewhere in this volume, has criticized my article " 'Sitting on a Man' " (Van Allen 1972) and my arguments there about systems of stratification. Her comments have helped push me to relate the economic effects of colonialism to its

Missionary Influence

Christian missions were established in Igboland in the late nineteenth century. They had few converts at first, but by the 1930's their influence was significant, though generally limited to the young (Leith-Ross 1939: 109–18; Meek 1957: xv). A majority of Igbo eventually "became Christians," for they had to profess Christianity in order to attend mission schools. Regardless of how nominal their membership was, they had to obey the rules to remain in good standing, and one rule was to avoid "pagan" rituals. Women were discouraged from attending meetings where traditional rituals were performed or where money was collected for the rituals, which in effect meant all *mikiri*, *ogbo*, and many other types of gatherings (Ajayi 1965: 108–9).

Probably more significant, since *mikiri* were losing some of their political functions anyway, was mission education. The Igbo came to see English and Western education as increasingly necessary for political leadership—needed to deal with the British and their law —and women had less access to this new knowledge than men had. Boys were more often sent to school than girls, for a variety of reasons generally related to their favored position in the patrilineage, including the fact that they, not their sisters, would be expected to support their parents in their old age. But even when girls did go, they tended not to receive the same type of education. In mission schools, and increasingly in special "training homes" that dispensed with most academic courses, the girls were taught European domestic skills and the Bible, often in the vernacular. The missionaries' avowed purpose in educating girls was to train them for Christian marriage and motherhood, not for jobs or for citizenship. Missionaries were not necessarily against women's participation in politics; clergy in England, as in America, could be found supporting women's suffrage. But in Africa their concern

political effects in an explicit way. I remain convinced, however, that ideology and consciousness should be treated as independent factors that can directly influence the form of economic and political developments, and that can be changed directly by "consciousness-raising" as well as indirectly by changes in economic structures.

was the church, and for the church they needed Christian families. Therefore, Christian wives and mothers, not female political leaders, were the missions' aim. As Mary Slessor, the influential Calabar missionary, said: "God-like motherhood is the finest sphere for women, and the way to the redemption of the world."* As the English language and other knowledge of "book" became necessary to political life, women were increasingly cut out and policy-making became less public.

Economic Colonialism

The traditional Igbo division of labor—in which women owned their surplus crops and their market profits, while men controlled the more valuable yams and palm products and did more long-distance trading—was based on a subsistence economy. Small surpluses could be accumulated, but these were generally not used for continued capital investment. Rather, in accord with traditional values, the surplus was used for social rather than economic gain: it was returned to the community through fees and feasts for rituals for title-taking, weddings, funerals, and other ceremonies, or through projects to help the community "get up." One became a "big man" or a "big woman" not by hoarding one's wealth but by spending it on others in prestige-winning ways (Uchendu 1965: 34; Meek 1957: 111).

Before the Pax Britannica, Igbo women had been active traders in all but a few areas (one such was Afikpo, where women farmed but did not trade).† The ties of exogamous marriage among patri-

* For the missionaries' views and purposes, see Ajayi 1965, Basden 1927, Bulifant 1950, Maxwell 1926, and Livingstone n.d.

† It is an unfortunate accident that the Afikpo Igbo, with their strong sexual stratification, have been used as examples of "the Igbo" or of "the effect of colonialism on women" in widely read articles. Simon Ottenberg's "Ibo Receptivity to Change" is particularly misleading, since it is about "all" Igbo. There is one specific mention of women: "The social and economic independence of women is much greater in some areas than in others." True, but the social and economic independence of women is much greater in virtually *all* other Igbo groups than it is in Afikpo, where the Ottenbergs did fieldwork. There are said to be "a variety of judicial techniques" used, but all the examples given are of men's activities. There is a list of non-kinship organizations, but no women's organizations are listed. Sanday's otherwise useful and thought-provoking article (1973) both takes the Afikpo as "the" Igbo and exaggerates the

lineages, the cross-cutting networks of women providing channels
for communication and conciliation, and the ritual power of female members of patrilineages all enabled the traditional system to
deal with conflicts with relatively little warfare (Anene 1967: 214ff;
Green 1947: 91, 152, 177, 230–32). Conflict also took the nonviolent
form of mutual insults in obscene and satirical songs (Nwoga 1971:
33–35, 40–42); and even warfare itself was conducted within limits,
with weapons and actions increasing in seriousness in inverse proportion to the closeness of kinship ties. Women from mutually
hostile village groups who had married into the same patrilineage
could if necessary act as "protectors" for each other so that they
could trade in "stranger" markets (Green 1947: 151). Women also
protected themselves by carrying the stout sticks they used as pestles
for pounding yams (the same ones carried in the Women's War).
Even after European slave-trading led to an increase in danger
from slave-hunters (as well as from headhunters), Igbo women
went by themselves to their farms and with other women to market, with their pestles as weapons for physical protection (Esike
1965: 13).

The Pax increased the safety of short- and especially of long-
distance trading for Igbo women as for women in other parts of
Africa. But the Pax also made it possible for European firms to
dominate the market economy. Onwuteaka argues that one cause
of the Women's War was Igbo women's resentment of the monopoly British firms had on buying, a monopoly that allowed
them to fix prices and adopt methods of buying that increased
their own profits at the women's expense (1965: 278). Women's
petty trading grew to include European products, but for many
women the accumulated surplus remained small, often providing
only subsistence and a few years' school fees for some of their chil-

---

amount of change in female status that female trading brought about. Phoebe
Ottenberg, Sanday's ultimate source on Afikpo women, described the change in
female status as existing "chiefly on the domestic rather than the general level,"
with the "men's position of religious, moral, and legal authority . . . in no way
threatened" (1959: 223). For examples of precolonial female trading in Igboland
and elsewhere, see Little 1973 (particularly p. 46, n. 32); Uchendu 1965; Van
Allen 1974b: 5–9; Dike 1956; and Jones 1963.

dren—the preference for sending boys to school further disadvantaging the next generation of women (Mintz 1971: 251–68; Boserup 1970: 92–95). A few women have become "big traders," dealing in £1000 lots of European goods, but women traders remain for the most part close to subsistence level. Little is open to West African women in towns except trading, brewing, or prostitution, unless they are among the tiny number who have special vocational or professional training (for example, as dressmakers, nurses, or teachers) (Boserup 1970: 85–101, 106–38). The "modern" economic sector, like the "modern" political sector, is dominated by men, women's access being limited "by their low level of literacy and by the general tendency to give priority to men in employment recruitment to the modern sector" (Boserup 1970: 99).

Women outside urban areas—the great majority of women—find themselves feeding their children by farming with their traditional digging sticks while men are moving into cash-cropping (with tools and training from "agricultural development programs"), migrant wage-labor, and trading with Europeans (Boserup 1970: 53–61, 87–99; Mintz 1971: 248–51). Thus, as Mintz suggests, "while the economic growth advanced by Westernization has doubtless increased opportunities for (at least some) female traders, it may also and simultaneously limit the range of their activities, as economic changes outside the internal market system continue to multiply" (p. 265). To the extent that economic opportunities for Africans in the "modern" sector continue to grow, women will become relatively more dependent economically on men and will be unlikely to "catch up" for a very long time, even if we accept education as the key. The relative stagnation of African economic "growth," however, suggests that the traditional markets will not disappear or even noticeably shrink, but will continue to be needed by the large numbers of urban migrants living economically marginal lives. Women can thus continue to subsist by petty trading, though they cannot achieve real economic independence from men or gain access to the resources needed for equal participation in community life.

It seems reasonable to see the traditional Igbo division of labor in production as interwoven with the traditional Igbo dispersal of political authority into a dual or "dual-sex" system. It seems equally reasonable to see the disruptions of colonialism as producing a new, similarly interwoven economic-political pattern—but one with stronger male domination of the cash economy and of political life.

To see this relationship, however, is not to explain it. Even if the exclusion of women from the colonial Native Administration and from nationalist politics could be shown to derive from their exclusion from the "modern" economic sector, we would still need to ask why it was men who were offered agricultural training and new tools for cash-cropping, and who are hired in factories and shops in preference to women with the same education. And we would still need to ask why it was chiefly boys who were sent to school, and why their education differed from that provided for girls.

Victorianism and Women's Invisibility

At least part of the answer must lie in the values of the colonialists, values that led the British to assume that girls and boys, women and men, should be treated and should behave as people supposedly did in "civilized" Victorian England. Strong male domination was imposed on Igbo society both indirectly, by new economic structures, and directly, by the recruitment of only men into the Native Administration. In addition, the new economic and political structures were supported by the inculcation of sexist ideology in the mission schools.

Not all capitalist, colonialist societies are equally sexist (or racist); but the Victorian society from which the conquerors of Igboland came was one in which the ideology that a woman's place is in the home had hardened into the most rigid form it has taken in recent Western history. Although attacked by feminists, that ideology remained dominant throughout the colonial period and is far from dead today. The ideal of Victorian womanhood—attainable, of course, only by the middle and upper classes, but widely believed in throughout society—was of a sensitive, morally superior being who was the hearthside guardian of Christian virtues and sentiments absent in the outside world. Her mind was not strong enough for the appropriately "masculine" subjects: science, business, and politics.* A woman who showed talent in these areas did not challenge any ideas about typical women: the exceptional woman simply had "the brain of a man," as Sir George Goldie said of Mary Kingsley (Gwynn 1932: 252).† A thorough investigation of the diaries, journals, reports, and letters of colonial officers and missionaries would be needed to prove that most of them held these Victorian values. But a preliminary reading of biographies, autobiographies, journals, and "reminiscences," plus the evidence of statements about Igbo women at the time of the Women's War, strongly suggests that the colonialists were deflected from any attempt to discover or protect Igbo women's political and economic roles by their assumption that politics and business were not proper, normal places for women.‡

When Igbo women forced the colonial administrators to recognize their presence during the Women's War, their brief "visibility" was insufficient to shake these assumptions. Their behavior was simply seen as aberrant and inexplicable. When they returned to "normal," they were once again invisible. This inability to "see" what is before one's eyes is strikingly illustrated by an account of a visit by the High Commissioner, Sir Ralph Moor, to Aro Chukwu after the British had destroyed (temporarily) the powerful oracle there: "To Sir Ralph's astonishment, the women of Aro Chukwu solicited his permission to reestablish the Long Juju, which the women intended to control themselves" (Anene 1967: 234). Would

* The fact that Englishwomen of the "lower classes" had to work in the fields, in the mills, in the mines, or on the street did not stop the colonialists from carrying their ideal to Africa, or from condemning urban prostitution there (just as they did at home) without acknowledging their contribution to its origin or continuation.

† Mary Kingsley, along with other elite female "exceptions" who influenced African colonial policy (e.g., Flora Shaw Lugard and Margery Perham), held the same values that men did, at least in regard to women's roles. They did not expect ordinary women to have political power any more than men expected them to, and they showed no particular concern for African women.

‡ For examples of this attitude among those who were not missionaries, see Anene 1967: 222–34; Crocker 1936; Meek 1957; Kingsley 1897; Perham 1960; and Wood 1960.

Sir Ralph have been "astonished" if, for example, the older men had controlled the oracle before its destruction and the younger men had wanted to take it over?

The feminist movement in England during the colonial era did not succeed in making the absence of women from public life noted as a problem that required a remedy. The movement did not succeed in creating a "feminist" consciousness in any but a few "deviants," and such a consciousness is far from widespread today; for to have a "feminist" consciousness means that one notices the "invisibility" of women. One wonders where the women are—in life and in print. That we have not wondered is an indication of our own ideological bondage to a system of sex and class stratification. What we can see, if we look, is that Igbo men have come to dominate women economically and politically: individual women have become economic auxiliaries to their husbands, and women's groups have become political auxiliaries to nationalist parties. Wives supplement their husbands' incomes but remain economically dependent; women's "branches" have provided votes, money, and participants in street demonstrations for political parties but remain dependent on male leaders for policymaking. Market women's associations were a vital base of support for the early National Council for Nigeria and the Cameroons (NCNC), the party that eventually was to become dominant in Igbo regions (although it began as a truly national party). And though a few market-women leaders were ultimately rewarded for their loyalty to the NCNC by appointment to party or legislative positions, market women's associations never attained a share in policymaking that approached their contribution to NCNC electoral success (Bretton 1966: 61; MacIntosh 1966: 299, 304–9; Sklar 1963: 41–83, 251, 402). The NCNC at first had urged female suffrage throughout the country, an idea opposed by the Northern People's Congress (NPC), dominated by Moslem emirs. Soon, however, the male NCNC leadership gave up pushing for female suffrage in the north (where women have never yet voted) in order to make peace with the NPC and the British and thus insure for themselves a share of power in the postindependence government. During the period between independence in 1960 and the 1966 military coups that ended party rule, some progress was made in education for girls. By 1966, consequently, female literacy in the East was more than 50 percent in some urban areas and at least 15 percent overall—high for Africa, where the overall average is about 10 percent and the rural average may be as low as 2 percent (MacIntosh 1966: 17–37; *West African Pilot*, April 29, 1959; Pool 1972: 238; UNESCO 1968).

Exhortations to greater female participation in "modern life" appeared frequently in the newspapers owned by the NCNC leader, Nnamdi Azikiwe, and a leadership training course for women was begun in 1959 at the Man O' War Bay Training Centre, to be "run on exactly the same lines as the courses for men, with slight modifications," as the *Pilot* put it. The motto of the first class of 22 women was, "What the men can do, the women can" (Van Allen 1974b: 17–20). But there was more rhetoric than reality in these programs for female emancipation. During the period of party politics, no women were elected to regional or national legislatures; those few who were appointed gained favor by supporting "party first," not "women first." Perhaps none of this should be surprising, given the corruption that had come to dominate national party politics (MacIntosh 1966: 299, 612–14; Sklar 1963: 402; Van Allen 1974b: 19–22).

Biafra and Beyond

On January 15, 1966, a military coup ended the Igbos' relationship with the NCNC: all political parties, and therefore their women's branches, were outlawed. A year and a half later—after the massacres of more than 30,000 Easterners in the North, the flight of more than a million refugees back to the East, a counter-coup, and the division of the Igbo-dominated Eastern Region into three states—Biafra declared herself an independent state. In January 1970 she surrendered; the remaining Igbo are now landlocked, oilless, and under military occupation by a Northern-dominated military government.* Igbo women demonstrated in the streets to protest the massacres, to urge secession, and, later, to protest Soviet involvement in the war (Ojukwu 1969: 91, 143, 145–46, 245). During the war, the women's market network and other women's organizations maintained a distribution system for what food there was and provided channels for the passage of food and information to the army (Uzoma 1974: 8ff; Akpan 1971: 65–67, 89, 98–99, 128–30). Women joined local civilian-defense militia units and in May 1969 formed a "Women's Front" and called on the Biafran leadership to allow them to enlist in the infantry (Uzoma 1974: 5–8; Ojukwu 1969: 386).

During and after the war, local civilian government continued to exist more or less in the form that evolved under the "reformed" Native Administration. The decentralization produced by the war has by some reports strengthened these local councils, and the absence of many men has strengthened female participation (Peters 1971: 102–3; Adler 1969: 112; Uzoma 1974: 10–12). Thus, at tragic human cost, the war may have made possible a resurgence of female political activity. If this is so, women's participation again stems much more from Igbo tradition than from Western innovation.

It remains to be seen whether Igbo women, or any African women, can gain real political power without the creation of a "modern" version of the traditional "dual-sex" system (which is what Okonjo argues is needed) or without a drastic change in economic structures so that economic equality could support political equality for all women and men, just as economic stratification now supports male domination and female dependence. What seems clear from women's experiences—whether under capitalism, co-

---

* The attitude of the Northern emirs who now again dominate the Nigerian government is perhaps indicated by their order in June 1973 that single women get married or leave Northern Nigeria because Moslem religious authorities had decided that the North African drought was caused by prostitution and immorality. Landlords were ordered not to let rooms to single women, and many unmarried women were reported to have fled their home areas (*Agence France-Presse*, as reported in *The San Francisco Chronicle*, June 23, 1973). In late 1975 the military government appointed a 50-man body to draft a constitution for Nigeria's return to civilian rule. As of this writing women's protests have produced no changes in its membership.

lonialism, or revolutionary socialism—is that formal political and economic equality are not enough. Unless the male members of a liberation movement, a ruling party, or a government themselves develop a feminist consciousness and a commitment to male-female equality, women will end up where they have always been: invisible, except when men, for their own purposes personal or political, look for female bodies.

Luo Women and Economic Change
During the Colonial Period

MARGARET JEAN HAY

THE LONG-TERM economic result of colonial rule in western
Kenya was the impoverishment of the African rural areas through
the withdrawal of resources that were required to subsidize the
development of the European sector of the colonial economy. Yet
at the same time that British colonial officials were extracting
capital and labor from the rural economy, they were insisting that
African cultivators maintain (if not actually increase) their level
of agricultural production. African families were expected to meet
all their staple food requirements through their own production;
and the artificially low wages paid to African workers meant that
in many cases rural families had to supply foodstuffs to labor
migrants in the towns as well. They were also expected to continue
the production of surplus commodities for sale or export. Declining soil fertility, increasing population pressures on the land,
and the fragmenting of landholdings in the later colonial period
made it even more difficult for Africans to maintain agricultural
productivity.

The real burden of coping with this nearly impossible situation
in the rural areas of western Kenya fell on the women, who remained at home while their husbands and sons sought outside
employment. This paper will examine the responses of a particular
group of Luo women, the women of Kowe, to the changes imposed
by the colonial economy. Through a continuous process of experimentation and innovation in agriculture and in trade, these women

managed to meet the economic demands of the colonial economy
and in a broader sense to stay even.*

Kowe, the focus of the present study, is an administrative sublocation about four square miles in size in Seme location, former
Central Nyanza District. It is the name, and the home, of a Luo
major lineage (*oganda*) whose members trace their genealogical
relationship back six to eight generations to a common ancestor,
Owe. As a major lineage, Kowe is one part of a larger maximal
lineage (*piny*) called Seme, whose members cooperated for military
and political purposes and did not intermarry. Within Luo society,
however, the major lineage is the largest geographical or kinship
area in which the corporate group functions in the political,
judicial, and economic spheres. It is also the major corporate
landholding unit. At the same time, Kowe is made up of three
smaller minor lineages, which became increasingly differentiated
as a result of colonial experiences. When the British imposed
colonial rule on western Kenya, they tried as far as possible to
base their regional administration on the existing forms of social
and political organization. In this way Seme and Kowe came to
exist both as lineage units and as administrative divisions.

An area of undulating plains and low rolling hills, Kowe is
covered with short grasses and occasional trees, and its slopes are
dotted with scattered homesteads. Expanses of arable land are
interrupted by patches of sandy soil and hillsides too steep or
too rocky for cultivation. In 1969 the sublocation had a population
of about 3,000, and thus a density of about 750 people per square

* The principal research on which this paper is based was carried out in
Kenya between 1968 and 1970 under a grant from the Foreign Area Fellowships
Program. The University of Wisconsin made possible a brief stay in Britain
during the summer of 1970; and a summer stipend from the National Endow-
ment for the Humanities with a supplemental travel grant from the University
of Wisconsin enabled me to return to Kenya in the summer of 1973. I am grateful to all of these institutions for their support, and I hasten to note that none
of them should be held responsible for any errors or misrepresentations. An
earlier draft of this paper was presented at the 1974 summer workshop in
African economic history at the University of Wisconsin, and I have benefited
from the comments and suggestions made by other members of that workshop.
Paul Lovejoy and Steven Feierman deserve particular thanks for their con-
structive criticism.

mile.* The movement of the people of Kowe into their present homeland is just part of the historic migrations of the Luo people, whose origins are said to be in the Sudan. During the eighteenth and nineteenth centuries, the people of the Seme lineage were moving along the shores of the Kavirondo Gulf (the finger of water that pushes into western Kenya from Lake Victoria), competing for territory with other maximal lineages. Population pressures and conflicts with other groups finally forced them to turn inland, away from the lake, and to expand gradually into the higher, wetter areas to the north. In general, their movements kept them out of range of the British and of the other European powers who were actively expanding their influence over much of East Africa in the late nineteenth century.

The punitive expedition led by two British officials in 1899 made clear the fact of British colonial rule to the people of Kowe and other Luo areas along the northern shore of the Kavirondo Gulf. This expedition was both a demonstration of British military strength and a retaliation for certain "outrages" committed by the Luo of Sakwa, Uyoma, and Seme. Remembered by the people of Seme as "the war with the Europeans," it resulted in the death of about 100 men and the capture of nearly 600 cattle and some 8,000 sheep and goats. For most Luo, this "war" represented their first contact with the British—and it was clearly a very traumatic one. Soon after this demonstration of force, the British imposed "chiefs" on each Luo maximal lineage and began to collect through them a "hut tax" of two rupees.† Thus we can take 1899 as the year

* An average household in 1969 probably consisted of five persons, with rights of use over roughly five acres of land. Only two of these acres were arable, on the average; the other three were either grazing land or rocky hillsides. Most families probably owned four or five head of livestock, and their landholdings were divided into two or three separate parcels. In many cases the head of the household worked regularly outside Kowe. See Margaret Jean Hay, "Economic Change in Luoland: Kowe, 1890–1945" (unpublished Ph.D. dissertation, University of Wisconsin, 1972), chap. 1.

† Interestingly, the influence of Indian traders in East Africa led the British to introduce Indian rupees and annas rather than pounds and shillings as the first official currency. The rupee was equal to one shilling and four pence at the time of the first hut tax. Some years later the official currency was changed to British sterling.

that marks the effective beginning of British colonial rule in this region.*

In the first decade of colonial rule, the demands of colonial officials were relatively slight, rarely going beyond payment of the annual hut tax. Informants do not recall any great difficulty in meeting this initial tax through the sale of produce or livestock, though clearly such sales would ultimately affect capital accumulation. Nor is there any evidence before 1910 of the two major forces that were to affect Luo society during the remainder of the colonial period: labor migration (whether forced or voluntary), and missionary activity. The economy of Kowe at this time was still based on pastoralism and agriculture, although *Apamo,* the great rinderpest epidemic of the early 1890's, had decimated the people's herds and required both immediate and long-term adjustments in the balance between the two sectors. Families that once had been famous for their wealth in cattle found themselves after the epidemic with only a few head or none at all.

The people of Kowe had recently moved north from the lakeshore at the time of *Apamo,* and the epidemic accelerated their efforts to exploit the greater agricultural potential of their new environment, an area marked by higher altitudes, greater annual rainfall, and an abundance of wild game. Though agriculture had traditionally been the province of women, one result of the *Apamo* was that some men in Kowe became increasingly involved in agriculture in an attempt to rebuild their herds. Ogumbo, one of the most influential men of his day, and others became devoted farmers, producing a surplus of grain on their own fields (as distinct from those cultivated by their wives) that they exchanged for sheep and goats, and eventually for cattle. But others remained aloof and waited for better times. The theoretical division of labor between men and women was fairly clear-cut during this period and can be expressed in the formula "pastoralism is superior to agri-

* See Hay 1972, pp. 77–82, for a discussion of this "war with the Europeans" and the striking differences between British and African accounts. A general introduction to the history of British colonial rule in Kenya may be found in Brett 1973, Wolff 1974, and Wrigley 1965.

culture as men are superior to women." Men were primarily responsible for tending livestock and arranging for livestock transactions; young boys did the actual herding under the supervision of the older men. In agriculture, it was the duty of men to clear the fields and break the surfaces for first cultivation. They also built houses, granaries, and fences, and defended the homestead in case of attack. Women were responsible for housework and child care, and stored and cared for the food supply. In addition, they did most of the planting, weeding, and harvesting of crops, and cleaned and repaired the walls and surfaces of the houses and granaries.

In practice, the man's role in agriculture varied a great deal from one household to the next. Generally, wealthy men—particularly those with many wives—scorned work in the fields, whereas poor men might help their wives with most of the agricultural tasks.* The association of women with agriculture and men with livestock and wild game is mirrored in a series of food taboos that prevented Luo women from eating chicken, eggs, milk, sheep, rabbit, hippo or elephant meat, and other kinds of game as well.† Customs that reserved many of the high-protein foods for men must have had some effect on women's health, fertility, and agricultural productivity.‡

The agricultural system of Kowe around the turn of the century was characterized by a rudimentary wooden-hoe technology, shifting cultivation, and the rotation of crops. The main crops included sorghum, the historical staple of the Luo, finger millet, barley, sesame, sweet potatoes or yams, pumpkins, beans, green gram,

* Interviews with Elijah Owe (22/1/70), Joan Arwa (19/4/70), and Isaya Mbori (24/2/70), Kowe Historical Texts (KHT). (These are the transcripts of my interviews, on deposit with the History Department at the University of Nairobi.)

† The men of Kowe were more active in hunting around 1900 than they had been previously, a fact that reflects both the abundance of game in the newly settled area and the devastation caused by the rinderpest epidemic.

‡ Similar food taboos for women are a common feature of many African societies. Though they have been studied primarily in terms of their ritual significance, further research is surely needed to explore the implications for health and production. See, for example, O'Laughlin 1974 and Douglas 1966.

and a number of vegetables. Maize was probably a recent introduction around 1900, and it still had a rather limited use. The
new environment permitted a second annual agricultural season
during the so-called "short rains," and the people of Kowe were
still experimenting with the possibilities of this second season
in the 1900–1910 period (Hay 1972: chap. 4).

It is often observed that "women were the traders" of precolonial Luo society, presumably because of their right of safe
passage even in time of war.* Yet this is an oversimplification,
for women were primarily involved in the local trade in grains
and other foodstuffs, including chicken and fish. In the late nineteenth century and up until 1919 or so, the women of Kowe took
a very active part in expanding trade links both north (with the
Luyia) and south (with the lakeside Luo of southern Seme). The
market at Kondik, in the heart of Kowe, was a famous one in this
north-south trade, and it capitalized on the environmental differences between the regions and provided a favorable middleman
position for the people of Kowe. In years of good harvests, or in
seasons of famine or shortage, the women of Kowe were active in
this local trade in foodstuffs; but it was not yet a major part of
their day-to-day economic activity. When the women judged that
the recent harvest guaranteed a comfortable surplus of grain
beyond what their families would need, they would take this surplus to other areas that had not been so favored and exchange it
for sheep or goats, which they could raise and later exchange for
cattle. In times of relative shortage, the women would reverse the
process—taking chickens or goats to other areas where they could
buy grain to feed their families. Thus the women's trade in foodstuffs tended to be a seasonal rather than a regular activity.

Trade in other goods, such as crude iron or iron products, cattle,
poison, shields, and headdresses, was the preserve of men. This
trade ranged broadly throughout the Luo areas of Central Nyanza,
because the environmental differences that gave rise to the north-
south axis of trade in foodstuffs did not apply to these goods. British

* Interviews with Hosea Pala (July 12, 1973) and Mathayo Otieno (August 9,
1973), KHT.

control and the relative peace it imposed facilitated the long-distance trade in cattle and iron goods; these new opportunities were also monopolized by the men.

In the patrilineal and patrilocal society of the Luo, land was the most easily acquired factor of production. By custom, a man would apportion plots of land to his sons as they married and established households of their own—the remainder being distributed among them at his death. In principle, each son would receive approximately the same amount, and the fields he was given would come from the specific gardens farmed by his mother.* Land was abundant in northern Seme around the turn of the century, however, and most men acquired fields simply by clearing virgin tracts rather than by inheritance. In fact, many men moved their homesteads from place to place within a radius of a few miles to exploit the fertility of the virgin soil and the best pastures.† A given field was planted only two or three years in succession and then was left fallow for eight to ten years.

Labor, not land, was the limiting factor of production well into the early colonial period, and this contributed to the high social value of polygyny and the desire for numerous offspring. Women's labor was the critical element in determining the standard of living of the household; and marriage thus represented the most significant form of investment for a man, requiring as it did the expenditure of considerable capital in the form of bridewealth. Whisson has shown how investment in wives was the critical first step for someone aspiring to become *ruoth*, or "chief" (Whisson 1961: 7–8). Nineteenth-century descriptions of wealth and wealthy men reflect the labor value of women and not simply the ownership of live-

* A man would assign specific fields to each of his wives, according to her abilities and her needs (largely determined by the number of her children). Women never held permanent rights in land, since a husband could reassign garden plots if he saw fit.

† Though the modern boundaries of Kowe (drawn by the British) encompass only four square miles, before the colonial period the people of Kowe had ranged over a much broader area. It is possible to trace both the location of abandoned homesteads and the history of use of individual pieces of land through oral data. See, for example, Samili Olaka's description of the different homestead sites occupied by Ogumgo and Ochola (interview of 15/10/69), KHT.

stock. A wealthy man (*okebe*) lacked nothing. In addition to owning cattle, sheep, and goats, he possessed stores of food, many wives,
servants, clients, and children. His home boasted abundant oil,
sesame, and grains of all kinds. At sowing time, people obtained
millet seeds from him. In times of famine, he was generous and
distributed grain to his less fortunate neighbors. In these ways he
became famous as a person of wealth and substance (Mboya 1938:
165). Such a reputation might well lead to a position of social
prominence and political status. This interpretation of wealth
emphasizes the importance of the wives' role in agricultural production and in childbearing; it goes far beyond simple descriptions
of the size of a cattle kraal.

The woman's consent to marriage was not vital. Indeed, an
element of force was implicit from the earliest stages of the preparation of the marriage contract. A woman was "taken by force"
(the Luo term is *yuayo*) to the home of her husband. She was
expected to cry out and to do all in her power to resist accompany-
ing the groom's relatives. If she was genuinely unhappy with her
husband, she might run away and return to her parents' home,
but it was extremely difficult for her to break her contract without
jeojardizing her chances of any future marriage. Only when she
could demonstrate unusual cruelty or mistreatment would her
parents not force her to go back to her husband.

To a certain extent one may object that this is ritualized behavior. The evidence would suggest, however, that in a number
of cases the bride's reluctance was quite genuine. Patricia Rading'
Obure described her own marriage in 1920 (interview, 14/4/70,
KHT):

I was taken by force [*noyuaya*], as was the custom. After Obure and I had
met, his people sent a number of cows, then they came and took me by
force. After I had spent three days with him, I was taken back home
with a lot of food, and a goat was slaughtered. I stayed at my parents'
home for some time, and then Obure's relatives met me again at Luanda
and brought me back here. I ran away again. I did not like my husband
because he was just an old man whose wife had died. That was why I used
to run back home. I kept running away, and my family kept forcing me
to return; and I did this until I got tired, and then I just stayed here in
Kowe. I cannot remember how long I lived with Obure before he died,

but when he died, I had produced seven children. I was then taken by another man [leviratic marriage] and we produced three more children. . . . Of the ten children, five lived and five died.

The new bride spent several years in the home of her mother-in-law, helping with both household and agricultural work there. After she had given birth to two or three children, preferably male, she moved into a home of her own and assumed her full status as wife and mother. She would continue, however, to help her mother-in-law with such tasks as weeding and harvesting. Each wife was responsible for producing enough grain to feed her family through the year. It was her right, however, to dispose of any surplus from her own fields as she saw fit, and a number of women accumulated livestock through trade. A woman regarded these cattle as her own, and in most cases kept them aside for later use in her own sons' bridewealth payments. There is an element of investment as well as sentiment in this process: her sons' wives would help with the heavy agricultural tasks for the rest of her life. Moreover, the practice of polygyny ensured that a woman's economic security rested with her sons and not with her husband. A wife, in fact, could not inherit from her husband, although she could inherit from her sons.*

This possibility for capital investment, as well as the element of competitiveness among co-wives anxious to retain their husband's favor, encouraged the women of Kowe to maximize production through various means. Experimentation and innovation in agriculture was an ongoing process among these women, and can be traced back at least to the 1890's, when the women of Kowe were learning the best means to incorporate the newly possible short-rains crops into the agricultural cycle. There has been a constant process of trying out new seed varieties and new techniques encountered either through visits to friends and relatives or through normal market activity—a process that has been generally overlooked by scholars. One notices that the Luo grow millet

* See the minutes of the Local Native Council discussion of March 12, 1940, pp. 8–9, in Ag KSM 1/642, Kenya National Archives (KNA). The forms Ag KSM, DC/CN, and PC/NZA, as well as the numbers that accompany them, refer to specific files in the Kenya National Archives.

and sorghum, and historians confirm that a variety of sorghum
was the staple food of the Nilotes as early as AD 1000 (Ogot 1967:
41). This kind of information led colonial officials to conclude that
the Luo had grown the same crops "from time immemorial," and
were not about to change. Yet this image of static agriculture
neglects the many different varieties of grain that are and have
been grown, some varieties having disappeared altogether as others
have gained in popularity. In conversation, some men admitted
that they could not keep up with all the different varieties that
had been grown and advised me to ask their wives.* Because the
rules of lineage exogamy dictate the choosing of wives from other
maximal lineages, and because Luo society is patrilocal, the wives
of Kowe come from many areas with widely differing agricultural
patterns. The exchanges of visits between lineage members united
by marriage facilitated the diffusion of new seeds and techniques
whenever wives returned periodically to their home areas and their
brothers or sisters came to visit in return. Cowpeas (*nyamageta*)
are just one example of new seeds that were brought back to Kowe
by women visiting relatives in other areas.† Many women mentioned visits to Luyia markets to the north of Kowe as being a primary source of information about new seed varieties and even
new crops. This ongoing process of innovation and experimentation made possible increased production and some capital investment during the early colonial period, but it was to become crit-
ically necessary in order to maintain even a fixed standard of living
in the steadily deteriorating economic conditions after 1930.

From 1910 to 1930 British colonial rule increasingly affected life
in Kowe through two principal agencies. First, the district administrative officials who collected taxes ensured the flow of labor
for plantations and other European industry and began to inter-
fere in local economic life. And second, the Church Missionary

---

* See, for example, interview with Joel Omino (July 22, 1973), KHT.
† Interview with Joan Arwa (9/4/70), KHT. This process still goes on today.
In visiting families in Seme over a period of several years, I have frequently
seen the conversation turn to new seeds which the woman has encountered and
purchased and tried. In most cases, her visitors will ask to try the seeds and she
will give them some to take home.

Society station at Maseno (about five miles to the north) managed to convince a number of men and women from Kowe to become self-conscious innovators in economic as well as religious activity. Both church and state indirectly promoted or accelerated economic stratification within Kowe.

The development of labor-intensive plantation agriculture in the White Highlands after 1908, the construction of roads and railways, and the need for African soldiers and porters in the First World War all accelerated the demand for African labor, though this demand was not accompanied by a willingness to pay reasonable wages. In response to settler agitation, British officials devised a number of ways to force labor out of the African reserves. These included curtailing the land available for African agriculture, increasing taxation, developing contract-labor systems with penalties for infringement, and providing official support for private labor recruitment.* When a private employer needed laborers in Nyanza Province, he obtained a note of authorization from the local District Commissioner. A recruiting agent then entered the reserves and presented his credentials to the chief or headman, who in turn provided the required number of men. Uncooperative chiefs or headmen were reprimanded, fined, or even dismissed. The men of Kowe remember the era of forced labor with a great deal of bitterness, particularly the years between 1910 and 1922. Under pressure from Chief Nyawara or his headmen, young men were sent to European coffee or sisal plantations in the Highlands and along the coast. These jobs were unpopular because of the difficult work and low wages, which was why European farmers found it necessary to rely on forced recruitment to fill their labor needs. Though this article will emphasize the role of rural women in coping with the adjustments made necessary by the colonial economy, it is worth noting that the men who were forced to leave home suffered hardships of their own on the plantations and in the mines.

In addition to the practice of forced recruitment, which declined

* Recent accounts of this period in Kenyan history include Chapter 6 of Brett 1973; Wolff 1974; and Colin Leys, *Underdevelopment in Kenya* (Berkeley, Calif., 1975), pp. 28–50.

after 1922, oral data indicate that a tradition of voluntary labor migration began as early as 1912 when a group of friends started off together for Kisumu, motivated by curiosity and a spirit of adventure. They were also apparently bored by looking after goats. One found a clerical job in Kisumu; the others went to work on European estates at Kampi ya Moto, near Nakuru.* By 1930 a large number of men had left Kowe at least once for outside employment. Almost all were between the ages of fifteen and twenty and unmarried when they first sought employment. More than half of this group stayed away for periods of fifteen years or more; of the remainder, many finished their original contracts and returned to Kowe, never going out to work again (Hay 1972: 170–73). Two distinct groups stand out among the long-term labor migrants. In the first were the sons of the most prominent men of the late nineteenth century—young men who had been educated at the Church Missionary Society (C.M.S.) school at Maseno and generally had made a commitment to European values and life-styles. These men usually found good jobs with government departments or private firms and thought of themselves as town-dwellers. The second group consisted of sons of poor or client families, and sometimes orphans—i.e., those with limited resources in land or stock. Long-term wage labor gave them a chance to improve their economic position, and particularly to acquire stock for bridewealth payments.

This growing export of labor from the province might be thought to have increased the burden of agricultural work for women. As early as 1910, administrators lamented the fact that Nyanza was becoming the labor pool for the entire colony, and complained that the area was being drained of "the best of its youthful cultivators." Yet the short-term migrants of the 1920's were usually unmarried youths, who played a relatively minor role in the local economy beyond occasional herding and the conquest of cattle in war. Furthermore, the short-term labor migrants could and often did arrange to be away during the slack periods of the

* See, for example, interviews with Omindo Ayieye (3/12/69), Johana Ming'ala (10/10/69), and Jeremiah Hokaka (13/4/70), KHT.

agricultural cycle.* At the same time, long-term migrants often took their wives and families with them during this period, in contrast to the tendency to leave families behind in Kowe that predominated after 1945. Thus labor migration in the period before 1930 actually removed little labor from the local economy and did not significantly alter the sexual division of labor.

In fact, the evidence indicates that one particular group of men—those who had become Christians—assumed a greater share of the agricultural labor than ever before during this period. Although the man's role continued to be largely a matter of individual predilection, informants recall that a number of men began to share almost all the agricultural activities with their wives. From the first, the C.M.S. school at Maseno emphasized the virtues of hard work and agricultural training as well as religious instruction.†

Early in 1906, the first C.M.S. missionaries arrived in Nyanza and established a "school for the sons of chiefs" at Maseno, north of Kowe. The Anglican Church and the education it sponsored played an important role in the history of Kowe throughout the colonial period. When the missionaries asked Chief Nyangaga of Seme to send several boys from his location to be boarders at their new school, the elders of Kowe purposely selected two boys from poor and relatively weak families—one an orphan, the other from a client family—to be among the first Luo students at Maseno. Their plans backfired, however; for when Samili Olaka (whose family were technically *jodak*, or "clients") returned to Kowe after 1910 to teach others what he had learned, his first convert was Yona Obara, son of Ogumbo, a lineage elder who was one of Kowe's most influential men. With Olaka's help, Obara established a day school at his home around 1912, and the two men together worked to teach others the fundamentals of Christianity, reading, and writing. These early teachers convinced many of their friends and relatives to attend services at their home and at Maseno.

* See the Kisumu District Quarterly Reports for December 1910 (p. 24) and March 1910 (p. 24), both in DC/CN 1/5/1, KNA.
† Interviews with Agutu Owili (23/1/70), Thomas Akuku (15/1/70), and Elijah Owe (22/1/70), KHT. See also John Lonsdale, "A Political History of Western Kenya" (unpublished manuscript, p. 192); and Richards 1956: 16–18.

Besides helping their own wives in the fields, these early Anglicans often contributed their labor as a means of persuading women to attend church services and instruction. Joan Arwa, one of the first women in Kowe to join the Anglican Church, recalled how she first became involved (interview, 19/4/70, KHT): "When a well-dressed Christian found an old woman carrying some firewood, he would help her carry it. Then the woman would say, now this boy has done me a great favor, I must go to this meeting too. And when they found me grinding, they would help me too, then tell me to go to church the next day. After Obara helped me to grind, he would light the fire and cook and give me food to eat. Then he gave me a piece of cloth to tie around my waist, and the next day I went to church."

Perhaps because of their close contacts with the European missionaries at Maseno and with different administrative officials and private employers, these early Christian men and women became conscious of their potential role as pioneers and innovators and committed themselves to economic change. Between 1910 and 1930, it was usually these people who first experimented with new crops and implements. They tried white maize, cassava, groundnuts, improved varieties of sorghum and beans, vegetables, fruit and hardwood trees, imported iron hoes, hand gristmills, and ox-drawn plows (all of which were ultimately incorporated in the local economy), and even cotton, coffee, and tobacco (which were not).

The same Christian education and literacy that brought jobs, status, and ultimate wealth for the men tended to bring difficulties and hardships for the women. Sofia Odero and Rose Orondo remember being stoned on the way to classes. Rebecca, one of Yona Obara's sisters, recalled that when she went to live with her husband in Kano, she was the first woman there to read or to wear a dress. Partly because she bore no children, but also because they thought she "gave herself airs," her in-laws scorned her. When she ran back home to Kowe they did not pursue her, and she remained in her parents' home until she died (interview, 15/10/69, KHT).

The early Christians led the other women of Kowe during the 1920's in adopting the innovations necessary to adjust to the colonial economy. Loye Elizabeth, the senior wife (*mikayi*) of Ogumbo, was famous throughout the lineage for her wealth and for her skills as a dancer and singer. People praised her as *wuon bel*, "owner of the sorghum," because her granaries were always full. The other women in her homestead recall that Loye's home practically overflowed with sesame, ghee, and other signs of prosperity. She accumulated a large herd of cattle on her own through the sale of her surplus crops. Through the persuasion of her son, Yona Obara, she became the first woman in Kowe to convert to Christianity. When she burned her *chieno* (the tassel of sisal fiber around her waist that identified her as a married woman) and began to wear European cloth, it caused a major disruption within the home. Ogumbo drove her from the house he had built for her, and later apparently sought help from various sorcerers to destroy both Loye and her son. But she persevered and further enhanced her reputation as a skillful cultivator by her experiments with white maize, cassava, groundnuts, and other new crops. It was often through her that other women in the area first acquired new seeds or cuttings and learned to work the new crops into the agricultural cycle.* Loye Elizabeth was the first woman in Kowe not to tear off her clothes and wail at the death of her husband, and she refused to be taken in leviratic marriage by one of his kinsmen. After Ogumbo's death, Loye succeeded him as *Jagolpur* ("the one who begins cultivating"); her undisputed skills in agriculture won her acceptance in a position normally occupied by men.

In the years between 1910 and 1920, women like Loye were able to accumulate large herds of livestock through the sale of their agricultural surplus. After 1919, however, local markets of the type at Kondik dried up and eventually disappeared, depriving women of what had been an important means of acquiring independent wealth. In part this decline of local markets reflected the relative lack of famines and food shortages during the 1920's (Hay 1972: 111–15). But it also reflected the increasing importance of cash in the colony's economy—cash that was needed to pay taxes

* Interviews with Julius Otieno (21/4/70), Joan Arwa (9/4/70), and Evelyn Ming'ala (13/4/70), KHT.

and to buy imported cloth, iron hoes, and other consumer goods. This desire for cash brought about a change in the focus of market activity from local barter markets, such as Kondik and Kipasi, to larger official "trading centers." The organization of these trading centers reflected the tendencies toward racial segregation inherent in British policy. Only Indians were licensed to buy and bulk African produce for export and to sell imported manufactured goods. Indians alone could erect permanent stalls in the trading centers; Africans were restricted to the smaller local open-air markets, which were thought to be their "proper sphere of activity."

The amount of time required to reach the trading centers at Luanda, Konyando, or Akala made it difficult for women to trade there regularly, and thus the initiative in trade passed temporarily to men. Women would still occasionally take their foodstuffs to these centers; but it was men who exploited opportunities to purchase salt, soap, or other high-value–low-bulk products from the Indian traders on a regular basis, and who then walked with them from homestead to homestead in Seme and sometimes in Gem, the maximal lineage that bordered Seme to the northwest, as well.

During the 1920's it seemed that the people of Kowe might successfully adjust to the demands of the colonial economy without sacrificing the vitality of the local economic systems. The worst abuses of forced labor had been corrected, and many of those who sought outside employment took their families with them to Nairobi, Nakuru, and Mombasa. The migrant elite (those whose education allowed them to take well-paying jobs) frequently invested their earnings in Kowe. Men and women alike experimented with new crops, techniques, and equipment that promised to open a new era of rural development and prosperity. Yet somehow this hopeful picture vanished, replaced by the discouraged conviction that agriculture was a dead end and that education for white-collar jobs was the only sensible investment. By 1945, Kowe had begun to be a society of women, children, and old men. Both capital and labor investment in agriculture were reduced to a minimum, and women worked intensely just to meet their subsistence requirements.

Though this transition occurred over the entire period between 1930 and 1945, its greatest force was felt in the early 1930's, when a series of related disasters wiped out the optimism of the 1920's. The world depression affected economic life in Kowe both through the severe drop in prices for food and cash crops, and through the loss of jobs as European employers tried to cut their losses. The devastations caused by swarms of locusts led to a prolonged famine in 1931 and 1932, known locally as *Nyangweso* (the Luo word for hoppers, locusts that have not yet grown wings). Drought caused a further, localized famine in 1934. The government organized a program of famine relief that was entirely financed, to the great indignation of the Luo, out of funds they had collected over a number of years to pay for the construction of a nonsectarian school.* For the people of Kowe, the prolonged years of famine emphasized the importance of wage labor as the only reliable means of income. In order to pay taxes, which district officials adamantly refused to postpone during the years of famine, and to buy food, the people of Kowe were forced to sell most of their livestock. Pastoralism never again became a viable part of the local economy.

The beginning of gold mining in Kowe in 1934 provided badly needed job and trading opportunities at this time of depression. Although perhaps not very significant from a colonywide perspective, the development of these mines brought some relief to the local economy. At the height of operations, D. K. Williams's "Kiboko Mine" employed several hundred people and regularly bought milk, produce, chickens, and prepared foods from the women of Kowe. The period of gold mining, although it lasted only a brief five or six years, established two basic trends that have dominated the local economy ever since: labor migration as the normal pattern of behavior for men under fifty; and trade and marketing as a regular part of a woman's daily life.

On the whole, the gold mines drew upon men who had not pre-

* Interviews with Julius Otieno (21/4/70) and Agutu Owili (23/1/70), KHT; Minutes of the Local Native Council meeting of 30 June 1931, p. 4, in PC/NZA 4/1/1/1, KNA; and Central Kavirondo District Annual Report, 1932, p. 18, DC/CN 1/6/1, KNA.

viously left Kowe for employment and brought them permanently into the labor market. The pattern of recruitment reflected the early growth of internal economic stratification, which was already apparent. Of the three minor lineages that formed Kowe, the people of Kamuga and Kachienga (who lived closest to the mines) provided the bulk of the mine laborers. These minor lineages were the last to be involved in the Anglican Church (and the first to leave it for other, independent churches), and thus were slower to take part in labor migration. At the same time, members of Kakal, the third minor lineage and the one that included most of the early Anglicans, felt that they had already specialized as skilled "outside laborers" and were scornful of employment opportunities at the mines.*

The women of Kowe began to trade in increasing numbers after 1933, particularly as they explored the market potential of the mines. No organized market existed at Kondik in those days, so women might take chickens or some sweet potatoes and walk to one of the southern markets, such as Akala, which was then known as Ober. However, it soon became clear that the gold-mining areas offered a regular market for produce and prepared foods. The women of Kowe began to take milk, vegetables, meat, eggs, chickens, and prepared foods such as porridge (*nyuka*) or maize and beans (*nyoyo*) and walk around the camp looking for buyers. The prices paid were very low, perhaps fifty cents for a large basket of vegetables or twenty cents for a bottle of milk, but for the women it represented an important opportunity to obtain a cash income. Those who lived in the vicinity of the mines often went twice every day, at midmorning and again in the late afternoon, whereas those farther away might go only twice a week.†

The Second World War further intensified the labor drain from the local economy, both through the extensive conscription of young men and through the increasing use of unpaid communal

* Interviews with Evelyn Ming'ala (16/3/70), Mathayo Orwa (2/4/70), Laban Okanja (15/4/70), and Japhath Omula (1/12/69), KHT.
† Interviews with Julius Otieno (21/4/70), James Athiambo (20/11/69), Ragen Kornel (22/4/70), Thomas Akuku (15/1/70), and Evelyn Ming'ala (16/3/70), KHT.

labor for bush-clearing and the construction and maintenance of roads, bridges, administrative camps, and so on. Wartime conscription claimed about one man from every homestead and tended to draw in those men who had previously remained at home.* (This was natural, since regular employment outside Kowe was a valid reason for escaping the draft.) The cash payment given to each soldier upon demobilization was a great boon to many men from poor families, who were thus able to buy cattle for bridewealth, to purchase a plow, or to enter local trade. Though some retired permanently from wage employment and managed to meet their recurring cash needs through local activity (such as plowing for hire), most of the men who had been conscripted eventually returned to the labor market.†

The long-term absence of men had an impact on the sexual division of labor, with women and children assuming a greater share of the agricultural work than ever before. Before 1930, much of the work on European farms had been seasonal, and men often had gone out to work only during the slack periods in the agricultural cycle. As double cropping became more common, however, and as agriculture as a whole became more intensive to make up for declining yields and the loss of soil fertility, these slack periods dwindled away; but the men continued to leave Kowe for outside employment in ever-increasing numbers.

The thirties represent a transition period with regard to the sexual division of labor, and it was clearly the women who bore the burden of the transition in rural areas. They met the problem by adopting labor-saving innovations in agriculture and reinvesting the labor saved in other economic activities, primarily trade. These changes did not, however, bring about the sudden and dra-

* The burden of conscription fell very unevenly on the members of this community, since the number of men in a homestead could vary widely. Though a typical homestead might have included an older man in his fifties with three or four married sons, in some cases the father might have died leaving only one son, whose absence through conscription could mean disaster.

† Interviews with K. L. Hunter, former Provincial Commissioner (19/5/69), Onyong'o Okaka (10/4/70), and Elijah Owe (22/1/70), KHT. Wrigley has written that the soldiers' family allowances were a major factor permitting the entry of Africans into retail trade at the end of the war (Wrigley 1965: 264).

matic rise of a group of women "peasant capitalists" in western Kenya. On the contrary, these women were forced to innovate in order to cope with a steadily worsening economic situation. Most of them ultimately managed to maintain—although not necessarily to improve—their standard of living.*

In the late 1930's and during the war years, some of the absent men began to "work with money"—that is, they sent their wives money with which to hire someone to help with clearing, hoeing, or weeding. In other words, these migrant laborers would pay substitutes to perform their normal share of the agricultural labor. And in the case of men who hired plow teams for their wives, the substitute was more than equal to their former labor contribution, since a plow team could dig up in a day or two the amount of land that a man and his wife might have hoed for many weeks.† "Working with money," however, tended to be a characteristic of the labor elite; and it was not something that the women of Kowe could count on. They were forced to adopt patterns of innovation in agriculture that reduced the required labor inputs. Many women began to plant cassava in the 1930's, for example, not only because of its drought-resistant qualities, but also because cassava flour could be added to sorghum flour to "stretch" it.‡ This was also the time when white maize began to compete with sorghum as the major starchy staple. Leaving taste preferences aside, white maize had the advantage of maturing more rapidly and permitting two crops a year (in both the short and long rains), whereas sorghum could only be grown during the long rains. The adoption of white maize thus helped spread labor inputs through the agricultural year and helped even out the peaks of labor demand.

* A. G. Hopkins has shown that a number of the earliest cocoa farmers around Lagos were also motivated by difficulties. In this case, the men were trying to cope with enormous commercial debts by shifting to a different economic niche. Hopkins argues that "innovation as a reaction to accumulating difficulties rather than a response to increased profits" may be a particular subcategory of innovation in colonial economies (Hopkins 1974: 24).

† Interviews with Evelyn Ming'ala (13/4/70) and Isaya Mbori (14/4/70), KHT.

‡ The increasing importance of cassava also reflected the declining fertility of the soil.

Other innovations were also valued primarily because they saved labor rather than because they permitted greater production. This was true of improved hoe blades, hand or water-powered grinding mills, and ox-drawn plows. When their husbands did not provide these conveniences, some women invested their own profits from trade in them. The overall effect of innovations between 1930 and 1945 was to reduce the investment of labor in agriculture and in food preparation and to reinvest it in wage employment for the men and in trade for the women.

Important changes also occurred in the social conceptions of agriculture and of its relation to economic security. Cultivating the land no longer seemed a viable means of acquiring wealth, which it had been in the past when men and women together had worked to produce large grain surpluses that could be converted into additional wives, cattle, and prestige. One probable element in this new equation was the intensification of rural poverty, which undermined feelings of egalitarianism and communal responsibility. Differences in wealth had certainly existed in the precolonial period, but the relative abundance of land in its own way had guaranteed each family a certain minimum income. Harvesting a bumper crop of maize or sorghum is public knowledge, whereas cash profits from trade and outside wages are not nearly so visible. It is difficult to refuse to lend money for school fees or for taxes when a kinsman asks; it is virtually impossible to refuse to give grain. Thus for some members of the community to have accumulated large grain surpluses (in the hopes of turning them into profit) at a time when others could no longer provide for their own subsistence needs—and when some were even losing access to land altogether—would have been extremely awkward. A sign of the times was the disappearance of the individual granaries that had dotted nineteenth-century homesteads; women began to store their grain in tin drums or gunnysacks, inside their houses and out of sight.

By 1945 a large number of people had come to feel that real economic security lay in formal education and long-term wage employment outside the home. The function of agriculture, in turn, came to be seen essentially as a holding operation. It was to continue to provide the basic elements of subsistence—food for the family in Kowe and often for the absentee laborers as well— and to guarantee a home and a place in the community that could be reactivated when necessary.

Women shared these new attitudes as well. They no longer exerted themselves to build up considerable surpluses of staple foods, but raised just a bit more than they thought the family would need in the coming year. The rest of their time was spent cultivating other crops for market, or developing a marketable craft (making ropes, pots, pipes, reed mats, and so on), or, finally, making regular visits to markets within a five- or ten-mile radius.

After the gold mines closed, the involvement of women in market activity did not decline. Instead, they began to range farther and farther afield, regularly visiting markets up to ten miles away from home. Again they took advantage of the environmental differences between north and south, buying bananas from the Luyia areas to the north and selling them in areas where they did not grow owing to insufficient rainfall, or buying fish from the lakeshore markets and carrying them farther inland—to give only two examples. The early 1940's saw the reestablishment of the local market at Kondik with permanent buildings and a fixed schedule, which made it once again an important locus of trade along the north-south axis. A pattern developed whereby the women traded in the open-air produce market in the center and the men bought the permanent shops surrounding the market as an investment (though they sometimes allowed their wives to run the shops). This economic segregation probably reflected the difficulty women faced in accumulating sufficient capital on their own.

By 1945, then, basic patterns of economic life had been established in Kowe that neither the later colonial officials nor the independent Kenya government have done much to alter. Because of such problems as overcrowding, the fragmentation of landholdings, and the declining fertility of the soil, and because the Luo people have been foremost in organizing and supporting political opposition to the Kenyatta regime, the economic disparity between

Seme and the more prosperous sections of the Gusii, Luyia, or Kikuyu regions seems to have increased.

The absence of adult men is even more striking today than it was in 1945, and the women of Kowe continue to cope with the problems discussed above. Most women probably make even greater sacrifices than before to ensure their children's education, skimping on their own food and clothing in order to invest their savings in school fees. Some daughters of Kowe have managed to acquire a secondary education and have gone out to join their brothers and fathers in urban employment. A few women have found new and prosperous opportunities at home: two are now joint owners of a store at Kondik Market that sells milk, soft drinks, fabric, kerosene, and a wide range of consumer goods. It is considered unusual and even unnatural for women to go so far in business on their own, but they seem to be managing quite well. Following the traditions established by Loye Elizabeth a generation earlier, these two women, Rose Orondo and Hilda Anyango, are staunch supporters of the local Anglican Church.

In conclusion, this paper has emphasized the role of Luo women in adopting economic innovations to resolve particular problems—primarily the need to maintain a certain level of food production despite the large-scale withdrawal of male labor from the rural economy and the increasing pressures of taxes, declining soil fertility, and the fragmentation of holdings. Luo women have long taken part in an ongoing process of experimentation and change in agricultural crops and techniques. Since the 1930's the women of Kowe, in particular, have adopted a wide range of labor-saving innovations in order to reduce the time invested in agriculture and to reinvest the time saved in trade. In the context of the steadily deteriorating economic conditions of the colonial and postcolonial periods, they have largely succeeded in maintaining both their agricultural production and their limited opportunities for capital accumulation.

Ga Women and Socioeconomic Change in Accra, Ghana

CLAIRE ROBERTSON

STUDIES OF women who play prominent political roles in African countries can give a false picture of the nature and direction of change in African societies. Such women, who often owe their positions to marriage or government tokenism, are usually part of the educated elite, and are thus atypical (Little 1973: 196–98). In these studies societies appear to be "Westernizing" at an appreciable rate, though in fact it is only the elites that are doing so. Of course, some scholars have taken the position that elites are the most important groups to study because they act as pacesetters for the rest of the population (Caldwell 1968: 18). But this attitude contains the implicit assumption that economic factors will permit the vast majority of Africans to better their condition and approach or attain the comfortable life-style of the elite minority. Yet such an assumption seems overly optimistic in view of current and projected economic conditions across much of Africa. Instead, it seems likely that the gap between the elite and the rest of the population will widen, especially if the former practice family planning and the latter do not. Moreover, it is not clear that the imitation of surface aspects of Western culture indicates a change of basic values at any level of society.

For these reasons, I have chosen to study the changes that have occurred during this century in the socioeconomic status of a non-elite group of women—the Ga women of Ussher Town, Central Accra, Ghana. These women make ideal subjects for studying socioeconomic change in an urban setting. As a coastal people living in an area that became the terminus for one of the main trade routes from the interior to the sea, the Ga experienced longer and more intensive contact with Europeans than almost any other people in Africa. Although their capital until 1680 was inland at Ayawaso, about twenty miles northwest of Accra, they had been participants in the trade in European goods since the fifteenth century (Dickson 1969: 68). The Ga have been fixed in the area where they are now—along the West African Atlantic coast from the Densu River to the Chemmu lagoon and north to the Akwapim hills—for more than a thousand years (Ozanne 1962: 66), and they have probably been urbanized to some extent ever since Ayawaso (probably their first town of any size) was founded in the late sixteenth century.

Until the nineteenth century, the contacts of the Ga with Europeans were primarily economic, for they functioned as middlemen in the trade with Ashanti to the north. But then they began to have a more intensive contact with European culture through education. In the 1820's Methodist missionaries arrived in Accra. Although they were not the first ones to come, they were ultimately to have the greatest impact. By 1839 they had set up a boys' school with 60 pupils and a girls' school with twenty pupils in Accra (Debrunner n.d.: 2, 6). From that time on, increasing educational opportunities were offered to people in Accra, and the Ga were not slow to take advantage of them. Nonetheless, European-style education principally affected men, not women, until after World War II (Robertson, forthcoming). And despite relatively early, intensive, and positive contact with Europeans, the Ga even today are not "Westernized" but display a complex syncretism of European and indigenous patterns in their social, economic, cultural, and religious life. For example, although the majority of the Ga are nominally Christian, the traditional Ga religion coexists with Christianity, and many people believe fervently in both.

Another factor that makes the Ga appealing for a study of social and economic change is their concentration in one place: they are a relatively small group of people (they formed only 3.5 percent of the total population of Ghana in 1960), and they are concentrated in Accra (15 percent of all the Ga in Ghana lived in Central Accra in 1960). Consequently, whatever the effects of urbanization, the Ga can be expected to have experienced them to their fullest extent (Kilson 1966: 20).

The 223 women I surveyed for this study were inhabitants of a small section of Central Accra centered on Bukom Square, Asere quarter, which is a large, dusty, bare spot surrounded by houses. In the olden days the Ga men met there before setting off to war. In the afternoons and evenings there is a market at one side of the square, but the main market serving the area is Salaga Market, two blocks away. The houses, or compounds, are jammed together around the square and sprawl in all directions. Some have two stories, but most are one-story affairs composed of an original house and numerous additions made at various times out of various materials. Except for narrow paths there is virtually no space between houses, so it is extremely difficult at times to distinguish where one compound ends and another begins.

This neighborhood is probably the site of the most ancient settlement of Ga at Accra. The earliest date of settlement at Accra is not known, but the site seems to have been well populated by the fifteenth century. Present-day Central Accra developed not from one center but from a series of contiguous settlements formed at different times by different peoples. Now, of course, the original settlements have grown into a continuous whole, but they preserve in their customs traces of their different origins. There are seven quarters that make up what is now known as Central Accra. Asere, Abola, and Gbese are supposed to be the oldest and most traditionally Ga of the quarters. Tradition has it that a fourth quarter, Otublohum, was originally settled by Akwamu and Denkyera, peoples who at one point controlled Accra politically. These four quarters together make up what is called Ussher Town, which is the area the Dutch claimed as their jurisdiction in the seventeenth century. The other three quarters of Central Accra—Alata (or Nleʃi), Sempe, and Akanmadze—are supposed to be of more recent origin. (Alata was settled by Nigerian workers imported to build a European fort.) The last three are commonly referred to as James

Town, which was the original area of British jurisdiction in Accra. Of these seven quarters Asere is by far the largest in population and area (Dickson 1969: 50; Manoukian 1950: 67; Amoah 1964: 19).

Ga women, like women of other West African peoples along the coast, have been involved in trading since as long ago as we can determine. Though the trade in such commodities as slaves, gold, and ivory was conducted mainly by men (McCall 1962: 697), the trade in fish and vegetables was always conducted by women; moreover, women probably took up the trade in small luxury items from the beginning of contact with Europeans. De Marees described in 1600 some of the commodities traded by the coastal women as "Linnen, Cloth, Knives, ground Corals [beads], Looking-glasses, Pinnes, arme Rings, and Fish." He went ahead to describe these women traders as "very nimble about their businesse, and so earnest therein, that they goe at least five or six miles every day to the places where they have to doe" (De Marees 1600: vi, 286–87). In 1853 Cruickshank noted women's devotion to trading in Accra: "The whole population are traders to a certain extent. It is the delight of the African women to sit in the market-places under the trees, exposing their wares for sale, or to hawk them through the streets from door to door, and from village to village" (Cruickshank 1853: ii, 280–81). In 1856 Daniell listed the commodities traded by women as plantains, bananas, peppers, limes, oranges, groundnuts, local soap, pineapples, flax, tobacco, okra, cassava, kenkey (the Ga staple food made from fermented corn dough) and other corn foods, soursops, berries, shallots, palm oil, shea butter, kola nuts, dried and fresh fish, smoked deer and goat meat, beads, earthenware, guns, copper basins, and local and imported cloth (Daniell 1856: 29). This list is still largely accurate, if we add both a greater variety of vegetables (lettuce, cauliflower, carrots, tomatoes, and avocados, most of which were introduced by Europeans) and more imported goods (margarine, toys, toilet paper, pots and pans—in fact, almost anything imported into Ghana). Though it is still true that the majority of Ga women deal in foodstuffs of some sort, as Wolfson has noted (1958: 164), the trade in imported goods has become increasingly important.

How important market trading was and is as a profession for the Ga women of Accra is indicated by statistics from the censuses. In 1911, when the first attempt to record women's professions was made, 75 percent of the 4,000 women in Accra District whose professions were recorded were traders. In 1921, in the Accra Municipal Area, the corresponding figure was 65 percent; in 1948, for the city of Accra only, it was 88 percent; and in 1960, for Ussher Town only, it was 78 percent. Also in 1960, 73.2 percent of all Ga women in Accra were listed as "sales workers." The 1921 figure is probably too low since the census distinguished between makers and sellers of food, a distinction not usually valid (many women do both).

Not only do most Ga women in Accra trade, but they dominate local trade in many commodities. In 1953, they formed 73 percent of all people of both sexes, and 89 percent of all women, engaged in commerce in Accra (Acquah 1958: 68). The areas in which they exercised the greatest dominance were in the trade of cloth, vegetables, fish, meat, provisions, prepared food, and hardware. Even though by 1960 the Ga were only 39 percent of the total population of Accra, Ga women formed 52 percent of the stallholders in the city's markets (Nypan 1960: 14, 28). The stallholders are the most powerful group of market women in terms of their influence on prices and their control over who is allowed to trade in the market. The activity of Ga women trading in Accra, then, is vitally important in the economy of the town.

Before turning to examine the sorts of changes that have occurred in the socioeconomic position of Ga women in this century, we must first understand some features of Central Accra Ga society as it existed in the late nineteenth and early twentieth centuries, and as it has continued to exist into the present. In Ga society, clan affiliation rights are traced patrilineally (people usually take their father's surname), inheritance rights cognatically (people inherit property from both parents), and residential rights bilaterally (people usually have the right to live in the compound where their parent of the same sex lives). The prevailing residential arrangement in Central Accra is that women live with their female matrilateral relatives, and men with their male patrilateral relatives, so that the area is a honeycomb of separate male and female compounds.* When a woman's husband wants her, he usually asks her to come see him that night. She usually prepares his food in her compound and sends it to him by one of the children. Normally, he is supposed to give her support money to pay for the food and clothing for the conjugal family. The small children and girls stay with her, and boys usually go to live with their father somewhere between ages six and ten, thus perpetuating the system.

This residential arrangement obviously has important economic overtones, in that it facilitates the organization of the women's cooperative trading and production ventures. But as Hajnal has pointed out, it is difficult to say whether the marriage pattern evolved as a result of economic pressures or vice versa. "In societies where the household is the principal unit of economic production as well as consumption . . . the marriage pattern is tied in very intimately with the economy as a whole. . . . The economic system influences the marriage pattern through the arrangements by which the economic basis for the support of a couple and their children is established. It is equally true that the marriage pattern influences the economic system" (Hajnal 1965: 132).

Up until the last quarter of the nineteenth century, fishing and farming were the most important occupations of Ga men. Before the Accra area became built up in the 1930's, many women helped their husbands with farming when they were not trading, and their trading usually included the sale of their husbands' agricultural surplus or fish (Field 1940: 62–63). Preparation or processing of food products for market took place in the women's compounds and involved members of several generations, with the older women instructing and supervising the younger ones. The women's compounds were also the scene of the local processing necessary for the imported-goods trade. The most important component of that trade through the end of the nineteenth century was beads, but in this century the focus has changed to cloth. In former times

* A third arrangement also exists whereby siblings of both sexes live together, expressing the frequently strong ties between siblings. It is numerically less important than the other patterns, however.

the cooperation of large numbers of female relatives in a business enterprise was necessary, and wealth was based on the number of people whose services one could control; but today, in a process that has been going on in southern Ghana for some time, wealth is increasingly coming to be defined in terms of the assets one controls (real estate, money).

With this background, let us examine what changes have been taking place in Ga women's socioeconomic roles. In addition to my survey of 223 Ga women in Ussher Town, Central Accra, I conducted intensive interviews with 72 of these women ranging in age from 36 to 98 (this will be called the "small survey" here). What follows is a partial distillation of some of the findings of both surveys (for more complete results, see Robertson 1974). The changes I discuss have had the paradoxical effect of making the Ga women simultaneously more economically independent but less qualified in terms of their training to make a success of that independence.

One major change I noted in Central Accra was a reduction in cooperation between spouses in economic enterprises. Ga women used to process and trade their husbands' fish and agricultural produce as a matter of course; this is still the common practice in Ga settlements outside Accra. Mills-Odoi (1967: 123–24) and Azu (1966: 105–6), in their respective studies of the fishing communities in Labadi and Teshie, two Ga villages east of Accra, noted the continued importance of cooperation between spouses in carrying on the industry. Husbands caught and wives marketed the fish, an arrangement that was conscientiously cooperative. One woman in my survey described it in this manner.

Q. Who contributed most to the support of your children?
A. Both of us contributed, but he put in more since he was the man. As long as he could afford it he provided the money for meals. When he was unable to, then I bought the food with my own money. That was generally the life at Faana [fishing villages] because there was nothing like a monthly pay packet in the fishing community.
Q. Was your husband anxious at times because he thought that you were too preoccupied with curing the fish?
A. No, not at all. He acknowledged my work then as a joint venture in the interest of our marriage. There were times when he had to put in a helping hand, especially when the fish were plentiful.

TABLE 1

Occupations of 108 Husbands of 72 Women, by Age Group of Women*

Occupations of husbands	Age group of women	
	60 and over (percent)	Under 60 (percent)
Fishing, farming, unskilled labor	27.3%	20.0%
Artisans (skilled labor)	28.5	47.5
White-collar workers	39.2	30.0
High-status traditional (chief, etc.)	5.0	2.5
TOTAL	100.0%	100.0%

* Some men had several occupations and are listed in more than one category. The relationship of the husbands' ages to the ages of the wives remained fairly constant over time: the husbands were usually 7 to 10 years older than their wives.

Because of the urbanization of Accra, and the corresponding decrease in the number of people involved in fishing and farming there, the possibilities for cooperation between Central Accra wives and their husbands (who might live elsewhere) in these spheres are lessening. Table 1 shows the change in occupations among the husbands of women in the small sample.

Those involved in fishing and farming—especially farming—diminished in numbers. Among the husbands of younger women, only 2 percent were farmers; among those of women 60 and over, 13 percent were farmers. Many men are now artisans and clerks, and these occupations do not lend themselves as well to patterns of husband-wife cooperation. The process whereby large numbers of men are becoming skilled laborers and clerks began in the late nineteenth century and has continued into the present. Where I did find men involved in cooperative enterprises with their wives, they were usually self-employed. Self-employed men accounted for the husbands of 48 percent of the women aged 60 and above and 35 percent of the women under 60, which suggests that wage labor may reduce the possibilities for cooperation. The trends toward there being fewer farmers and fishermen and less self-employment are not necessarily coterminous; that is, there were self-employed men in all categories listed in Table 1. But both trends lead in the same direction: the possibilities for economic cooperation between spouses are reduced.

Another change shown in Table 1 is the lower occupational status of the husbands of the younger women in the small sample. Because many men who make good in white-collar jobs move out of Central Accra to the suburbs, the proportion of men in the other categories looms larger than it did previously; the percentage of husbands who were white-collar workers went down in the younger age group, whereas it went up among men in the general population of Accra and of Ghana because of the economic boom of the 1950's. The largest single category of occupations of husbands of women in the older group was white-collar workers. For younger women's husbands, however, the largest category was artisans, and this indicates a fall in status. More poor men now become artisans than farmers or fishermen in Central Accra. (Of course there are large variations in the income of white-collar workers and artisans, but it was impossible to obtain sufficient information to break these categories down by income.) I will return to the significance of this change for the women's economic status later, after further consideration of cooperation between spouses.

In my intensive interviews I learned that even where possibilities existed for women to cooperate with their husbands in economic endeavors, the women often did not take advantage of them. In the past it was often felt that a wife had an obligation to sell her husband's produce, but this seems no longer to be the case. Of the 72 women I spoke with, only one woman in nine under age 60 had ever cooperated with her husband in some sort of work; by contrast, more than half of the women 60 and over had engaged in some cooperative venture with their husbands. Why was this? In a few cases the women said they found that their husbands were not catching the type of fish they specialized in selling. This may be indicative of a general trend whereby purely economic considerations are coming to play a larger part in the relationships between fishermen and fishsellers than personal considerations. And this trend among the fishermen and fishsellers may represent a tendency toward the attenuation of mutual economic obligations of spouses in all fields of endeavor. In short, economic cooperation between spouses seems no longer to be an ideal.

Another aspect of this decrease in cooperation was the mutual

suspicion between spouses concerning sharing knowledge of business dealings. Women did not like to let their husbands know the
intimate details of their businesses. Only women who got along
extremely well with their husbands trusted them with knowledge
of their profits. One woman, who by all accounts had a good husband, explained her cautious attitude in this way. "Once a husband
gets to know about the finances of his wife, the man begins to be
tight with money toward the wife. He will not be willing to meet
some of the financial responsibilities he has previously been shouldering. Therefore, a safe attitude is to keep the man in the dark."
Other women told me of cases where men had quit giving support
money to their wives when they found out how much their wives
were making. The women therefore pursued a conscientious policy
of keeping their husbands ignorant of their profits.

This policy even has affected women's getting business capital
from their husbands, which is an established practice (Mills-Odoi
1967: 122; Field 1940: 55). Some women said they did not want to
get capital from their husbands lest they be expected to account
to them for its use.* Several women stated that the only time
women had to let their husbands know about their profits was
when the husbands had supplied the capital.† One proudly claimed
that she had never quarreled with any of her husbands over money
because "no one has any cause to quarrel with you over money
unless that one has financed you and you have wasted the money."
A stronger reason for not wanting to get capital from the husbands,
however, was the commonly expressed fear that if the husband
provided capital he would discontinue support money. One woman had a husband who "once gave me capital for work with the
understanding that with it my monthly pocket allowance would
cease. He wanted me to maintain myself from the profits. I made
it plain to him that it would not work, for I should have to eat

* Elkan noted a similar sentiment among Ganda women in Kampala with
respect to receiving economic support from men. Walter Elkan, *An African
Labour Force*, East African Studies No. 7 (Kampala, 1956), p. 42.

† This was confirmed by High Court Justice Annie Jiagge in an interview on
March 14, 1972, and by a case in the *James Town Mantse's Judgment Book*,
pp. 382–83. This last is in the possession of the present Ga Mantse (Paramount
Chief of the Ga), Nii Amugi II.

into the very capital. In the end I was proved right. The business did not last long."

Though the younger women in the small survey got less support from their husbands than the older women had received from theirs, more younger women than older ones had received business capital from their husbands. Forty-one percent of women under 70 had received business capital from their husbands, compared to 16 percent of those 70 or over. This change may be one manifestation of a divergence in attitude between the men and the women. Whereas men may make the demands described above when they provide capital, women zealously defend their economic independence. Although many of the women in the younger age group received capital from their husbands, not one cooperated with her husband in a business where he supplied the capital. These women were also not in the habit of making confidences about their profits. Another reason capital was less popular than support money was that it was not viewed as a free gift, but rather as a loan. One woman described getting capital from her husband in this manner.

Q. When you thought you needed capital and approached your husband, did he assist?
A. Yes.
Q. And what happened to the capital afterwards?
A. It was refunded at the appropriate time because it was a loan.

She was unenthusiastic about borrowing capital and stressed that it was better not to tell husbands about profits so that they would not quit giving support money. The men may find giving capital a more satisfactory way of providing support because it gives them a claim on their wives' profits, and because they can demand its return; obviously, the women would rather have support money with no strings attached.

In this zealous defense of their economic independence, the women of Central Accra may be fighting a last-ditch battle against a general shift in the pattern of financial arrangements between marriage partners. When cooperation between spouses was the rule rather than the exception, it was often the women who handled the money end of transactions. In the fish and vegetable

trades, where cooperation was most common, the women sold
the goods for cash, of which they then returned a portion to the
men (the cost price). Their opportunities for turning this situation
to their adavntage must have been great. No wonder that in
accounts of the relative economic power of men and women in
Ga fishing villages the women seem to have been generally better
off than the men.* Under changed conditions, the women even
seem to have improved their position in the village of Teshie,
according to Azu. "Moreover, because the money the women now
make comes directly from their own efforts and they cannot in any
way be said to be dependent on their husbands, their wealth is
seen as theirs alone; this has led to an increase in the status of
those women who have 'made it' in the modern industry. The
psychological state of the men in front of this growing strength
of the women is one of hostility and frustration. They say that now
no man can compel his wife to come and sleep, and that the women
do not give their husbands the same devotion and respect as they
did in the past."†

But in Central Accra the women's position relative to that of the
men has worsened. With increasing numbers of men earning salaries and doling out occasional allowances, the source of the "conjugal" income has come under their exclusive control. In the
former situation, where women handled the cash transactions in
joint ventures, the men had a rough idea of the value of their products and could demand a fair share; but in the current situation,
where men are bringing in salaries whose size they often hide from
their wives, the women are at a great disadvantage. Illiterate
women are often wholly ignorant of the market value of their
husbands' skilled labor or literate skills, so they have no way of
estimating the men's income. Nonetheless, they maintain their
attitude of independence: "let him do his work and I will do

* This seems to have been true in several villages near Accra: Tema before
resettlement, Teshie, and the old parts of Labadi. See G. W. Amarteifio, D. A.
Butcher, and David Whitham, *Tema Manhean, A Study of Resettlement* (Accra,
1966); Azu 1966; and Mills-Odoi 1967.
† Azu 1966: 107. There, too, the women were less dependent on their husbands for fish than previously because of the mechanization of the fishing
industry.

mine." Their chief concern was that their husbands continue to contribute support money; as long as the amount of support was up to their expectations, they did not express much concern about their husbands' total income.

Indeed, the practice of spouses' owning separate property in marriage was and is recognized by the local courts, both of Ga customary and British-Ghanaian law.* A woman's property cannot be seized to pay the debts of her husband, or vice versa. She does not ordinarily inherit any of her husband's property, unless she can prove that he gave it to her while he was alive, or unless she can get the court to enforce her right to inherit a fifth of his estate in an Ordinance marriage.† The Ga courts will uphold a woman's right to be maintained from her husband's estate. A woman can act on her own behalf before any court as creditor, debtor, contractor, head of a lineage, administratrix of an estate, and guardian of children; and she does not need the consent of her lineage or husband to do so. In spite of the disadvantage of illiteracy, women have not been slow to defend and extend their rights, and have even taken advantage of some rights granted them under Ordinance marriages that they ordinarily would not have had.‡ For example, in going through Accra District Court records I found that women have become increasingly willing to bring debt cases

---

* The Ga courts were operated by the Ga chiefs and had functions roughly equivalent to our petty courts, except that they dealt with most matters having to do with Ga customary law, especially concerning marriage (see following). They were subordinate to the British-imposed higher courts, which dealt with cases involving large sums of money and matters of British law. These courts are now the Ghanaian courts.

† Ghana National Archives, SCT 17/4/22, 545–46 (cases Nov. 2, 1900). SCT 2/6/5, 34, *High Court Judgment Book*, Part I (case July, 1914). SCT 2/6/16, 441–42, *High Court Judgment Book* (case May 26, 1933). *James Town Mantse's Judgment Book*, 27, 40, 102 (cases Oct. 15, 1919, and 1922). A. N. Allott, *Essays in African Law* (London, 1960), p. 217. Ordinance marriages were originally intended for Europeans wishing to marry in the Gold Coast. They were rarely performed for Ghanaians, and usually only for elite couples. None of the people in my survey had had one.

‡ R. J. H. Pogucki, *Report on Land Tenure in Customary Law of The Non-Akan Areas of the Gold Coast Colony, Part II: Ga* (Accra, 1968; issued originally in 1954), pp. 29–30. SCT 2/6/2, 180, *High Court Judgment Book* (case Oct. 20, 1895). SCT 17/6/1, 118 (case 1895). ADM 37/4/2, 157–58 (case Feb. 28, 1930). SCT 2/6/5, Part I, 59 (case Sept. 25, 1914). *James Town Mantse's Judgment Book* (case Nov. 2, 1921). A. N. Allott, *Essays in African Law* (London, 1960), p. 221.

in recent years. And when they were sued for debt they usually put up a good fight. For example, one woman who got entangled with a Lebanese moneylender in 1939 fought him to the High Court and managed to get her debt reduced from £504 to £281.* In collecting overdue rents women often resort to the courts, too.

Because spouses most commonly keep their property entirely separate, any money given by one spouse to the other is usually regarded as a loan subject to repayment. However, the recognized institution of support money might make it difficult for men to regain money given to their wives for safekeeping (a former practice) or for trading. For instance, one man sued his ex-wife for the value of goods he had given her to sell, but she responded that he had quit giving her support money so she did not owe him anything. She won.† But because women have no fixed obligations to their husbands, they usually can recover—by legal means if necessary—any money given to their husbands. In the small survey I found that in 27 percent of marriages women claimed to have helped their husbands by lending them money at one time or another. If relations were amicable between spouses, women found refusal to give an interest-free loan difficult. They viewed it as part of the reciprocal obligations of spouses. After all, their husbands had given them children (i.e., support in old age and indirect rights in property). One woman expressed it this way.

Q. Do women maintain men at times?
A. Yes, many do that. A man may lose his job; if that happens the woman should necessarily provide for the upkeep of the man. The pity of this situation, however, is that the men often turn out to be ungrateful. They sack the woman and attempt to get married to a fresh woman as soon as they become re-employed.
Q. Did any quarrels arise between you and any of your husbands?
A. One, the second, tempted me immensely, but I managed to avoid a clash by allowing him to have his way because of our four children. He was in need of money and I lent him some. After all, today his children are maintaining me.

* SCT 2/6/19, 124–29, *High Court Judgment Book* (case Aug. 8, 1939). The money unit used here is the British pound, which was the official Ghanaian currency until 1965.
† SCT 17/4/16, 557 (case Sept. 19, 1895).

Other women were more hardnosed about lending money. One woman, asked if she lent money, said "Yes, at 50 percent interest [per month]. But for my husband, only 30 percent."

In fact, lending or giving money to husbands was one form of expenditure women made that they did not often publicize, both because there is a Ga ethic against lending and because lending often led to marital troubles when loans were not repaid. Some women bore lasting grudges against ex-husbands who had gone off without repaying loans. One court case dealt with a man who had quit supporting his wife and owed her £51. She then kicked him out of her house (where they had been living), whereupon he attempted to sell it illegally in her absence.* However, there are not many women who are in a position to lend money to their husbands now.

In fact, the relative economic positions of men and women appear to have changed, and women's lending of money to their husbands was probably a feature more of the old system than of the new. The new model with which the women of central Accra are often presented is that of their suburban sisters, who are more likely to be living with their husbands, under their economic control and/or supported by them. Fragmentary evidence seems to indicate that Ga living in the Accra suburbs are moving toward a residential and marriage pattern of a type more familiar to Westerners—although not necessarily Western European in nature (the external forms may look similar, but the internals of the situation may operate in a radically different manner). Further research is needed before we can say for certain whether this is so. There are indications that in the suburban situation a man may demand more information about his wife's finances because he is contributing to them but may not furnish her with similar information—partly to keep open his option for having "outside" women without his wife's knowledge. Faced with this model, the Central Accra women tend to equate financial dependence on a husband with high-status marriage, so that they sometimes view it

* SNA 11/704 (case Nov. 9, 1920).

TABLE 2

*Percent of Women Owning Different Types of Property,
by Age Group of Women*

Property owned	Age group of women	
	50 and over	Under 50
Houses	27%	8%
Farms and/or unimproved land	47	33
Boats and/or nets	5	0
Jewelry	54	50

as desirable. Meanwhile, the erosion of their economic position has also made increased support from their husbands desirable, although it is not often forthcoming. In fact, the younger women in the small sample showed noticeably higher expectations of support from their husbands than the older women did.

Evidence of the deteriorating economic position of the younger women in the small sample can be found in Table 2, which shows the distribution of property ownership by age group. Of course it could be argued that the younger women will naturally own less property than the older ones because their careers have been shorter. However, the women in their fifties were one of the most prosperous groups; many had built their houses at least ten years before, when they were in their forties during the prosperous 1950's. The women in their forties, on the other hand, showed no signs of planning to build houses; moreover, few of them owned land on which to do so. In 1971 Sai noted that it was becoming increasingly difficult for women to build houses, and that most women who did build houses had traded for thirty or more years (pp. 47, 104).* This evidence cannot be regarded as conclusive, but it may be indicative of relative poverty on the part of the younger women.

* Spending money on houses is probably the best indicator of prosperity among women traders. Real estate is the most popular form of investment for Ghanaians; 75 percent of the women in my small sample said that they would buy land and build a house if they had the money to do so. Today, most land that is bought is in the suburbs of Accra, and the houses that are built there are very often rented out to bring in income.

The women's economic position cannot be described only by their assets; we must also consider their liabilities. Women have to meet a variety of financial responsibilities beyond the universal expenses for food and clothing. Of the 72 women in my small survey, 82 percent were spending money on the education of their children; 70 percent had loaned money to relatives; 70 percent were enrolled in some form of savings association requiring regular deposits; 36 percent had invested money in land; 26 percent had invested money in houses; and 6 percent had loaned money to nonrelatives. It is noteworthy that only a minority could afford to invest in real estate. In their expenditures these women contradicted this statement by Field (1940: 54) about Ga women's economic position: "In the matter of money there are probably no people on earth whose women are in such an enviable position as the Ga. A woman's financial responsibilities are almost negligible, but the occasions on which she makes financial claims are legion. She also makes money by her trading, and no one can touch this money." Of course, Field was talking mainly about women in the fishing communities around Accra in 1940, but even so she ignored the kind of financial help to husbands mentioned earlier, which was probably more important in small fishing communities than in Accra. The pattern of expenditures adduced above clearly shows the importance of women's obligations to their children for education and to their relatives for loans.

The top item of expenditure was for education. In the small survey the education of 50 percent of the children of the informants was financed primarily by their mothers, that of 37 percent by their fathers, that of 6 percent by female relatives, and that of 4 percent by male relatives. It may be objected that the women were overestimating their own role in paying for education. In my experience, however, they were more likely to underestimate it, since some shame was involved in admitting that a husband did not support his children as he should have. The husbands were supposed to pay for their children's education. Schooling is regarded as an investment, since the educated are expected to repay the cost of their education many times over by earning more than uneducated people would and by supporting their sponsors in old age. One woman said, "My children were educated through the sweat of my brow. The children are my assets."

Lending money to relatives was a high-risk investment, but a person usually got back services, if not always money. One woman felt that she had been amply repaid by her younger sister for the money she had donated for her education and business capital, since her sister gave her small sums of money from time to time and contributed to her expenses for induction into the traditional Ga priesthood. Sixty-six of the 72 women in my small sample claimed to have helped support relatives other than children and grandchildren: 61 percent said they supported their mothers; 3 percent, their fathers; 21 percent, their sisters; 3 percent, their brothers; 35 percent, their sisters' children; 23 percent, their brothers' children; 30 percent, other matrilateral relatives; and 6 percent, other patrilateral relatives. Mothers were the relatives most often supported by women; this confirmed the data on the percentage of women who said that their daughters were helping them (57 percent). This situation verifies Field's statement (1940: 56) that "a woman and her mother in the matter of money are one person, just as a man and his father are one. 'They have one money-bag.'" Whereas for the men this may no longer be true, it certainly held for the majority of women in my sample. Mother-daughter ties seemed to be the strongest links, both socially and economically, that the women had. Some women stated that they tried to become self-supporting as early as possible so their mothers would not have to support them, and that they then gave some of their earnings to their mothers. Older women often tried to keep working as long as possible so that their daughters, who were hard-pressed caring for their own children, would not have to provide support for them. Even much of the support to other matrilateral and patrilateral relatives evidenced in the percentages cited above went to "mother substitutes"—usually the mothers' sisters and their children, or else the fathers' sisters. In fact, slightly more women helped their fathers' female relatives than helped their own fathers. Support, then, usually goes matrilaterally for the women and patrilaterally for the men. Old men must rely primarily on their sons for help, evidently; but women get more help from their sons than men get from their daughters. I found court cases in the National Archives where mothers and sons bailed each other out of debt but none involving fathers and daughters.*

Help for (or from) the children of siblings most often took the form of a woman's accepting one or more daughters from a sister to bring up. Women occasionally exchanged daughters with a sister, and childless women were sometimes given daughters by a sister as foster children. In the same way, a woman with no daughter might have begged and received one from a sister or brother. Twenty-nine percent of the women in the small sample had sent a child to a relative to care for, either temporarily or permanently, and 44 percent took care of the daughters of a sister or brother. Only 11 percent took care of sons belonging to a sibling, which was about the same proportion (9 percent) that cared for daughters belonging to friends. Because girls are more useful than boys in providing women with economic help, it was usually daughters who were sent to other female relatives. This practice was one aspect of the apprenticeship system whereby young women learned the rudiments of trading.

The final item in the women's pattern of expenditures I want to comment on is savings. The older women in my small survey tended to keep their savings in the form of jewelry or cash hoards. Jewelry was often used as collateral for business loans, so it was hoarded in preference to money. But hoards are extremely susceptible to robbery, as several women in my survey discovered. For this reason other forms of saving were becoming increasingly popular. The younger women, in particular, were partial to bank or post office accounts.† But among women of all ages the *susu*, or rotating credit system, was the most popular vehicle for saving. Sixty-seven percent of the women in the small survey reported that they were using it or had used it at one time.

* SCT 2/6/12, 264, 266–67, *High Court Judgment Book* (cases Nov., 1928).
† Twenty-five percent of the women in the small survey claimed to use or to have used bank accounts, and 9 percent post office accounts.

The practice of *susu* is relatively recent, having developed during and after World War II in conjunction with the growth of voluntary associations.* *Susu* takes many forms among the Ga. Most often it is performed as a function of a voluntary association, the most popular one at present being Nyemimei Akpee ("Siblings' Society"). Members meet once a week and pay fixed amounts of money into a pool that is given to a different person each week in a set order. Two shillings a week (20 pesewas, or U.S. $.15) might be the cost of a share; and a woman with one share will get the fund once during each full rotation. Obviously, the number of members in a *susu* is an important consideration; where the *susu* is large, women often take two or more shares in order to get the pool two or more times in the course of one rotation (which may take several years!). (For a further discussion of rotating credit associations, see the paper by Barbara C. Lewis elsewhere in this volume.)

In addition to providing a vehicle for saving, the voluntary associations offer the women a means of making business and social contacts. They are a good forum for the exchange of information on business techniques and prices, and they also serve as a recruiting ground for partners. Their informal functions are analogous to those of Rotary and similar organizations. Ga women are the main participants in associations of this kind in Accra, and may have established them partly in an effort to widen their business links outside the context of their lineages. Certainly the voluntary associations perform more functions than the lineages, and we may view their development as another manifestation of the increase in women's economic independence.

In summarizing the economic position of Central Accra Ga women, we find that economic independence for women does not necessarily improve their economic status. For the great majority of women, conditions in the economy as a whole have a far greater

---

* The first references to it I found in the court records were in 1945. ADM 37/4/9, 391, 468 (cases Sept. 1 and Oct. 1, 1945). *Susu* is a corruption of the Yoruba word for the same institution, *esusu*. W. R. Bascom, "The *Esusu*: A Credit Institution of the Yoruba," *Journal of the Royal Anthropological Institute*, 82, no. 1 (1952), pp. 63–69.

impact on their relative prosperity than the matter of whether or how much they are cooperating with their relatives or spouses in economic enterprise. Though the reduction in economic cooperation has made it possible for some women to make more economically "rational" business decisions, only the large traders seem to have profited significantly by the change. Most of the traders make only enough to get by.*

In fact, it is possible that the economic position of most Central Accra women has deteriorated in comparison with that of their predecessors. Because of the signal importance of education today as the principal route to economic success and high status, young women are anxious to educate their children. Coupled with the high cost of education, though, is the fact that husbands are increasingly tending not to fulfill their support obligations, partly because Central Accra men tend to be in less remunerative occupations than their predecessors. Thus the burden of educating children has fallen heavily on the women. Also, a relatively high divorce rate (48 percent of the marriages of the women in the small sample ended in separation), and the fact that men often did not support children of a previous marriage, meant that many women had to rely primarily on their own resources to provide even the basic necessities of life for themselves and their children. Then, too, men frequently gave financial obligations to their lineages higher priority than those to their wives. Also, some men with the best of intentions simply could not provide support money because of periodic unemployment or a poor catch. For all these reasons the young women of Central Accra, who now have more surviving children than their predecessors did (an average of about seven per woman), often have a heavy financial burden in simply feeding and clothing their children, much less educating them.

At the same time, trade conditions have become increasingly monopolistic in the two most profitable lines pursued by women—fish and cloth selling. In the latter field, it is difficult now for a

---

* Sai 1971, p. 9, said that the profits of the average trader were not substantial enough to raise her living standard. Nypan 1960, p. 40, claimed that half of the traders had a daily turnover of £2 or less.

small trader to get started in a business because of the amount of capital required to obtain a passbook (a credit account) with a large firm in order to get cloth and imported goods to sell. The mechanization of the fishing industry in the 1950's and the establishment of the State Fishing Corporation in the 1960's have resulted in monopolistic supply conditions that are not to most women's advantage. The reduction in economic cooperation does not help the women combat these conditions either. More husbands may give business capital, but the amounts given are smaller; and the husbands' capabilities of giving support money have been reduced because of their declining economic status. Meanwhile, because of the intervention of education for women, young women's reciprocal economic bonds with their mothers are being loosened; the educated daughters are often unwilling to engage in trade, which they consider to be too low in status to suit their aspirations. Thus many no longer cooperate with their mothers in compound-based businesses. Although this reduction in economic cooperation has created more economic independence for these Ga women, it has probably worsened their financial position.

Central Accra, which in the past often belied its appearance of being a slum, is now perhaps becoming one—a ghetto of people who have few options for getting out. Now it is a refuge not only for the workers who rent rooms there, but also for the Ga women who can live there rent-free in their mothers' compounds. As wealthier people move out, the mutual contacts between the suburbs and Central Accra, which might once have alleviated the poverty of some in Central Accra, have become attenuated. Central Accra no longer has to the same extent the mix of rich, comfortable, and poor that it once had; the departure of the first two groups in large numbers has left the area increasingly just poor. Meanwhile, the women look desperately for means to support their children when their husbands do not fulfill support obligations. These children now expect to be educated and pressure their mothers to pay for it; and the women do pay, in part because they themselves have high expectations of economic betterment through the agency of their children. However, with a bad unemployment problem in Accra, their hopes are likely to be dashed as they watch their sons go unemployed and their daughters become prostitutes. They then must accept gratefully whatever the daughters can earn.

"When jobs in modern industry, in modern trade, and in offices are held exclusively or overwhelmingly by men, the productivity, attitude, and outlook of men and women begin to diverge. . . . Economic progress benefits men as wage earners in the modern sector, while the position of women is left unchanged and even deteriorates when competition from the growing modern sectors eliminates the traditional enterprises carried on by women. . . . This pattern of sex roles, with men doing the skilled and supervisory work and women in the unskilled and subservient jobs, so dominates the developing and industrialized countries alike, that it is often regarded as 'natural' by both men and women alike." (Boserup 1970: 139–40.) Though opportunities for women as skilled laborers or clerks are perhaps better in Ghana than in some other countries, there is still a large gap between men and women; and this gap is not closing, because men had a head start in formal education. Fewer girls than boys complete secondary school, and therefore a girl looking for a clerical job will probably have to compete with many boys, some of whom are bound to be better qualified for the job than she is. In addition, women working in offices have to contend with sexual overtures from male co-workers, who regard such "emancipated women" as fair game. This tendency has driven some women back into market trading, which offers free choice in matters of personal contact and flexible hours. No wonder, then, that Kilson saw the modernization process as reinforcing the Ga cultural bias toward belief in male superiority (1966: 107). Economic "progress," such as the mechanization of the fishing industry and its concentration of the supply of fish in a few hands, does not necessarily mean prosperity for everyone. And economic independence for women can sometimes mean that women's economic position is worse, not better.

The Limitations of Group Action Among Entrepreneurs: The Market Women of Abidjan, Ivory Coast

BARBARA C. LEWIS

THE INDUSTRY and economic independence of African market women have been frequently noted—and with good reason. Market women are tough entrepreneurs who sometimes surpass their male counterparts in the panoply of petty trade so characteristic of African city life. Active participants in the volatile and competitive commercial sector, they strive to protect their economic interests and better their economic status. But though these efforts have gained the attention of political observers, they have not always been crowned by internal harmony or external success. Organizations of market women have proved far more difficult to maintain than the many voluntary associations grouping co-ethnics or residents of the same neighborhoods.

This study focuses on a specific group of market women, the traders in the Treichville quarter market in Abidjan, the capital of the Ivory Coast. These women have sought, through collective action, (1) to provide a regular and systematic means of accumulating capital, (2) to cut the costs of goods acquired from suppliers, and (3) to defend their interests in conflicts with administrative authorities. These same women also participate in group activities outside the market; here we can observe the impact of their differing cultural backgrounds in defining strategies by which shared goals are achieved. The comparison between associational activities in and outside the marketplace will suggest what impedes market women's efforts to achieve shared goals and thus, in more general terms, will suggest the limitations of voluntary group action.*

A brief discussion of the peoples of the Ivory Coast will provide a frame of reference for what follows. For the purposes of this paper, I have distinguished between two "regions" in the Ivory Coast—the north and the south. The lush tropical vegetation of the south gives way gradually to savanna and grassland as one proceeds farther north, and the peoples indigenous to each region have very different social and economic backgrounds. Though as many as 60 ethnic groups have been enumerated in the Ivory Coast, my discussion here focuses upon "northerners" and "southerners." The northerners I refer to are Dioula, members of the Manding ethnic cluster located across much of the West African savanna.† Islam and trade are the identifying features of the Dioula community, whose precolonial commercial networks linked the fringe of the forest to the south with points as far north as Timbuktu, as far east as Nigeria, and as far west as Senegal. Permanent Dioula communities existed in the north of the Ivory Coast at the time of the French conquest, but the new commercial opportunities in the forest that developed during French colonial rule have attracted vast numbers of Dioula to all the new towns in the south. It is noteworthy that Dioula women, unlike the cloistered women of some Muslim groups, are allowed to share fully in various commercial activities.

Among the southerners, most of whom are animists, are the Lagoon peoples of the coast, the Akan of the eastern Ivory Coast and neighboring Ghana, and the Krou to the west. The Krou, who historically have formed dispersed and insular communities, were latecomers to the commerce triggered by the European presence on the coast. The Akan people of the Ivory Coast, related to the Ashanti in Ghana, shared in the political and economic expansion

* This research was made possible by a grant for the summer of 1970 from the Social Science Research Council. I also wish to express my gratitude to the Mayor of Abidjan, M. Konan Kanga, and his staff, who generously lent this research their full support.

† For a discussion of the origins of the Dioula and of the contemporary Dioula community in the Ivoirian south, see Lewis 1971: 273–307.

of the precolonial Ashanti kingdom. They too, like the Lagoon peoples, have long been active in commercial agriculture and trade, which spread north from European coastal centers in the Ivoirian east and Ghana. The matrilineal structure of the Akan (and some Lagoon groups) gives women special status and autonomy from their spouses. These historical and structural features appear to explain why the women of these eastern groups have assumed a more lively role in commerce than the Krou women from the west have done.*

Abidjan, the chief port and political capital of the Ivory Coast, has drawn thousands of migrants over the past 25 years and has grown from a city of 17,500 people in 1936 to one with a population of over 850,000 in 1975. It has attracted peoples from throughout the Ivory Coast and neighboring countries, and now houses numerous Muslims, including the Dioula, as well as animists and Christian converts from among the Krou, Akan, and other southern groups. Though women of all these groups participate in petty trade, the Dioula and Akan women are particularly well represented in retail marketing.

The Treichville quarter market, Abidjan's largest, is one of the most impressive in West Africa. Not yet a decade old, its two-story, opensided concrete building occupies nearly a city block. Hundreds of men and women trade here and in the surrounding space. Some have booths; others sit behind tables; but the majority, sellers of foodstuffs that they purchase for little and sell for slightly more, sit on small wooden stools with their goods beside them on one or two square meters of rented space. Though sellers are grouped by product, no systematic or complete ethnic specialization results, except in the case of the Gouro pepper sellers, who have a near monopoly. But even though all the major trading sectors are ethnically heterogeneous, ethnic feeling is still strong. For example, the seamstresses, who included members of over half a dozen

---

* Generalizations regarding the southern women are difficult to make, as traditions vary, even among the Akan. The broad distinctions between northerners and southerners presented in the course of this paper are explanatory hypotheses; the work of other scholars will reveal whether there are significant ethnic differences in the urban networks of southern women.

peoples, often arrange their seating behind the long tables at which they work so that co-ethnics are side by side. And each of the four ethnic groups engaged in selling fish has its own marketing system. There is also a tendency toward ethnic specialization in the production and marketing of certain prepared foods—for example, *attiéké* (steamed manioc similar to couscous), which is made and sold largely by women of the Lagoon peoples.

The reasons why no clear pattern of ethnic specialization has evolved are many and complex. For one thing, the non-Ivoirians who dominated market activity during the colonial period are still an important presence in the marketplace, though political pressures have reduced their dominance. For another, spaces in the market are not wholly controlled by the women who trade there and cannot be passed on routinely to kin or friends of the same ethnic group, though this is occasionally done. Places in the market are obtained through the Treichville mayoral office; and since ethnic monopolies are in official disfavor in the Ivory Coast, any attempt by one ethnic group to monopolize a given sector at the expense of another group (or other groups) will not find a sympathetic response among the licensing officials. Moreover, women do not always sell goods from their home areas.

Space in the market is so limited, and the number of unemployed or underemployed women desiring to sell there is so great, that getting a place is a greater barrier to success than getting goods to sell. Those determined to gain an official allocation of space must pursue several strategies. Naturally, one such strategy is for a woman to keep checking with kin or friends within her own specialty in the hope of finding someone willing to share a space or about to leave the market. She will have to take what she can get, and this can often mean switching to a new line of commerce if a space becomes available in another sector. One seamstress turned to selling yard goods, because the one place she was able to find was in the yard-goods sector. Of course, a woman with the good fortune to have official connections may find the public authorities more effective in locating her a desired place. Others may offer the municipal clerk in charge of seating and fee collection a gift to encourage him in his efforts on their behalf. But the clerk must be careful and diplomatic in placing a newcomer. Should he attempt to place a stranger among established sellers without first clearing the matter with them, they can be an imposing force. Similarly, sellers often vigorously defend the place of a neighbor when she takes a trip and leaves her place empty. And if a seller moves away, her neighbors are likely to have candidates for the newly available place. Thus the market's predominant tone is one of intense competitiveness: each woman has struggled, maneuvered, and even bribed her way onto "her" space, and her keenest desire is to maximize returns for the money and energy she has expended.

With the help of my interpreter, I interviewed 44 women from nine different sectors.* The goods they sold ranged from low-profit items (e.g., peppers and yams) to manufactured goods (e.g., toiletries), fresh and smoked fish, and cloth (both indigenously dyed cloth and imported prints). During the mornings we introduced ourselves to sellers in the market and arranged to talk with them at home in the relative calm of the late afternoon or evening. In most cases, my interpreter was able to overcome the initial resistance prompted by what many saw as our desire to steal their trade secrets. As a result, over the period of my research I obtained a complete view (1) of the interplay between the women's changing business and family situations and their associational ties; (2) of the goals and strategies that brought them to the marketplace; and (3) of how they managed their earnings to meet family obligations and improve their economic and social status.

Associational Ties in the Market

In the market the women acted largely, although reluctantly, as individual entrepreneurs. "Here," they said, "it's each for herself." Peer-group organization among sellers had little effect in satisfying their business needs. They acquired their goods through individual

---

* Mme. Solange N'Guessan Zoukou, herself a sociologist, was far more a collaborator than an interpreter. Her insights, enthusiasm, and patience were fully as precious as her linguistic skills.

140   BARBARA C. LEWIS

ties with more or less regular suppliers, from whom they sometimes obtained credit. They spoke often of the desirability of collective wholesale buying, but in the few cases where it had been tried, it had failed.

Similarly, they spoke regretfully of past unsuccessful efforts to form savings associations with neighboring sellers in the market. These associations were usually of the "rotating credit" type, as they have become known.* Though many variations have been described in the literature, a rotating credit association can be defined basically as a group of persons who agree to make regular contributions to a fund, which becomes the property of each contributor in rotation. By joining such a group, each member assumes or creates an obligation to save a certain amount of cash over a period of time—cash that she might otherwise dissipate. Money seems to "burn a hole" in the pockets of market women perhaps even more than in ours. The extended family and the strong tradition of cooperation and reciprocity place enormous pressure on anyone with cash on hand to aid a needy kinsman or co-ethnic. By joining a credit association, a woman ensures herself the opportunity of disposing of a large sum of money, whether to make a major personal purchase, to meet a high-priority family obligation (such as paying a child's school fees), or to expand her commerce by making a large capital investment. But though such credit associations are self-help banking arrangements that involve no fee or extra cost, the order in which members receive the fund is a source of unequal advantage. Those earliest in the cycle of distribution receive, in effect, an interest-free loan that they repay over time. This advantage is financed by those at the cycle's end, for whom the system works in a manner little better than simply

* Clifford Geertz, in "The Rotating Credit Association: A 'Middle Rung' in Development" (1966: 420–42), emphasizes the adaptive welfare and commercial functions of these institutions but does not elaborate upon the nature of authority and cohesion by which they are maintained. For an extensive survey of the literature on rotating credit associations that describes structural variations found on several continents, see Shirley Ardener, "A Comparative Study of Rotating Credit Associations" (1964: 201–29). Both Geertz and Ardener describe associations with more extensive hierarchical structures and more complex loan and interest arrangements than any I found in Abidjan.

storing their savings under a mattress would. Also, it is possible that the group will break up before the cycle is completed: thus members whose turns come later in the rotation both provide cost-free loans for the others and risk losing their savings. These tensions and uncertainties have caused many market women to become disenchanted with this mode of saving.

Some market women have thus turned to an alternative scheme by which they "contract" with someone to make regular deposits that they subsequently receive as a lump sum. This has been labeled the "ambulatory banker" system. Since their appearance in the market, ambulatory bankers have largely replaced collegially organized and managed rotating credit associations. The new system does not permit individual sellers to profiteer at their peers' expense, but it also significantly reduces their potential for collective action and their material benefits. Each participating seller has a small card, marked off like a month's calendar, on which her banker writes her name and the amount she has agreed to deposit every day for that month. At the close of each market day, the bankers pass through the market with their black briefcases to collect deposits from each of their clients, marking each one's deposit on her card and returning it to her. The transactions are brief and businesslike; the bankers are in a hurry and the sellers are weary and ready to go home. Each participant will get an amount at the month's end equal to the sum of her deposits minus one-thirtieth, or one day's deposit, which is the banker's fee. Like rotating credit associations, the ambulatory banker system compels members to save on a regular daily basis; but unlike the rotating credit associations, the ambulatory banker system results in the loss of a small part of each seller's savings in fees.

The impersonal nature of the ambulatory banker system frees participants of the interpersonal tensions that have plagued the rotating credit associations. However, deposits with a banker are less secure than they are in an association. Participants in the banking system rarely know where the banker lives or have any information concerning his property holdings or identity that would enable them to track him down should he fail to appear at the month's end. Moreover, banker and client rarely share ethnic ties. But this makes little difference, for respondents told me that the banker who runs away with his depositors' money shows no special consideration for those of his clients who are his co-ethnics. The women worry about their savings; all give examples of bankers who have absconded with funds. Some so victimized have found another, and they hope honest, banker. Some hedge their bets by saving with several different bankers, whom they select on friends' recommendations or after having seen them in the market for several months. The women complain of the risk involved, but they accept this regular and convenient mode of saving *faut de mieux.*

The ambulatory banker system is a much more beneficial arrangement for a very few prosperous cloth sellers than it is for the petty trading majority. These big traders, habitually dealing in hundreds of dollars worth of stock, are known businesswomen with property assets in addition to their assets from commerce. Their profits permit them to deposit as much as $25 daily with their banker. And he in turn is willing on occasion to advance them their entire month's savings on the fifth day of the month. Thus, for a $25 daily deposit, a seller can have an advance of $725. One exceptional cloth seller saves $25 a day with one banker and $50 a day with another; her bankers regularly grant her the advance they grant to others occasionally, so that she gets a working capital of $2,175 on the fifth day of the month.* However, only big savers like these are granted advances. The far more numerous small-scale traders using the same bankers are unaware of this

---

* The French West African Franc, or CFA, is the Ivoirian currency; the exchange rate at the time of my research was approximately 390 CFA = U.S. $1. I have used the round figure of 400 in converting the data. Although the Ivory Coast is prosperous relative to many other African states, the average annual income per capita is only about $400. This underlines the importance, in local terms, of the amounts of capital that big traders handle. If a woman "saves" $75 per day, only part of that amount will be profit, for much of it will cover her operating costs. Nonetheless, in her context, she is unquestionably in the big leagues.

service, which apparently means that it is not an option open to them.*

Sellers using the ambulatory bankers are well aware that they pay one-thirtieth of their savings each month for a service they theoretically could have free through a rotating credit association formed with other sellers. But they nonetheless use the more impersonal banking arrangements. Several said they did not want to expose themselves to the quarrels and insults that peer-group savings associations seem inevitably to entail. Members connive to be first to receive the fund, or one is delinquent in her payments and gives unconvincing excuses. No respondents cited the bad character of a particular ethnic group as the source of trouble, although if a respondent said a particular Baoulé or Dioula had been intolerably egotistical, the ethnic group mentioned was not the respondent's own. However, undertones of ethnic tension are minor. The women's experience has convinced them that inevitably some member will prove unreliable or troublesome in any group set up among neighboring sellers in the marketplace.

It is pertinent that despite negative experiences with rotating credit associations in the market, no respondent claimed to have lost the money she put into the fund. We can conclude that the sometimes heated arguments, though in themselves a real objection, also reflect a broader competitive tension generated by every member's concern that some other member might benefit unequally. If, for example, members contribute daily to the fund but distribute it biweekly or monthly in order to let a larger sum accumulate, the person trusted to keep the fund enjoys a ready source of capital for short-term investments. The problem is not her reliability but rather her relative advantage as a merchant in direct competition with other members. Similarly, to be last to receive the fund, or to cede one's turn to a member claiming an

---

* Whether these bankers use their funds for short-term loans is an intriguing problem. Certainly the market women who use the fund solely for savings purposes are indirectly financing the loans enjoyed by the big traders. But I suspect that the bankers still have a margin of liquid capital before the month's end that they invest, thus augmenting their profits from clients' fees.

emergency, requires not just generosity or trust but a willingness to assume a temporary disadvantage vis-à-vis fellow traders. Thus many sellers participate outside the market in credit associations structurally identical to those they shun in the market. Others use one or more ambulatory bankers, and still others do both.

Perhaps even more than they regret their inability to make rotating credit associations in the market work for them, market women regret and resent their inability to make collective buying arrangements succeed. These efforts have included a far greater number of sellers than the ten to fifteen typically involved in a rotating credit association, and the direct costs of these failures have been borne by the traders themselves.

Several of the most dramatic of these efforts took place over a decade ago, in the early 1960's. In one, a deputy in the national parliament organized most of the cloth sellers into a purchasing cooperative. All members paid a fee to establish a fund with which to buy cloth directly from producers. But in the turmoil that followed two alleged attempts to assassinate President Houphouët-Boigny in 1963, the deputy heading the cloth sellers' cooperative was detained, the cooperative dissolved, and most of the funds that had been collected disappeared. Although the cloth sellers still talk of organizing to bypass wholesalers, they have never initiated another effort. Each one seems instead to seek gratification in reporting—as proof of her superior talent—how much credit her supplier has been willing to give her.

A similar endeavor was initiated among the retailers of fresh fish. In 1960, a dynamic woman organized a buying cooperative to displace intermediaries handling fish at the Abidjan port. The retailers established a fund to guarantee payment for fish the cooperative purchased wholesale and distributed for retail sale. But many sellers failed to reimburse the fund as they sold their stock, and the cooperative went bankrupt. The members held their *présidente* responsible for their lost membership fees, and she has repaid them over the last nine years out of her earnings. Now she plans a new cooperative with greater sanctions for defaulting members. These were the only cases of cooperative buying efforts I discovered at the Treichville market; as we have seen, both failed shortly after their creation.

Another kind of organization by trading sector that has appeared sporadically is the emergency fund. When a seller or a seller's close kinsman dies, colleagues in her sector often (but not always) spontaneously contribute money for funeral costs and for the maintenance of surviving family members. This occurred among the seamstresses at the market while I was conducting my research. After this particular instance, a respected member of the group initiated a series of meetings with the aim of establishing a permanent fund for such situations. Members agreed to contribute each month, and the kitty was to be used in the case of any death "in a seller's family." But the broad definition given by some members to a death in the family led to disagreements and defaults in payment. At my departure, many seamstresses had withdrawn from the association and the organizing core was attempting to gain agreement on a workable set of statutes.

Certain issues have periodically aroused market women to pressure municipal authorities. One perennial issue is the desire to exclude non-Ivoirian women, "who take our places in the market." Another is the favoritism of municipal officials who give places to functionaries' wives, "who don't really struggle for their livelihood the way we do." But the municipal authorities' "betrayal" in twice increasing the rental fees women pay for their spaces in the market has elicited the greatest response.

When the new market was built and opened in the early 1960's, the mayor's Treichville delegate informed market sellers that their rental fees had to be raised to pay for the new market; however, he promised that the fees would be reduced after a few years. Then fees were increased a second time. Bitterness toward the Treichville mayoral delegate was particularly strong among older sellers, who observed that they had supported him long ago when he was "small," but now that he was a "big man" he had forgotten them. When the fee was raised for the second time, sentiment ran high throughout the market. Sellers organized and selected delegations by section. The Gouro pepper sellers alone claim to have had a

clearly preestablished leader—a senior member of the group who
was a leader in Abidjan's Gouro community. Thus the Gouro were
immediately ready to act. The other sellers in the pepper section
followed their example and chose additional representatives to
join the Gouro. Cloth sellers rallied behind one of the older traders,
whose brother was a national minister. In other sections, leaders
were chosen because they spoke French or had personal connections. The external orientation of the sectors and the lack of internal structure in delegate selection are conspicuous.

The mayoral delegate claimed that he was powerless to reverse
the decision but promised to speak to his superiors. After a long
and fruitless wait, each of the sellers' delegations began to tap the
connections of its members in an effort to gain access to those in
power. The seamstresses created a fund to facilitate their entrée
with municipal officials—to no avail. The cloth sellers were the
most persistent: when they were refused audiences with higher
municipal authorities, they made two visits to President Houphouët-Boigny's sister—also to no avail. Finally they established
a travel fund and sent their delegation up-country to the president's village, where he was then resting. But again they failed—
the eruption of "student troubles" demanded the chief of state's
full attention.

Months passed as groups of sellers awaited audiences with various officials. By the time of the "student troubles," the traders'
movement had lost momentum. Some older traders insisted that,
if they could just get past the *"égoïstes"* surrounding the president,
their sacrifices in the early days of the Party (le Parti Democratique
du Côte d'Ivoire) would be remembered and their cause righted.
But the majority of sellers ceased to believe that they could bring
about a reduction in fees. Though their response to the fee increase had been energetic, their organization had been fragmented.
Faced with numerous administrative brush-offs, they were without
strategy or confidence. Thus the larger political system—from the
municipal to the national level—has shown itself extremely un-
responsive to sellers' efforts to protect their interests. Successful
encounters with such external authorities might well have enhanced and encouraged internal organization among the sellers.

But the absence of such reinforcement is not adequate by itself to explain the lack of internal cohesion among market women. Before we can offer any further explanation, we must consider women's associational ties outside the market. An understanding of how and why women's organizations have succeeded there will go far toward clarifying why they have failed in the market context.

Associational Activities Outside the Market

Nearly all the sellers I interviewed belonged to at least one association outside the market that met regularly and required financial contributions. But two very different patterns appeared, one among the Dioula women from the north, the other among women from the various peoples of the south. The Dioula participate in a variety of associations that nonetheless are all characterized by fixed contributions distributed to each member in turn. Associations of southern women (chiefly women of the Akan, Lagoon, and Krou peoples), however, do not always entail the same explicit quantitative balance between a member's obligations to the group and her own material gain. This difference between northerners and southerners is not absolute; but despite the small sample size, the tendency is unmistakable. Most southerners belong to associations in which individual contributions need not be—and are not expected to be—strictly equal to benefits received. In contrast, *all* Dioula women customarily participate in some form of association where expenditure and gain are explicitly balanced.

Associations among northerners. The Dioula women's associational activities were both more extensive and more varied in purpose than those of the southern women. Nearly all Dioula belonged to a type of association formed to cover the financial obligations surrounding marriage or the birth of a child. Women join a *furu moni* (marriage association) to cover the costs of a daughter's wedding; and the particular association joined reflects the financial means of its members, for the amount of the contribution required varies. Since a member can draw on the fund only once before it makes the rounds, there is a saying that "if you have two daughters the age of puberty, you know you must join two associations." A young wife will join an association appropriate to her concerns: a *djigi moni* or *safina moni* (birth or soap association). In these, each member must contribute regularly a fixed amount of soap or cash. (According to respondents, a piece of black soap was the traditional offering in villages before the advent of the money economy.) A woman may draw on the fund when she has a child, but again only once per rotation cycle. The minimum amount of cash required in Abidjan was equal to about $0.25; fancier associations required two lengths of cloth, designated toiletries, infant clothes, or cash amounting to $10 or $15.

These associations are usually headed by an old and respected member of an important family, who keeps track of contributions, settles disputes, and sees that things run smoothly. Young women starting a *safina* or *djigi moni* often formally request an older woman to be the "mother" of their association. Though her actual role in the association is largely ceremonial, her presence suggests that good membership is learned and requires guidance.

Dioula women also form *diaou moni* (commerce associations) or *wari moni* (money associations), which exist to provide capital savings for individual use. Although this type of *moni* is surely the creature of the modern trading economy, the strict principle of rotation is unchanged. The distribution of funds may be accompanied by a gathering of the members. In one case, members of a *diaou moni*, all cloth sellers, met for the distribution of the two-yard lengths of cloth each had contributed. Here socializing was clearly a secondary purpose, for meetings were short—"long enough for members to see what quality of cloth you have given, for you will get the same when your turn comes." Frequently there is no meeting at all, and the *présidente* sends her *griot* around to collect the fund and distribute it.

The Dioula birth and wedding funds are joined only by Muslims, because the ceremonies surrounding marriage and birth have religious content. They are not restricted to persons from a certain region or Dioula subgroup. Although all Dioula have a strong attachment to their region of origin, whether it be in the northern Ivory Coast, Mali, or Guinea, they see themselves as members of a centuries-old ethnic diaspora. Islamization and the recent intensification of mobility have strengthened the underlying bonds of shared culture that give these strangers in Abidjan a strong sense of unity. Women of financial means and social status frequently belong to half a dozen different *moni*, which vary not so much in function as in membership. Every woman belongs to at least one association from her region of origin (and perhaps even to a *moni* of her clan from that region), but she may also belong, for example, to a Malian group, to a group of Dioula from her Abidjan quarter, and to a group of Dioula planning to go to Mecca. In conversation, a Dioula woman conveys not only that she has considerable resources enabling her to meet all these obligations, but that her social network is broad and includes some relatively elite circles. For her, association memberships are as much a mark of achieved success as they are a means of attaining greater wealth and status.

The apex of financial success and moral achievement comes with participation in associations formed to fund pilgrimages to Mecca. Here the monthly contribution is great ($15 to $30) and is made by 30 to 60 men and women. One or more pilgrims are chosen by chance each year, and these people are ineligible to win again until the rotation is completed. Because of this, wealthy people may join more than one association, or they may contribute to one association two or three times the required amount in order to win that many times before one rotation is complete. Most members send at least one older kinsman to Mecca before taking his or her turn; this personal sacrifice for one's elders merits the highest praise among the Dioula.

These pilgrimage funds require particularly strong and reliable leadership, not only because the sum is great but because it must be banked for a year. The *président(e)* of such an association accordingly must be morally reliable and financially secure. This does not mean that the *président(e)* cannot use the capital fund for personal business ventures; rather, it means that no matter what misfortune may occur in business, he or she will be able to raise the full amount when the drawing takes place.

Associations among southerners. The southerners I interviewed included women of the Baoulé, Bété, Adioukrou, Agni, Appollo, Gouro, and Ebrié peoples. They form associations not to celebrate births or marriages but rather to assist each other in paying for funerals, hospitalization, or similar things. With the exception of some Protestant church groups, associations of southerners usually are based on ethnic ties—sometimes to the extent that all members are from the same ethnic subgroup or canton. Contributions are made either on the basis of ability or at an agreed-upon rate, and the principle of rotation is not present. Because the funds are earmarked for particular misfortunes, one member may receive them several times before another receives them once. One religious association, Saint Michel, attracted two respondents because, they said, it arranged very beautiful funerals. In their eyes, this association fills much the same need as other explicitly traditional ethnic associations.

Despite the variation in ethnic traditions among southerners, their associations share key features distinguishing them from the *moni* so popular among Dioula women. For one thing, southerners have little latitude in choosing one association over another—a woman simply joins the local association of people from her region of origin. (But in one case, a respondent living in Treichville joined the association of her co-ethnics in another quarter of Abidjan because more of her kin lived there than in Treichville.) For another, there is no suggestion that southerners select or accumulate memberships to express social prestige or realize social mobility, as some Dioula women do. Moreover, leadership (as a means of attaining status) probably plays a more important role in southerners' associations than in the more egalitarian *moni* of the Dioula. Leaders notify members of meetings and pressure or even sanction members who miss meetings or lag in their contributions, yet they are not compensated by any particular material benefits. Because the calculated balancing of individual costs and gains characteristic of the Dioula *moni* is absent in these associations, they are held together solely by membership solidarity and social morality. In no case do associations of southerners provide members with capital that they can use for commerce or for other elective purposes.

In addition to the religiously exclusive Dioula associations and the ethnically exclusive associations of southerners, there is another class of associations outside the marketplace. These are rotating credit associations, whose workings I described earlier in discussing their role within the market. Generally modeled on the Dioula *moni* principle of rotating distribution, these associations facilitate individual capital accumulation. Nearly a third of the southern women I interviewed had participated or were participating in them, and all the southerners knew how they worked. One Baoulé, for example, joined some neighboring Dioula women in a *wari moni* in which funds were collected daily and distributed monthly. Another reported that while living in an up-country town, she joined an association of market sellers that included other southerners and Dioula. Another southerner, a civil servant's wife who owns a big stall in the market, joined a large rotating credit association in the neighborhood where she lived. Founded by a Dioula, the group was multiethnic but included only women who lived in that distinctly bourgeois quarter. In this case, the criterion of residential quarter (indicating household income and emerging class status) was the basis of recruitment (rather than religion or ethnic origin), and this was reflected in the gracious ambiance of monthly meetings and the substantial financial obligations of membership. Not all rotating credit associations are so exclusive, though most have specific criteria for participation. But what is noteworthy is that such groups seem always to be initiated by Dioula women; the southerners have not borrowed the *moni* institutional form from the Dioula and made it their own.

Conclusions: Interest-Group Formation Reconsidered

What conclusions can we draw from this examination of associations outside the market in assessing the relative weakness of sellers' organizations in the market's commercial context?

We have seen that Dioula women's associations readily lend

themselves to the satisfaction of explicitly individual goals as distinguished from collective ones—indeed, the various types of *moni*
rigorously balance individual contributions and benefits, thus both
regulating self-interest and rendering it socially acceptable. However, the ceremonial and religious context of most Dioula organizations and the strong sense of cultural unity among all Dioula
keep the centrifugal forces of individualism in check and prevent
the breakup of associations. Yet the Dioula women have not per-
fectly resolved this inherent conflict between individual aggran-
dizement and group cohesion. *Wari moni*, in particular, are more
subject to internal conflict than *djigi moni* or *furu moni*, whose
religious underpinnings are explicit.

Associations of southerners contrast with those of northerners in
being more narrowly ethnic and almost exclusively group-oriented.
Southerners have negative attitudes toward quarreling among
peers, and they seem generally unwilling to tolerate the tensions
generated by explicitly ego-centered behavior in a group context.

How are these differences in orientation reflected in the marketplace? For one thing, Dioula women rely far less on the ambulatory
bankers than do southern women. Only about a third of the Dioula
women I interviewed saved with ambulatory bankers, whereas
roughly two-thirds of the southerners did. And I found that only
southern women made deposits with more than one ambulatory
banker. This can be attributed, of course, to the greater prevalence
of rotating credit associations outside the market among the Dioula
than among southerners. Since women who belong to *wari moni*
outside the market are free to invest the money they gain there
in their commercial ventures in the market, there is less motivation
for them either to enter market-based rotating credit associations
or to save with ambulatory bankers. Nonetheless, problems do
occur in *wari moni* (abuse of members' good will regarding order
of rotation or irregular payments), and this may explain why some
Dioula women, like the great majority of southern women, have
opted for the impersonal formality of the ambulatory banker
system.

With this background, what explanations can we offer for the weakness of women's associations in the market? Can we infer that Dioula market women are impeded by the southerners among them from achieving effective sellers' groups on the model of their *wari moni*? Or does the marketplace present a constellation of factors so intensifying self-interest that it overtaxes even the Dioula's ability to accommodate competitive individualism within an association depending on voluntary submission to group norms? Variations in shared cultural norms and situational stress combine in collective efforts both in and outside the market: What can the successes and failures observed teach us about the processes of group formation and maintenance generally?

Divisive forces in the marketplace that impede the growth of associational ties can be summarized briefly. First, individualism prevails as a function of the marketing situation itself. Competition with one's neighbor is immediate and visible: a client gained by one seller is a sale lost for her neighbor. Such competition is absent or attenuated among salaried office workers or neighbors in residential quarters: a salaried worker's pay does not increase as a fellow worker's pay declines; and neighbors, even when they are traders, are not competing for clients at home. Second, unequal access to economic and political resources enhances the competitive dimension among sellers. Some sellers enjoy greater capital, credit, and political resources than others owing to kinship or marriage ties. Such privileged sellers not only might feel less need for collaborative efforts; they are unlikely to give up easily a relative advantage that would disappear if, for example, they were to support a purchasing cooperative. Moreover, less well-off sellers resent these inequities and generally lack confidence in the good faith of their more privileged neighbors. Third, ethnic heterogeneity inhibits collective action. Outside the marketplace, the sellers' social networks are largely ethnically defined, i.e., ethnically segregated. Thus interethnic ties must be developed largely in the market itself—a difficult task, given the divisive forces already mentioned. The differing patterns of existing associational ties are an added obstacle to interethnic group action.

It is tempting to conclude that the Dioula organizational pattern

—with its relatively high tolerance of explicit self-interest in group activities—is more conducive to group organization in the market than is the southern pattern. A case study cannot prove or disprove the extension of this argument—that the southern organizational pattern is *the* impediment to greater collaboration among the sellers. However, the evidence suggests that such a view misconstrues the Dioula's organizational capabilities and misrepresents the nature of collective action itself. Indeed, the characteristic balancing of individual contributions and profit among the Dioula may *hinder* group action toward clearly *collective benefits*, that is, benefits enjoyed by all despite variations in contributions or expenditures. For example, group pressures to reduce space-rental fees in the market would benefit all sellers, even if most of the energy by which this was achieved were expended by only a few. Similarly, cooperative purchasing endeavors require disproportionate efforts on the part of the organizers, and the initial and equal contributions to a cooperative fund will never correspond precisely to each member's benefits. In short, most group endeavors ultimately yield benefits that are unequal to the energy, time, or capital each member invests, no matter how carefully individual costs and benefits are computed at the outset. The Dioula's individualistic orientation surely indicates their entrepreneurial ability, but it does not in itself enhance their organizational capability in all spheres.

The voluntary limitation of self-interest narrowly conceived is an explanation we readily accept with regard to groups engaged in unambiguously social and cultural activities. But it is equally a prerequisite for groups with economic goals. The analytic problem here is far-reaching. Contemporary social scientists often speak of interest groups when they mean simply persons working together to acquire some benefits that each desires. The rotating credit association, and in this context the Dioula *moni*, strikes a familiar cultural chord in us. It seems to be such an uncomplicated and reasonable arrangement, whose purpose makes such eminent good sense, that we might be tempted to take its creation and maintenance for granted. The legitimacy of associating for individual gain is a concept we probably share with the Dioula. But the desire for individual acquisition through the group is not, among the Dioula or among us, sufficient to sustain the group.*

Our inquiry becomes much more fruitful when we look beyond the group's explicit goals to characteristics that members share. The shorthand of "social categories"—whether social class, occupational group, or language (ethnic) group—is frequently used to denote shared status or shared situation, and thus the potential for collaborative effort. When these categories are recognized by members, we may appropriately speak of a group. But the formation of a purposive association requires several additional key elements. Group members must focus on a shared dilemma and perceive solutions through collective action. And when they reach agreement on common goals, they must act together with some confidence that each member can hold her own, can defend both her material self-interest and her sense of self, her dignity or self-esteem. This latter psychological requirement rests in some important measure on members' familiarity with one another. Behavior must be predictable: there must be an understanding both of how members will deviate and of how other members can bring corrective pressure to bear upon deviants. Without this understanding, members will suspect the intentions of others and feel uncertain that they can act to protect themselves.

Social confidence and self-confidence, both rooted in the familiar and predictable, are vital features of the foundation necessary when multicultural groups attempt to create an association. In such cross-cultural transactions, the boundaries of appropriate or even decent self-seeking must be established. Acceptable strategies for the pursuit of personal interest in one culture are improper in another. Any snag in the smooth functioning of the group becomes magnified, and interpersonal tensions become unmanage-

* Mancur Olsen, in *The Logic of Collective Action*, discusses the theoretical contradiction between rational (calculated) self-interest and the voluntarism that is the keystone of the group theory of politics. The analysis of voluntary associations presented here suggests the near impossibility of truly balancing members' costs and benefits in collective endeavors, thus affirming the inadequacy of rational self-interest as the basis of group action.

able. Then each member begins to focus anxiously on her individual investment, with the result that confidence in the endeavor's viability—the precondition for success—yields to negative expectations. Arguments ensue and withdrawal follows.

The effects of ethnic heterogeneity on associational behavior should not be overemphasized, however. The dominant individualism of the marketplace itself fosters psychological predispositions inimical to group efforts. Sheldon Wolin (1960: 328, 331) has observed in another context that entrepreneurial behavior is rooted not in a self-confident drive for autonomy and success but rather in a competitive anxiety that motivates each person to seek to confirm his or her superiority vis-à-vis his or her peers. The Abidjan marketplace—a situation of nearly perfect competition—both renders ethnicity inoperative as the basis for group action and works against the establishment of associational ties among sellers on any other basis. In settings where the competitive component is less in evidence (e.g., neighborhoods) associations may prosper. They may even be multiethnic, since where competition is not the salient factor cross-cultural relations are less likely to be strained by anxiety and negative expectations. In contrast, the marketplace is little conducive to associational innovation, but rather enhances individuation.

Rebels or Status-Seekers?
Women as Spirit Mediums in East Africa

IRIS BERGER

THROUGHOUT AFRICA women have played a prominent role in spirit-possession cults and ceremonies. Indeed, in the interlacustrine and Nyamwezi areas of East Africa—southern and western Uganda, Rwanda, Burundi, and northwestern Tanzania—their participation in other spheres of precolonial religious activity was severely limited. Recent anthropological explanations of this phenomenon have focused on the leverage that possession allowed women to exert in specific conflict situations. I. M. Lewis, for example, centered his wide-ranging comparative study *Ecstatic Religion* on tensions between men and women and found numerous cases where predominantly female spirit-possession cults functioned as "thinly disguised protest movements" against the male sex.* A study of female mediums in the interlacustrine and Nyamwezi regions, however, suggests that this "sex war" hypothesis defines only one aspect of the problem; for, in addition to supplying an antimale outlet, cults also offered large numbers of women initiates an unusual degree of authority in ritual situations and provided smaller numbers with long-term positions of high status.

Spirit cults in these two areas† centered on groups of legendary

---

* In addition to Lewis's work, see Wilson 1967: 366–78. Edwin Ardener (1972) discusses the problem of women and religion generally.

† In a widely followed series, the *Ethnographic Survey of Africa*, anthropologists have divided the interlacustrine cultures into three groups: (1) the western group (Nyoro, Toro, Nkore, Kiga, Haya, Zinza); (2) the southern group (Rwanda, Rundi, Ha); (3) the eastern group (Ganda, Soga). The Shi and Hunde of eastern Zaire are closely related in many respects to the peoples of the second group and share some of their religious institutions. The major peoples of "greater Unyamwezi" include the Nyamwezi, Sukuma, and Sumbwa.

heroes known collectively as Cwezi or Imandwa. Legends trace the cults of these deities to an early state in western Uganda whose rulers bore the name Cwezi. According to tradition, after the Cwezi kingdom declined, people began to honor the spirits of their former kings.* By the 1800's closely related religious movements spanned an area stretching southward from the kingdoms of Bunyoro and Buganda in modern Uganda to Buha, Unyamwezi, and Usukuma in northwestern Tanzania. In these southern sections of the cult area, as well as in the neighboring states of Rwanda and Burundi, the cults focused not on the Cwezi but on another set of spirits dominated by a legendary hero known alternately as Ryangombe (Lyangombe) and Kiranga. But the historical ties between the Cwezi and Ryangombe cults remains clear from their numerous common deities, their similarities in organization and mythical themes, and their large clusters of shared terminology. Most notable among the latter are forms of *-cwezi* or *-swezi* (e.g., *bacwezi, baswezi, buswezi*) and of *-band-* (e.g., *emandwa, imandwa, embandwa*), all of which refer, in different areas, to groups of deities and to cult members and the organizations that they formed.† The related verb *kubandwa*, which designates the initiation or training process for potential members, may apply to the entire religious complex.

Most of these cults were democratic in their inclusion of large numbers of people, both men and women, and most provided a central focus for religious activity in their respective societies. In

---

* See Iris Berger, *Religion, Myth and Kingship in Precolonial East Africa* (Tervuren, Belgium, forthcoming), for a detailed history of these spirit-possession cults.

† These terms illustrate the principles of word formation in Bantu languages, with each consisting of a stem and a prefix that indicates whether the word is singular or plural and to which of a number of classes of living and nonliving things it belongs. These vary, of course, from one language to the next. To take one useful example, Bunyoro is the name the Nyoro give to their kingdom; Lunyoro is their language; and the people call themselves Banyoro. The area of the Nyamwezi peoples, however, is Unyamwezi. Since modern scholarly usage tends to drop the prefixes in many cases, this paper will refer, for example, to the Nyoro, Nyamwezi, or Rwanda peoples and to the Cwezi or Swezi cults. On the map of East Africa on p. xii of this volume, though, the appropriate prefixes are used to indicate geographic areas.

Buganda and the nearby Sese Islands in Lake Victoria, however, elitist cults relied on small numbers of professional mediums;* and in Unyamwezi, the Swezi society formed only one of a large number of esoteric organizations that filled functions ranging from divination to snake charming. Such organizational divergences combined over time with differences in social, economic, and political settings to effect some variations in women's roles from one area to the next.

The peoples of the interlacustrine and Nyamwezi regions were similar in many ways. All were patrilineal, lived in scattered settlements rather than compact villages, and spoke closely related Bantu languages. Various combinations of agriculture and cattle-raising formed the basis of economic life. With the exception of the Kiga in southwestern Uganda, all the peoples of these two regions had some type of centralized political structure. The forms of political organization varied considerably—from large, relatively unified kingdoms (Buganda, Bunyoro, Nkore,† Rwanda, and Burundi) to clusters of small states (Buhaya, Buha, Unyamwezi, Usukuma, and Usumbwa). Nonetheless, all showed a relatively high degree of class division, sometimes between a ruling clan or family and commoners, sometimes between a minority of upper-class pastoralists and a majority of lower-class agriculturalists. In the latter cases stratification possessed an ethnic as well as a political dimension, with the upper and lower classes identified as Tutsi and Hutu, respectively, in Rwanda, Burundi, and Buha, and as Hima [Huma] and Iru, respectively, in Bunyoro, Nkore,‡ and Buhaya. Religious beliefs and practices reinforced the cohesion of both families and larger political units; but except for some of

* The separate cult of Nyabingi, a female deity who became particularly prominent in northern Rwanda and southwestern Uganda in the nineteenth century, also took on this form. I prefer the terms "democratic" and "elitist" to "cults of affliction" and "royal cults" suggested in T. O. Ranger and I. Kimambo, eds., *The Historical Study of African Religion* (Berkeley, Calif., 1972), p. 11. The latter term in particular is too narrowly defined to cover all interlacustrine cases. Most of these cults and spirits were known by forms of *-band-*.

† Nkore is the name of the traditional kingdom that formed the nucleus of the colonial district of Ankole.

‡ Some scholars have suggested recently that the spheres of activity of Hima and Iru in Nkore were too separate to constitute a class system. See Martin

the spirit cults and rituals performed at royal courts for the benefit of the entire kingdom, most religious observances occurred within either the nuclear family or the lineage (both of which were male-dominated).

In these predominantly hierarchical societies, women's positions depended on their status in the class system; a woman was inferior to a man of her own social level, but she was superior to one of lower status.* Nonetheless, by definition women occupied a socially subordinate place; although a few upper-class women attained considerable wealth and authority, men possessed political power, judicial rights, the right to inherit cattle and land, and, "indeed, ... [the right] to independent action outside the walls of the house." The few women who were able to rise above their sexually assigned standing did so by gaining the favor of a male superior, often by such means as manipulation, lying, or flattery (Albert 1963: 180). Women of all social levels were expected to be sub-servient and obedient, as the following quotation from Albert (1963: 180–81) makes clear: "Unlike a man, a Rundikazi [Rundi woman] in public does not speak, nor does she look you in the eyes. To each question, she answers *Ndabizi?* How should I know? In public, she lets it be thought that she knows nothing about poli-tics, or where her husband is today, or even the wedding date of her daughter. She is the modest and obedient wife of her husband, the mother of her children, the conscientious mistress of her house, who is always working. Whatever she does, she does within the limits of her various feminine roles." Throughout her life, a woman was subject to her father's will, despite the fact that after marriage she also had to obey her husband. A woman's reference to "my home" actually meant her father's kraal. Only over her

R. Doornbos, "Images and Reality of Stratification in Pre-colonial Nkore," *Canadian Journal of African Studies*, 12, no. 3 (1973); and Yitzchak Elam, "The Relationships Between Hima and Iru in Ankole," *African Studies*, 30, no. 3 (1974).

* I follow here Albert 1963: 179–215. She extends her conclusions to Rwanda as well as Burundi, and the scattered material on women elsewhere seems to sanction the extension to the other societies under discussion, too. An important recent study is Elam 1973. Unfortunately, however, he does not deal with pre-colonial religion.

younger sisters, her children, and her husband's subordinates did she possess any authority.

A set of well-defined attitudes delineating the differences between men and women lent ideological support to female subordination. The people of Burundi believed, for example, that women's greater strength suited them better for manual labor; but their clumsiness, lack of agility, inability to control their emotions, and proneness to jealousy left them generally inferior to men. And despite the recognition of their continual hardships in childbearing (the reason given for women aging more quickly than men), the male role in procreation was believed to be more important than the female. According to a local proverb, "Woman is only the passive earth; it is the man who provides the seed." Despite variations in detail, this general picture of female inferiority and subordination in Burundi also held true for the other societies in the interlacustrine and Nyamwezi regions.

Nevertheless, in the religious systems of these regions we find scattered references that indicate opportunities for women to rise above their general status of inferiority through various roles and activities. In the culturally related areas of Burundi and Buha, for example, both men and women might enter the hereditary profession of "rainmaker," *muvurati*. And in Heru, one of the six states of Buha, there lived a woman rainmaker (Kicharuzi, "the one who cuts water") whose fame as "the chieftainess of rainmakers" covered all of Buha and extended into neighboring Burundi. With ordinary practitioners as her subordinates, she acted on behalf of the chief of Heru in cases of severe drought (Scherer 1959). But it was the spirit-mediumship cults that offered women the greatest avenues for active participation in religious life. Raymond Firth (1950: 141) has defined spirit mediumship and distinguished it from spirit possession. "*Spirit possession* is a form of trance in which behaviour actions of a person are interpreted as evidence of a control of his behaviour by a spirit normally external to him. *Spirit mediumship* is normally a form of possession in which the person is conceived as serving as an intermediary between spirits and men. The accent here is on communication; the actions and words of the mediums must be translatable, which differentiates them from mere spirit possession or madness." Such possession is interpreted favorably as a sign that a god has chosen a person to be inhabited by him periodically for the good of the community. Thus, extending Firth's definition, spirit mediumship implies communication between the supernatural world and a particular social group for which the medium is an agent.

The bizarre (in European eyes) appearance and behavior of the interlacustrine mediums captured the attention of several early travelers to the area. Grant (1864: 292–93) described them at some length.

A class of mendicants or gentle beggars called "Bandwa," allied to the Wichwezee [Cwezi cult members], seem spread all over these kingdoms. They adorn themselves with more beads, bells, brass, and curiosities than any other race and generally carry an ornamented tree-creeper in their hands. Many of their women look handsome and captivating when dressed up in variously-coloured skins, and wearing a small turban of barkcloth. One man amongst them wore, from the crown of his head down his back, the skin of a tippet-monkey to which he had attached the horns of an antelope. They wander from house to house singing and are occasionally rather importunate beggars, refusing to leave without some present. A set of them lived near us at Unyoro and seemed to have cattle of their own so that they do not depend entirely on begging for subsistence. The natives all respect them very much, never refusing them food when they call, and treating them as religious devotees. Anyone may join their number by attending to certain forms; and the family of a Bandwa does not necessarily follow the same occupation. I knew one of them the captain of a band of soldiers. This whole country was once occupied by people of this class, called Wichwezee, who, according to tradition, suddenly disappeared underground.

Emin Pasha, a German who converted to Islam and changed his name while living in the Middle East, focused his attention more specifically on the female adherents, as the following extract shows (Schweinfurth et al. 1888: 285).

The most striking figures among the crowds of people loitering about here were the Wichwezi [Cwezi] sorceresses, a large number of whom are found at the court of every Wawitu [Bito, the ruling family of Bunyoro] prince. Clothed in bark cloths, yellowish brown or dyed black—one wore even the handsome *mtone*, a fine bark cloth with black patterns—so that the whole body is covered, they also not infrequently wear skins of goats or sheep, and occasionally [of] cheetah or otter, ... and adorn or disfigure their heads with objects of every conceivable description. These ladies are certainly not beautiful, and they would hardly be eligible for vestal virgins, but they are feared, and therefore venture to take many liberties. As is always the case where professional interests are concerned, they vie with one another in eccentricities. One at Rionga's [a local chief's] court grunted every minute; another sat down beside one of the company, wanted her shoulders rubbed and her head bent.

These accounts highlight the large numbers of women among the mediums, the nature of some of their activities, their striking costumes, and the respect they commanded from those around them.

The cults in which they participated centered on a mythologically defined pantheon associated with long-dead or legendary kings or heroes, natural phenomena, and particular occupations. Frequently the female spirits concerned themselves with women's activities, such as childbirth and agriculture. People consulted the gods on regular occasions as a precautionary measure, and on special occasions when difficulties arose that might have resulted from their neglect. It was felt that, if properly conciliated, the gods could ensure the health, prosperity, and fertility of their followers. Novices usually acquired the ability to intercede with the deities through a formal initiation ceremony, although sometimes direct possession rendered this unnecessary. A person's prolonged illness, for example, might be interpreted by a diviner as a particular spirit's signal of its choice of a medium. When a woman was "signaled" in this way, a ritual was conducted that taught her the necessary professional skills; the ritual also marked her rise to a new and higher social status and, sometimes, to membership in a new social group.

The underlying themes of these ceremonies stressed the initiate's passage through a "liminal" or "indeterminate" phase, one that Turner describes as having "few or none of the attributes of the past or coming state" (Turner 1969: 80–81). Following this phase comes admission to a new society that is superior to the profane one and separated from it by special regalia, a secret vocabulary, spirit possession, and esoteric knowledge. Within this new order, the adherent passed through the main stages of life—birth, childhood, marriage—suggesting the idea of a new ritual and spiritual life that paralleled ordinary existence, but on a higher plane. The indicators of this enhanced status varied from place to place. It was implicit everywhere in the intimate relationship to a group of spirits generally conceived of as kings or extremely important and powerful people. Explicit signs included food taboos similar to those of the upper classes, a view of non-initiates as minors incapable of full participation in community affairs, and possession of legal immunity or particular rights and privileges. This high status, however, was temporary and situational except in the case of professional mediums and priests attached permanently to temples. Others probably assumed their normal position between ceremonies, as indicated by the application of food taboos only to ritual situations.

The cults operated on several different social and political levels —from small localized kinship groups to royal courts—but all of these levels remained decentralized and independent both of each other and of political officials (but note that Buganda is an exception to this). The main rites usually took place among kinsmen or neighbors, although ceremonies also occurred at the courts of local chiefs and kings. Colonial rule disrupted activities at this latter level profoundly, however, making them difficult to reconstruct. Dancing, rhythmic music, mediums speaking in an esoteric language and dressing and acting the role of the possessing spirit all lent a theatrical quality to these ceremonies that has led Michel Leiris to describe similar rituals conducted in parts of Ethiopia as "living theater."

Accounts everywhere emphasize the predominance of women in these cults. Speke (1863: 266–67) described a visit to a District Chief of Rumanika in Karagwe, a former Haya kingdom in northwest Tanzania: "Many mendicant women, called by some Wichwezi, by others Mbandwa, all wearing the most fantastic dresses of Mbugu (barkcloth) covered with beads, shells, and sticks, danced before us singing a comic song, the chorus of which was long shrill rolling, coo-roo-coo-roo, etc. . . . Their true functions were just as obscure as the religion of the negroes generally; some called them devil-drivers, others evil-eye averters. But whatever, they imposed a tax on the people."* The early Church Missionary Society members in Buganda invariably described women as the mainstay and most enthusiastic supporters of the "Lubare [spirit] superstition";† a Catholic missionary in the early part of the twentieth century, writing of the people at the southwestern tip of Lake Victoria, depicted the Swezi as a secret society "to which most Bazinza women belonged";‡ and May Edel (1957: 146) termed the spirit cult among the Kiga of southwestern Uganda the *"emandwa* of the women." Elsewhere, too, observers have agreed on the large numbers of female members in spirit-mediumship cults, although rarely have they offered exact estimates, and although the balance of the sexes undoubtedly varied from one community and one deity to the next. In the Ankole District of Uganda, for example, *emandwa* initiates were "at least as likely to be female as male," whereas mainly women joined the more recent cult of Nyabingi. In Bushi, an area of eastern Zaire with close cultural relations to neighboring Rwanda, almost all young girls were dedicated to the deity Lyangombe before marriage. And women formed an estimated 95 percent of the members of the Benakayange cult, which developed in the early twentieth century in honor of a group of people killed by Belgian soldiers (Colle 1937: 199, 205–7).

This prevalence of female mediums is hardly unique. Lewis refers to a widespread form of possession, regarded initially as an illness, which is in many cases virtually restricted to women. He continues with a description that suggests the essential features of the East African cults (Lewis 1971: 30): "Such women's possession 'afflictions' are regularly treated not by permanently expelling the possessing agency, but by reaching a viable accommodation with it. The spirit is tamed and domesticated, rather than exorcized. This treatment is usually accomplished by the induction of the

---

* Speke's reference to a "tax" probably means the periodic gifts these women demanded.

† E.g., A. M. Mackay's letter of March 12, 1882, sent from Buganda to a Mr. Whiting in London and now in the Archives of the Church Missionary Society, London.

‡ *Chroniques trimestrielles de la Société des Missionaires d'Afrique (Pères Blancs)*, July 10, 1907, pp. 230–31.

affected woman into a female cult group which regularly promotes possession experiences among its members. Within the secluded cult group, possession has thus lost its malign significance."

Although only Lewis has devoted a full-scale study to explaining this phenomenon, most works on spirit possession attempt some analysis of the high level of female participation. Some concentrate on the psychological characteristics of possessed women: S. G. Lee, for example, attempts to relate possession among the Zulu of South Africa to particular personality types and forms of neurosis; he suggests that active and aggressive women tend toward possession (as diviners), whereas feminine and passive women report a history of crying accompanied by "an intense subjective feeling of fear, localized between the shoulder blades" (Lee 1969: 143). Aidan Southall, by contrast, writing on the Alur of northern Uganda, focuses on the external situations that may generate psychological distress. He views possession cults as offering women release "from the frustrations of ordinary life. . . . Married women usually have to live away from their own kin, among people who are relative strangers. Their status is inferior, their work monotonous and their diversions few. If in addition they fail to produce healthy children, in a society still subject to very high infant mortality rates, they fail in the chief matter which can compensate for their general disabilities and their prospects are correspondingly dim. It is hardly surprising that some women become keen devotees of spirit possession" (Southall 1969: 244–45).

It is difficult to assess whether such analyses might be valid for the interlacustrine and Nyamwezi cultural areas, especially since none of the research done on the *kubandwa* cults has offered any real psychological information about them. Moreover, I would be hesitant to interpret as "neurotic" a type of behavior that involved such large numbers of women in different societies and that was viewed favorably by those societies. Southall's assertions, in particular, would need to be tested by determining whether women themselves shared this view of their situation. Since few observers took any particular interest in the "femaleness" of cult members per se, we know little about such characteristics as the woman's average age at joining or her marital status. We also need information on the problems that women of different social classes faced at particular stages of their lives, on the lives of women who did not become cult adherents, and on changes over time in female participation in particular cults. Nonetheless, despite the lack of information on these and other important questions, we do have available considerable material on women's roles in the *kubandwa* cults and on the sources of the cults' appeal to them.

Most data point to the cults' primary concern with a number of female problems, most commonly sterility, childbirth, and marital difficulties, with an emphasis on the first of these. F. M. Rodegem (1971: 928) calls the cult of Kiranga in Burundi a "regenerative rite aimed at valorizing fertility." The main object of the traditional *mbandwa* cults in Bunyoro, according to John Beattie, is to assist women to bear children; consequently, many Nyoro attributed colonial government and missionary attempts to eradicate *mbandwa* to a desire to cause their gradual disappearance as a people (Beattie 1961: 13). Similarly, among the Sumbwa of western Tanzania, the traditional story of the death of Lynangombe, the cult's central spirit, records the hero's last pronouncement: "Whoever comes to my tomb to pray will be heard by me and I will help him in his trouble. . . . I will help women in their confinements and I will give children to barren women. Let everyone pray to me and I will help them" (Cory 1955: 924). Although Sumbwa husbands sometimes expressed uneasiness at their wives' joining the Swezi, the case of a nervous or barren wife always proved sufficient argument; to avoid domestic trouble, the men would pay the fees and ask no questions (Cory 1955: 927). Finally, Bösch, writing on neighboring Unyamwezi, describes the majority of female cult members as sterile (1930: 209). This stress on fertility would suggest that *kubandwa* appealed to younger married women of childbearing age and, perhaps, allowed women a religious alternative to the worship of their husbands' lineage ancestors.

Lewis argues that such therapeutic pretensions simply masked the cults' real aim of protest against the dominant sex, offering women both protection from male exactions and an effective ve-

hicle for manipulating husbands and other male relatives. He
terms such cults peripheral—that is, they play no direct part in
upholding the moral codes of the societies in which they appear,
and they are often believed to have originated elsewhere. (Their
counterparts, central cults, support society's moral codes and provide an idiom in which men compete for power and authority.)
In brief, Lewis sees peripheral cults as a feminist subculture generally restricted to women (though sometimes including lower-class
men as well) and protected from male attack through their representation of being a therapy for illness. Underlying this interpretation is the view that these movements stem from threatening or
oppressive conditions (physical or social) that people can combat
and control only by "heroic flights of ecstasy." These cults thus
represent an attempt to master an intolerable environment.

Both in myth and in practice, the East African cults shared some
of these features. Women among the Soga of eastern Uganda had
control over their husbands during possession (Lubogo 1960: 247),
and Shi women in polygynous marriages might feign seizure by
the spirit Chihangahanga in order to get rid of a rival. Colle cites
a case in which the deity said through the medium, "Yes, I will leave
her, but only if the concubine is driven out; if that other woman
is not driven away, . . . I will kill someone here" (Colle 1937: 187–
88). Possession by such a ghost was seen as harmful; it had to be
exorcised. Similarly, in the Rundi cult of Kiranga, a medium whose
husband threatened to beat her might simulate possession. "Kiranga is there, the husband tells himself, and he will prevent himself from harming her" (Zuure 1929: 65). A more recent Rundi
sect, Umuganzaruguru (from -ganz-, "to dominate," and -ruguru-,
"above"), attracted women seeking escape from their husbands'
domination. The "cure" for a wife's symptoms of trance, illness, and
crying included not only initiation but acceptance of the woman's
control over household goods and of her refusal to continue carrying loads; henceforth the husband had to provide her with a servant or transport loads himself (Rodegem 1970: 371–72).

Some of the Nyabingi myths express a similar theme. In an account of one, as told by Bessell (1938: 75), Kanzanira, a woman

possessed by the spirit of Nyabingi, met a woman named Rutajirakijuna.

[The voice of Kanzanira asked] "What is it that troubles you?" [Rutajira-
kijuna] replied: "My husband has thrown me out of his house and when
I went back to my father's house he refused to take me in." The voice
then asked if she were hungry and when she admitted it she immediately
found a basket of cooked peas and a gourd of beer at her feet. After
Rutajura Kijuna and the children had made their meal the voice commanded her to return to her father's house saying that it would protect
her, and at that moment the spirit of Nyabingi entered her.

On her return to her father's house she sat down beside one of his
granaries and proclaimed herself as the Nyabingi. Soon all the people
round about brought her gifts of food and beer. Seeing this her father
hastened to build her a hut and to set aside provisions for her. He also
provided several large baskets for the reception of the offerings. Eventually he found it necessary to build her many large granaries.

According to tradition, Kanzanira herself had relied on the
spiritual power of Nyabingi to exert pressure on her father, a
Rwandan subchief. The latter had called together his sons to con-
vey his last wishes to them; Kanzanira, excluded from the proceed-
ings, hid behind a screen to listen. When she was discovered, her
father ordered her killed. But her spirit returned to his house, crying out continually and demanding an explanation for her miser-
able treatment. Finally, asked what she wanted, she replied, "A
country to live in." So her father gave her Ndorwa in southern
Uganda. The spirit that had appeared and spoken with Kanzanira's
voice was that of Nyabingi (Bessell 1938: 74–75).

These examples definitely bear out Lewis's suggestion of the
power that spirit possession offers women in disputes with men,
although gaining advantages may describe the situation more accurately than engaging in "war between the sexes" (Curley 1973:
17). Defining the *kubandwa* cults as peripheral, however, poses
problems in terms of both the foreignness of the spirits and the
relationship of the cults to the moral codes of society. (Lewis defines public morality as concerning the relationships between
people and groups.) Although some of the gods in every culture
originated elsewhere, people remain conscious of the alien nature
of only the relative newcomers and firmly consider the older gods

as national spirits. Thus Lewis's characterizations of "unwelcome aliens originating among hostile neighboring peoples, or mischievous nature sprites existing outside society and culture" would apply only occasionally. And, despite regional variations, in most areas the cults were relatively thoroughly integrated into the established order, particularly in terms of ideological and organizational involvement with the existing rituals for family spirits. Thus, Lewis's theory does describe one way in which the interlacustrine and Nyamwezi spirit groups served their female adherents; but most of the cults also occupied a central enough position in religious life to render their characterization as peripheral inaccurate. Indeed, this very centrality probably explains the status elevation associated with them. And improvement of status must have been an element in the cults' appeal.

An additional factor may have been the authority and license of the ritual situation itself, which frequently offered women a share in the status and prerogatives of men. In Busoga, for example, where women normally could not sit on stools, all female mediums had their own skin seats and were treated as men during possession; afterward, however, they resumed their ordinary status and with it all the restrictions that customarily applied to members of their sex (Lubogo 1960: 247). During the Rundi ceremonies, women wore men's ceremonial dress (called *imbega*), sat on stools, carried spears, and had the right—ordinarily denied them—to judge in trials.* In Buha, a woman dressed as a man and treated as a great chief led the procession that completed the initiation ceremony. She bore the name Ruhang'umugabo (from *umugabo*, "adult male" or "husband"). During the procession, which involved gathering food and begging from people, people hurried from their houses and greeted her with the words, *"Ganza, mwami nven'-ongoma"* ("Greetings to you, great chief") (Van Sambeek 1949: 1, 72). In the Nyoro ceremonies to remove a yellow, frothy substance associated with thunder and lightning that could drop from the sky, "The women ... kept strolling up and down, holding and

---

* I learned this in an interview with four women in Burasira, Burundi, on March 6, 1970.

shaking their spears and shields like men at war ..." (Nyakatura, 1970: 60). Similarly, one of the female deities was named Rukohe Nyakalika Irikangabu, she "who wields shields like men." The Rwanda ceremony of *kubandwa* abolished sexual differences; all initiates, men and women alike, acquired a virile masculine quality, *umugabo* (Arnoux 1912: 844). Among the Hunde of eastern Zaire, the spirit Mbalala, which possessed women, carried a spear without "becoming a leper" (apparently the normal punishment for such a transgression of sexual boundaries); sometimes the possessed woman danced with a spear and shield "just as if she had become a man" (Viaene 1952: 405).*

A small body of material also suggests that the cults functioned as vehicles for expressing hostility against the social order in general or against particular people, especially superiors. Although none of the examples applies specifically to male-female relationships, it seems unlikely that women would have ignored such opportunities. In Rwanda, a list of highly unflattering or obscene names of spirits included Nkunda abatutsi, "I love the Tutsi" (in this context clearly an ironic expression of attitudes toward the upper class); and possessed persons had complete freedom to express any feelings they wished since others accepted these words as those of the spirit. Individuals bore no responsibility for their utterances. "They could speak inconsiderate words, abuse their parents or their superiors, without anyone dreaming of asking for compensation after the ceremony was finished" (Kagame 1967: 766). These instances are particularly interesting in view of the predominance of lower-class agriculturalists, Hutu, among cult members. In Buha, where the cult's social composition is unknown, possessed people behaved in a similar fashion. "Another only abuses everyone, even the chief of the country if he is present" (Van Sambeek 1949: 1, 79).

The explanation of this ritual rebellion probably lies in the concept of possession as a liminal state in which all ordinary rules

---

* Wilson (1967: 322, n. 4) suggests that women adopted male symbols in these situations because power and authority in their societies could be expressed only through "maleness."

of society are suspended—thus permitting such transgressions as criticism of superiors and men dressing as women and women as men. In Buha, for example, "Initiates who dress as their spirit say that they are no longer men, and they allow themselves many insults and even dishonest actions that they would not permit themselves in a normal state" (Van Sambeek 1949: 2, 53). The temporary nature of this state is of paramount importance; and leadership and prestige often accrue to the medium only while she is possessed. In this way women may be allowed possibilities for status, but the predominant ideas about female inferiority or about women's place in the established social order are not threatened. In fact, the theatrical nature of possession ceremonies may well reinforce this feeling that the occasion is out of the ordinary. Additional evidence in support of this interpretation comes from two facts: most female deities are concerned primarily with female activities (especially agriculture and fertility); and most are also conceived of in positions of subservience to men (usually as wives, daughters, sisters, and slaves of male deities). Although some female deities may have transcended such characterization, the Nyoro view of Nyabuzana probably expresses a general attitude. She had no hut dedicated to her, but "stays at the hearth because she is a woman" (Beattie 1961: 32, n. 9).

Despite anthropological interpretation of such rites as reinforcing the status quo, and despite the temporary nature of possession, mediums were highly respected members of their societies. Furthermore, the cults also provided them with access to more stable and institutionalized high-status positions. In the words of Max Gluckman, becoming a diviner is the "only way an outstanding [Zulu] woman can win general social prestige" (quoted in Lee 1969: 141). Robin Horton (1969: 42), writing on Kalabari communities in Nigeria, echoes a similar theme. "The fully-developed complex of possession roles typically figures a man: not just an ordinary man, but a man of wealth, power, and status. In adopting this complex of roles a woman is enabled, from time to time, really to 'be' what she has always yearned to be but never can be in ordinary normal life." Writing specifically on Bunyoro, Beattie (1969: 169) repeats this theme. "The social status of women in Bunyoro is low, as it is elsewhere in East Africa, and subservience and deference towards men is traditionally expected of them. But as mediums . . . they can command attention and respect, as well as providing themselves, if they practice divination, with a substantial source of income." Similarly, an Nkore source observes that women normally were not regarded as people and could neither possess nor inherit property; only certain "great witches" and princesses of the royal family were exceptions.* Others indicate that female mediums were trusted with tasks not ordinarily granted to women; thus, again in Nkore, the pickets and spies for cattle raids often were "women devotees of the spirit-king cult who circulated freely between the western Lacustrine kingdoms" (Stenning 1959: 15). This also points up the itinerant lives of many mediums, suggesting that at least some female *emandwa* possessed greater freedom and geographical mobility than did ordinary women. In addition, many were able to use their positions to accumulate relatively large amounts of wealth. In Bunyoro, by the 1950's, initiation might involve the payment of a fee as large as £20 and the provision of large quantities of beer and food. While this may exceed precolonial payments, a typical song of the ceremony goes: "You get plenty to eat [in the society of *babandwa*] and as well as that you put your hands in other people's purses" (Beattie 1957: 152–53). A Nyamwezi account asserts that the fees, paid in units of five (shillings, hoes, pieces of cloth) to become an ordinary initiate and in units of 50 to gain access to the higher levels, tended to make functionaries of the cult wealthy men and women.† These fees, however, also made access to higher levels of the cult difficult for anyone but the rich. Rundi, for example, usually were fairly old by the time they became mediums because of the wealth required;‡ and in Rwanda the funds

* Fr. Le Tohic, "District Book," Mbarara, Section 12, Ankole, Reel 2, Microfilm, Makerere University Library.

† District Officer Nzega to District Commissioner Tabora, "Baswezi Society," Tanzania National Archives, Secretariat File No. 19303, 26 November 1930, Ref. No. A/2/144, p. 2.

‡ Interview with Ambroise Buryeburye, Bujumbura, Burundi, February 27, 1970.

necessary to undergo the second stage of initiation made it less easily accessible to the poor (Coupez 1956: 135). But this requirement might explain the cult's particular openness to women as opposed to other low-status people, since a woman's access to her husband's resources gave her an asset unavailable to a poor man.* Again, however, essential data on male versus female acquisition through these positions are lacking.

A small number of women also were able to attain positions of national prominence. In the Mubende District of Kitara (the former Nyoro kingdom), the medium of Ndahura, the spirit of smallpox, possessed not only her own temple but an extensive domain. According to the earliest available description (Lewin 1908: 91–92):

Mt. Mubende ... was at one time a sacred place regarded by both Baganda and Banyoro with reverence and dread, for thereon dwelt Ndaula [Ndahura], the spirit of Smallpox, guarded by the priestess Nakaima of the Basazima or snail tribe, with her wand Nkinga made of a bull's tail studded with shells and beads. The spirit's home was in the midst of a lofty grove of huge trees perched on the highest peak of Mubende.... The priestess ... is still alive and it is said that when the spirit Ndaula takes possession of her, her face and hands become covered with smallpox marks which remain for a whole day.

The kings of both Bunyoro and Buganda treated the site with great respect, and Nakaima received offerings from both rulers on the occasion of smallpox epidemics or when they had queries that they wished the spirit to answer. Ndahura, through his medium, also played an important role in the accession ceremony of the *mukama*, "king," of Bunyoro; without this god's aid, the king "could not properly 'eat' Unyoro." Furthermore, the spirit's prestige exempted Mubende Hill from both Nyoro and Ganda attack.

Frequently, the main deities had women dedicated to them as wives, these women not being allowed to marry while in the spirit's service. By far the most important of these women was the official

---

* It would be interesting to know whether patrons in Burundi, Rwanda, and Buha provided the initiation fees for their clients. The terms patron and client here refer to the partners in a feudal-type contract somewhat like that in medieval Western Europe but based on cattle rather than land.

wife of Kiranga in Burundi, Mukakiranga. J. M. M. Van der Burgt
writes: *

> In Burundi, in which he was until now the uncontested master, Kiranga
> (the devil) possesses for himself two herds of cattle, each one presided over
> by an Ngabe, sacred bull. Satan also possesses as a fief his *iburunga*, or
> sacred mountain, administered by a Vestal called the wife of Kiranga. This
> priestess is, it is said, condemned to perpetual virginity. She enjoys great
> authority and is exempt from all dues to the king. Nonetheless the latter
> has her closely watched to prevent her from violating her obligations, in
> which case she would be put to death with all those of her family. She
> assumes her position at the same time as the king does; when the latter
> dies, she is condemned to take poison; if to the contrary she dies before
> him, she is replaced by another young girl.

Mukakiranga played a major part in the great national ceremony
of *umuganiro*, a yearly spiritual renewal of the kingdom in which
all Rundi participated. Together with the king, she presided over
one portion of the ritual; and she filled a crucial role in the remainder of it. "She and the king are equals and hold Burundi in
common. The king is the visible chief of it. Kiranga incarnates himself in his wife and, through kubandwa or initiation, she becomes
Kiranga in person" (Gorju et al. 1938: 45).

Though not equally central to national unity, the medium of
Mukasa, the god of Lake Victoria, also occupied an influential
female position, as shown by the account of an early missionary in
Buganda.†

> It is more than a month back, that we first heard of the intended journey
> to Rubaga (the capital) of one of the most noted Gods (or evil spirits)
> in Uganda, for the purpose of curing the king. This spirit is named
> Mukasa, and he is supposed to be the chief deity of the Victoria Nyanza
> on which lake he has his dwelling. This spirit has gone by the name of
> Mukasa for generations back and takes up his abode in some witch of
> great power or medicine woman. All the people, and especially the boat-
> man and islanders, hold this medicine woman possessed by the evil spirit
> Mukasa to work miracles, and the report spread that she was going to
> cure the king by speaking a single word only. The chiefs, especially the

---

* *Chroniques Trimestrielles de la Société des Missionnaires d'Afrique (Pères
Blancs)*, S-antoine de mougera, Ouroundi [Burundi], 3d trimestre, 1902, p. 79.
† Letter from George Litchfield to Mr. Wright, Rubaga, Uganda, January 3,
1880 (Archives, Church Missionary Society, Letters of George Litchfield, Nyanza
Mission, c/A6.0 15/1-23).

older and more influential of them, hailed her coming, and began to make every preparation to receive her with honour.

Although the immense power of the king by the mid-nineteenth century had reduced her independence, this medium remained among the more esteemed in the kingdom.

In Nkore, a female diviner, Nyabuzana, possessed land and a palace at Ibanda Hill in Mitoma. She performed ceremonies at each new moon and directed a four-day ritual of spirit worship that became an important part of the royal accession ceremonies. In addition, she functioned as a source of information to the king on the movements of his enemies and bewitched other chiefs to facilitate their defeat. Her prestige allowed her to walk about in her ceremonial dress and claim any cow she wished; no one refused, believing that the *emandwa* themselves had chosen the cattle (Williams 1937: 309; Gray 1960: 167–68; Bamunoba 1965: 95–96).

Much larger numbers of women could attain highly regarded positions as local mediums and priestesses. The Toro clan priestess, the *nyakatagara*, could communicate with one or two of the clan's Cwezi spirits. She directed the construction of shrines, advised on their maintenance, offered prayers on periodic visits to homesteads, and invited initiated cult members, singers, and musicians to participate in rituals. Generally, she shared the direction of ceremonies with the most important local medium, the *kazini* (Taylor 1957: 198–200). Nyoro group mediums, more commonly women than men, held such high status that even the household head, whose authority was unquestioned in all other matters, had to treat them respectfully at all times. Nyoro informants derive their title, *nyakatagara*, from the verb *okutagara*, "to be free to do what one likes, to be privileged." Beattie (1961: 15–18) doubts the accuracy of this etymology, but notes that the implication is plain. Among the Sumbwa, a leader of the female cult members organized the work of women and arbitrated in quarrels between them (Cory 1955: 936). One account from the Tabora District of Unyamwezi describes a woman named Kanunga as the Mtwale Mkubwa, Great Chief of the Swezi of Uyui; another account refers to the *mnangogo* and the *mnangogokazi*, the society's chief and chieftainess. Writing on Shinyanga District in Usukuma, a colonial officer noted that "women have equal status with men, and many female members of the Baswezi have been nominated in the past as chieftainesses."*

An even greater degree of female power prevailed in the cult of Nyabingi. In Rwanda and southwestern Uganda, the *bagirwa* (priests and priestesses) adopted the style of the interlacustrine kings, surrounding themselves with a large personal entourage, often armed; collecting tribute; and using or threatening to use physical violence to consolidate their positions. Some adopted still another prerogative of royalty and appeared publicly only on litters. In addition, of course, they cultivated a strong aura of supernatural power, both beneficial and malevolent. One account (Rwandusya 1972: 138) describes the arrival of the priestess Rutajirakijuna in Rukiga.

A mysterious woman, possibly from the country of Bahima, arrived in Rukiga. She was accompanied by hundreds of worshipers and ordered that she be taken to Kyante where she wanted a temporary court.

. . .

It is said that she was "Ekyebumbe" who could appear and disappear and could cause anything to happen. All the Bakiga feared to approach her for fear of death or other misfortune which could easily arise from being associated with such a personality. She was worshiped by many Banyarwanda but not at first by the Bakiga. After some time her fame grew wide and high, spreading like fire until King Rwabugiri IV of Rwanda came to learn about it. He ordered his representative in Bufumbira to investigate.

Though her conflict with the Rwandan king soon led to her beheading, during her life Rutajirakijuna achieved "an almost royal power" and always received the royal greeting, "Kasinje!" accompanied by hand-clapping. Eventually she changed her original name, Rutajirakijuna ("she who lacks support"), to Rutatangirwa omu Muhanda ("she who cannot be stopped on her way," i.e., the invincible) (Bessell 1938: 75).

Probably the most famous priestess was Muhumusa, who claimed

* Whether this refers to the Swezi or to other political units is not clear. J. W. T. Allen, Administrative Secretary, Lake Province, to District Commissioners in Province, 17 November 1954, Ref. No. s. 13/57, Hans Cory Collection, University Library, Dar es Salaam, "Baswezi" No. 45.

to be a wife of Rwabugiri, an immensely powerful nineteenth-century Rwandan king. One tradition records that after her son's succession as king had been successfully challenged in a civil war she fled to the north and gathered a group of adherents around her by personifying Nyabingi. But German support of the reigning king, Musinga, doomed her attempt to install her son as king, and she turned her attack against the Europeans. "As the Nyabingi she raised a large following both of Bakiga and Banyaruanda. Proclaiming herself the Queen of Ndorwa and liberator of it from the Europeans, in the course of 1911 she swept through the country, raiding, looting, and burning" (Bessell 1938; see also Des Forges 1972: 153–54). Another priestess, Kaigirirwa, participated in organizing the 1917 Nyakishenyi revolt in Kigezi District, which began with an attack on the local Ganda political agent and 63 of his followers. Eventually she was killed while resisting capture.

All of these instances of local female leadership occurred in religious movements that were relatively independent of lineage organization. This independence stemmed from the fact that in some areas the new cults eclipsed those of lineage ghosts, whereas in others they took the form of autonomously organized groups not based on kinship ties.* Since lineage cults represented the husband's family, perhaps their eclipse in itself enhanced the possibility of female religious participation. In Bunyoro and Toro the process was gradual, probably occurring over a period of several centuries; in Unyamwezi and Rukiga, on the other hand, it developed specifically as a result of historical changes during the nineteenth century.

In Bunyoro and Toro by the colonial period, the cult of family ghosts, *bazimu*, had been replaced as the basic religion by the cult of Cwezi *mbandwa* (Beattie 1961: 32, n. 5). Today, the cult of the *bazimu* in these areas either is not practiced at all or is of negligible importance. This trend correlated also with the breakdown of residential organization based on patrilineal descent groups (Beattie

---

* A largely female Shi sect, the Benakayange, also had a "great chieftainess," but no information is available about the sect's organization. See Colle 1937: 206–7.

1964: 143, 150). The *mbandwa* cults, in this situation, offered leadership possibilities to many women in their local cult groups, which, although loosely associated with patrilineal clans, had their own heads and stressed solidarity between initiates rather than between kinspeople.

In Unyamwezi, the divorce from lineage organization was even greater, for by the late nineteenth century secret societies (among them the Buswezi) had begun to fulfill many roles of kinship groups in assisting members in time of need. This trend resulted from people's dispersion through their large-scale participation in long-distance trade (Roberts 1970: 43). With both family and neighborhood organizations extremely fluid, and with geographical mobility high, the cults were dissociated from any kinship connections and came to form highly delineated, independent corporate groups. With this decline in the importance of kinship ties came the only instance in the area of women's involvement in cults of lineage ghosts; only here could they preside over the rites to honor deceased members of the group (Millroth 1965: 134; Bösch 1930: 137).

The Nyabingi cults of northern Rwanda and southwestern Uganda offer another instance of autonomously organized religious groups. By the late nineteenth century, these cults had successfully eclipsed those of *bazimu* and *emandwa*, both fully integrated with patrilineages (Edel 1957: 146). Here the historical setting was the attempts of the Rwanda state, and later the Europeans, to conquer politically decentralized areas. The new cults provided a new, militant form of organized resistance; and in these groups, centered on a female spirit, a number of famous women were able to exercise substantial power. Pertinent here, though, is the problem of institutionalizing female authority; for although women apparently acted as the chief priestesses in an early period, as the position acquired increasing power in the late nineteenth century male priests became more prevalent.* Thus, as in the Unyamwezi lin-

---

* I am indebted to Catherine Robins for this observation. May Edel, writing from the perspective of the 1930's, judged that female members were considered subordinate to male members (see Edel 1957: 154).

eage cults, women seemed to gain some positions only at times when they possessed relatively low value. This raises the question, impossible to answer from available material, of whether women participated more actively in the initial stages of spirit cults when possession might have been more spontaneous and less regulated than in later stages. It also suggests the possibility that the imperfect fit between the interlacustrine and Nyamwezi areas' religious movements and Lewis's definitions arises from the process of historical transformation by which peripheral cults may evolve into central ones. But although the data do point to a trend toward greater integration with older institutions over time, they do not necessarily verify a process of linear progression from one form to the other. Furthermore, it seems that in their possible historical role as peripheral, *kubandwa* cults have assumed more importance as a continuing vehicle for popular protest among both men and women than as a strictly feminist outlet. Although they allowed women a prominence not otherwise available to them and certain vehicles for pressuring men, other aspects of protest they embodied have been as much against a social order oppressive to men and women alike as against the specific subordination of women. The mobilization of Nyabingi followers against Rwandan and then European overlordship illustrates this theme, as does the cults' earlier involvement in resistance movements against the imposition of new state systems (see Berger forthcoming: chaps. 4 and 5). Nonetheless, deciding on the balance between these themes is difficult since the possibility exists that the latter appears dominant because of its association with militant revolts. Such actions become history, whereas the individual- and family-level conflict between the sexes goes unrecorded.

In conclusion then, regardless of religious or social structure, a small number of women everywhere emerged in institutionalized positions of religious leadership. Thus, as in most stratified situations, a few people were allowed to rise above their customary status without challenging the dominant ideology or structure of subordination. In the Ganda pattern of elitist cults, which lacked mass initiation, women's leadership positions were limited to these few. This may have held true in Unyamwezi as well since the Swezi was only one of numerous secret societies, in others of which authority and sometimes even active membership were limited to men.* Similarly, in the Nyabingi cults only small numbers of women leaders emerged.

Only in the democratic cults of the Nyoro-Ha area did large numbers of women participate actively in religious life. Although their exercise of power and authority was restricted to ritual situations, they could acquire wealth from their positions and apparently commanded respect at all times because of their religious powers. And here, as in the elitist cults, smaller numbers of women achieved institutionalized high positions either as national figures or, more frequently, as local religious leaders. Yet this religious form arose largely in the most highly stratified societies of the region.† This may explain the occurrence in a precolonial setting of a religious form usually associated with the late nineteenth and early twentieth centuries; for the oppression of these societies, like that of the colonial period, may have drawn together subordinate peoples into movements that offered at least occasional and temporary prestige as well as an institutionalized outlet for antisocial feelings. In this context, the form and function of women's religious participation corresponded with that of other low-status groups.‡

* A few references to women's societies do occur: the Bagota, for people who officiate in twin ceremonies; Wagoli; and Ba Shingoma. Little is known about them, however.

† Rukiga is an exception: the *emandwa* cults spread here from the surrounding kingdoms. But even here their strong association with women suggests that they took root primarily among a subordinate group in society.

‡ This conclusion is particularly clear for Rwanda and Burundi, the most oppressive of the interlacustrine societies. The cults' social composition in the north is less clear. In a historical context, however, subordination also might have involved the imposition of a new ruling dynasty.

From *Lelemama* to Lobbying:
Women's Associations in Mombasa, Kenya

MARGARET STROBEL

AN OUTSIDE observer, assuming the oppressed status of Muslim women and noting their widespread lack of education and non-participation in political campaigns, might well have been surprised at the scale of organization and concerted effort that marked the entry of Kenya's coastal Muslim women into politics in 1958.[*] During the struggle for coastal autonomy in the late 1950's, 100 Arab women from Mombasa successfully petitioned the colonial government in Kenya to protest discriminatory legislation that denied them the vote but gave it to women of other ethnic communities (Salim 1973: 229; interview with Fatuma Mohamed [BS, MWCA], 24.7.73). Having succeeded with their petition, the women began a registration campaign that lasted a full year and involved house-to-house visits by Arab women to explain to their neighbors what voting was and why Arab women should vote just like Asian, African, and European women (Shamsa Mohamed Muhashamy [IW, MWI], 29.11.72). This episode suggests a high level of feminist consciousness on the part of Mombasa's Muslim women, but closer study reveals different motivations. Although

---

[*] This article was first presented at the Annual Conference of the Historical Association of Kenya, on August 24, 1973, in Nairobi. It is based on fieldwork carried out between November 1972 and August 1973 in Mombasa with the aid of a Fulbright-Hays Doctoral Dissertation Research Abroad grant. Early drafts of this article received much appreciated criticism from Edward Alpers, Fred Cooper, Fatma Dharamsi, and Gary Nash. I conducted many interviews with Muslim women in Mombasa during my 1972–73 stay, and where such interviews are cited, the initials following an informant's name indicate the organizations of which she is (or was) a member. IW and BS stand for Ibinaal Watan and

these women have developed organizations that could be mobilized for feminist political ends, the consciousness directing their activities has continued to be influenced by ethnicity, prestige, and competition for social status as much as by a growing awareness of their needs as women.

Muslim women's motivation and ability to organize can be elucidated by studying the development of women's organizations in Mombasa from the 1930's to the present—from *lelemama* dance associations such as Ibinaal Watan and Banu Saada to newer organizations such as the Muslim Women's Institute and the Muslim Women's Cultural Association. Although political activity like the 1958 suffrage campaign has been infrequent, both the dance associations and the later organizations have mobilized women in pursuit of goals important to the Muslim community. In the 1930's and 1940's the dance associations provided entertainment and the mechanism for women to achieve high status; the later groups directed their attention to social welfare and education. Women brought organizational and leadership experience with them from Ibinaal Watan and Banu Saada when they joined the Muslim Women's Institute or the Cultural Association. This paper will discuss the functions, consciousness, continuities, innovations, and limitations of women's groups in Mombasa.

Mombasa Society

The social hierarchy of the East African or Swahili coast has evolved over hundreds of years of migration and interaction by various peoples.* In the 1890's Mombasa was already a cosmopoli-

---

Banu Saada, respectively, the two principal *lelemama* dance associations of Mombasa in the 1920's and 1930's; MWI and MWCA stand for the Muslim Women's Institute and the Muslim Women's Cultural Association, respectively. Dates are given in the form day-month-year. For the purposes of the current volume I have cited only the most important interviews; readers interested in greater detail are referred to my dissertation, "Muslim Women in Mombasa, Kenya, 1890–1973" (University of California, 1975).

* Some of the material in this section has appeared in slightly different form in my article "Women's Wedding Celebrations in Mombasa, Kenya," *African Studies Review*, 18, no. 3 (Dec. 1975), pp. 36–37. For historical background on Mombasa and the coast, see Berg 1968a ("The Coast from the Portuguese Invasion to the Rise of the Zanzibar Sultanate"), Berg 1968b ("The Swahili Com-

tan town with a population of 25,000, most of whom were Muslim.
The upper stratum consisted of wealthy slave-owning families.
This elite grew out of intermarriage between long-time coastal resi-
dents—the Twelve Tribes of Mombasa—and immigrants from the
Hadhramaut and Oman in Arabia. Ancestors of the present
Twelve Tribes (*Thenashara Taifa*) migrated between the fourteenth and seventeenth centuries from coastal communities north
of Mombasa. Some of the Twelve Tribes claim Persian origin.
Along with many Kenyan peoples, the Twelve Tribes were dispersed from the southern Somali coast by raiding Galla pastoralists.
Upon arriving at Mombasa Island, the Twelve Tribes formed
two segments, the Nine Tribes and the Three Tribes, between
whom successive Omani Arab governors mediated from the late
seventeenth century until 1895, when the British established a
Protectorate. The Twelve Tribes have been Muslim for centuries
under the influence of religious men from the Hadhramaut. Mi-
grating from southern Arabia in small numbers since the fourteenth century, these Hadhrami holy men and traders established
themselves in coastal towns. Other Arabs, from Oman, wrested
control of the coast from the Portuguese by 1700 and thereafter
settled as traders, administrators, and plantation owners. Their
migration increased after the Busaidi dynasty moved its capital
from Masqat in Oman to Zanzibar and conquered Mombasa in
1837. The Busaidi brought soldiers from Baluchistan and the
Hadhramaut for their garrisons. These three ethnic groups—the
Twelve Tribes, Hadhrami Arabs, and Omani Arabs (excluding the
soldiers)—formed the upper crust of Mombasa society at the turn
of the century.

The middle layers included some slave-owners among the traders, sailors, artisans, and laborers, who were drawn from the poorer
ranks of Twelve Tribes and Arab society. In addition, some freed

munity of Mombasa, Kenya, 1500–1900"), Berg 1971 ("Mombasa Under the Busaidi Sultanate: The City and Its Hinterland"), Berg and Walter 1968 ("Mosques,
Population, and Urban Development in Mombasa"), Cooper 1974 ("Plantation Slavery on the East Coast of Africa in the Nineteenth Century"), Prins
1952 (*The Coastal Tribes of the North-Eastern Bantu*), and Prins 1967 (*The
Swahili-Speaking Peoples of Zanzibar and the East African Coast*).

slaves rose to this level. On the bottom rung, slaves from the hinterland Mijikenda peoples* and from central and east Africa provided agricultural, maritime, and domestic labor. Ethnicity and
social status were not congruent, though Omani Arabs tended to
be on the top, African slaves on the bottom, and Twelve Tribes
people and Hadhrami Arabs scattered among the ranks of the
freeborn.†

British rule from 1895 to 1963 influenced social structure in
Mombasa in two major ways—through the abolition of the legal
status of slavery in 1907, and through the introduction of racial
categories that conferred differential rights and advantages.
Though legally freeing slaves, the 1907 law could not erase the
stigma of slave ancestry, which continues today. The government's
introduction of racial categories—European, Indian, Arab, and
African—contributed to conflict between the Twelve Tribes and
Arabs. Some Twelve Tribes members, unhappy with their classifi-
cation as "Swahili" and therefore "native" or African, claimed
that years of intermarriage with Arabs made them of Arab descent
and thus gave them the right to Arab status. Arabs rejected these
claims, and rival organizations (the Afro-Asian Association founded in 1927, and the Arab Association begun in 1928) destroyed
an earlier unity that had been based on hazy distinctions rather
than rigid categories (Salim 1973: 186–92). The political maneu-
verings of these groups are not within the scope of this paper, but
the discussion above indicates the complexity and intensity of
ethnic and status considerations among people who shared many
common features. The great majority were Sunni Muslims (Trimingham 1964: 53). Although they maintained certain customs and
dances of their countries of origin, they mixed these elements

* Mijikenda is the name by which the nine groups of peoples known during
the nineteenth and early twentieth centuries as the Nyika now refer to themselves. They live in the dry hinterland along Kenya's coast.

† This simplified outline of Mombasa society excludes the Indian ("Asian"
after 1947) population of Muslims, Hindus, Jains, and Goan Christians who, for
the most part, did not intermarry with the Arabs and indigenous Africans in
Mombasa. Similarly, the up-country African migrants that swelled the city's
population in the twentieth century were not a part of *lelemama* and have
been excluded from consideration.

freely in weddings when members of two different communities intermarried. The Swahili language was widely used by all but the most recent immigrants. As microcosms of the wider community, women's associations shared these ethnic and status tensions.

Lelemama Associations

Ibinaal Watan and Banu Saada are only two of over 40 women's associations devoted to dancing *lelemama*, a style brought from Zanzibar to Mombasa at the end of the nineteenth century. The heyday of *lelemama* groups was the period from 1920 to 1945, although the associations exist today on a reduced scale (see Topan n.d.). Members incurred huge expenses in the course of the associations' activities. Cattle or goats were slaughtered for a weekend picnic on a member's farm that culminated in a *lelemama* dance. Dancers lined up on a bench wearing identical *leso*, the traditional coastal dress,* or Omani-style smocks and trousers. Dancing sedately, they sang old favorites or newly composed songs that revealed the misdeeds of people in the community, publicly shamed individuals, or challenged rival *lelemama* associations by ridiculing their dancing abilities. Associations usually formed competing pairs, following a pattern common to coastal societies.† Success was measured not only in dancing ability and the originality of the songs, but also in the size of the audience and the lavishness of picnics and officers' installations. Occasionally the rivalry became vicious, as in the case of the Ibinaal Watan–Banu Saada competition held shortly after World War II, which is described in detail later.

As one would expect in a society very concerned about ethnicity and social hierarchy, the dance associations were not all equally

---

* *Leso* are pieces of printed cotton cloth about one meter by two meters. Bought in pairs, one *leso* is wrapped around the body and tucked under the armpits, covering the woman from breasts to calves. The second is worn around the head and shoulders for modesty, or wrapped around the waist or hips. Older women still wear only two *leso*. Girls and younger women wear Western dresses, sometimes tying a *leso* around their waist so that it reaches the floor.

† See, for example, Prins 1965: 272–74; and Lienhardt 1966: 374–86. The pattern of competing pairs appears also in men's brass bands, for which see Ranger 1975.

prestigious. The predecessors of Ibinaal Watan and Banu Saada—
Kingi, Kilungu, and Scotchi—had a male *beni* or brass band con-
tingent as well as a female *lelemama* section. These three associations, drawing from the elite and their followers in Mombasa's
Old Town, were most prestigious and most able to afford feasts
and competitions. In imitation of Kingi, Kilungu, and Scotchi,
similar associations grew up in the newer settlements of Mombasa
Island among people lower on the social scale, in some cases of
slave ancestry. In all associations, however, the leader had to be
able to afford an elaborate investiture ceremony.

The *lelemama* associations had two sets of titles, which could
be held simultaneously and for life. One type, reflecting Arab
social concepts and practices, were *usheha*, from the term *Sheik*
("ruler," "elder," "influential person"). At the top was the *Sheha*,
followed by her *Waziri* ("Ministers"). Other officers included
Wazee ("Elders"), each performing specific tasks. The *Mzee wa Jiko*
("Elder of the Kitchen") supervised cooking, the *Mzee wa Ngoma*
drummed, another *Mzee* invited guests to the gathering. To become *Mzee* one had to give a feast (*kupima mchele*, "to measure
rice") for important members of Mombasa's *lelemama* associations as well as for various categories of townspeople—carpenters, fishermen, midwives, masons, ironworkers, etc. The highest status went to *Mtenzi*, the woman who provided a cow to
be slaughtered for a feast.* Ibinaal Watan had from 40 to 50
Wazee, but only four *Watenzi*. These ranks were drawn from precolonial life and incorporated Arabic and Swahili words and functions.

In contrast to these was the second set of titles. Having acquired
one of the Swahili ranks, one could also hold a title associated with
jibli ("jubilee"), which clearly reflected British colonial influence.†

* The *Sheha* need not have slaughtered a cow, and thus she could be below
the *Mtenzi*. Fatma Saidi (IW), 18.7.73.
† Fatma Saidi (18.7.73) associated *jibli* with the coronation of a queen. Queen
Victoria's Jubilee in 1897 is almost certainly the origin of the Swahili term,
since the coast was sufficiently under British administration by that year to
have celebrated. Moreover, two coastal men actually attended Victoria's Jubilee
and no doubt informed their friends about it upon their return. Kenya Na-

The *Kwini* ("Queen") was surrounded by her court of *Maduki* ("Dukes") and *Maledi* ("Ladies"). In Ibinaal Watan there was a *Kanala* ("Colonel") and *Vaiz-Kanala* ("Vice-Colonel") in charge of land forces and an *Admirali* ("Admiral") and *Vaiz-Admirali* ("Vice-Admiral") in charge of sea forces. In practical terms their rank allowed them to order other women around. A *Daktari* ("Doctor") dressed in white pretended to give people shots. In other associations the *Daktari* oversaw food arrangements; a *Kashia* ("Cashier") collected dues; a *Kijumbe* invited guests; and a *Kamanda* ("Commander") directed the dancers. The details of these titles were closely watched. It is reported that the head of Kilungu was a *Sheha*, not a Queen, and that another woman gave a feast sufficient only to earn her the right to wear a half crown instead of a full crown.*

To receive either type of title one had to spend lavishly. One woman reputedly spent 10,000 shillings for this *heshima*, or respect (Fatuma Mohamed [BS, MWCA], 20.5.73). Upon receiving a title, a woman could expect the drumming to stop when she entered the dance area, a chair to be brought, and her orders to be followed by subordinates.

Not only in structure but also in other aspects, Ibinaal Watan and Banu Saada were characteristic of *lelemama* associations. These two were begun in the mid-1920's by the generation of the daughters of Kingi, Kilungu, and Scotchi. Their founding reflects the dissension that plagued—and continues to plague—the associations. Fatma Mwaita, the daughter of the *Sheha* of Kilungu, left Kilungu to join the rival Kingi, and then left Kingi to begin her own *lelemama* association. In taking the name Ibinaal Watan, Arabic for "daughters of the city," she imitated a men's regiment within Kingi called Ibn Watan, "sons of the city." Shortly thereafter she quarreled with Ibinaal Watan because she felt slighted at a wedding: each important person had received a separate tray

tional Archives (KNA), LMU/12, Tanaland Province Annual Report 1915/16, Provincial Commissioner to Chief Secretary, Nairobi, 5.7.16.
* The information in this paragraph came from interviews with several members of *lelemama* associations.

from which to eat, but she had not. Thus rebuffed, Fatma Mwaita
left Ibinaal Watan and started a rival group, Banu Saada.* Fatuma
binti Hassan, niece of the Bandmaster of Kingi, then assumed the
role of Queen of Ibinaal Watan. Banu Saada grew, and with it
grew the rivalry toward Ibinaal Watan.

Criteria for membership in these two associations are ambiguous.
Daughters of Kilungu members largely entered Banu Saada,
whereas daughters of Kingi joined Ibinaal Watan. Members of
Ibinaal Watan tended to come from the neighborhood of Old
Town called Mjua Kale, traditionally a Nine Tribes area; and
members of Banu Saada came from Kuze and Mkanyageni, traditionally Three Tribes neighborhoods. Ibinaal Watan had a large
proportion of Omani Arabs, and Banu Saada a relatively large
number of "Africans," "black people," or *manegro*.† Because of
their ties with the Twelve Tribes, Mijikenda women from the
nearby hinterland frequently were members. However, Indians
and up-country Africans did not join. Membership patterns did
not reflect rigid rules, but rather developed out of interactions and
relationships within Old Town. Arab and Twelve Tribes elites
formed associations with former slaves and servants of their families, with Baluchis who had intermarried, and occasionally with
Hadhrami women.‡ As one woman put it, "it was not a matter
of tribe; to join you had to be like us." This meant a Muslim, not a
recent arrival to Mombasa, and not a "raw" (*mbichi*) Mijikenda.
These are elusive but real cultural criteria: one had to feel at home
in the Old Town Arab-Swahili milieu. The single Christian mem-

* Banu Saada is also the name of the tribe of the Prophet's wet nurse Halima;
see Knappert 1970: 71.
† Zubeda Salim (IW) stated the tribal affiliation explicitly (31.5.73). Fatuma
Mohamed (BS) admitted the connections between associations and districts, but
denied tribal affiliations (20.5.73). Fatma Saidi (IW), the best informant regarding *lelemama*, said that Ibinaal Watan was mostly Nine Tribes. Banu Saada
was not so exclusive, but many members came from Kuze, a Three Tribes area
(18.7.73). The prejudice of many coastal Arabs, who consider themselves superior to others by virtue of status, religion, and ethnicity, is historical fact.
In discussing this prejudice my intention is not to stir ethnic hostility, but rather
to explain an important aspect of coastal life.
‡ Not many Hadhrami women entered *lelemama* associations—Aziza Omar
Abeidi (9.7.73).

ber of Banu Saada was accepted because she had mixed with Old Town people, come to their weddings, and visited in their homes.* Within the broad cultural framework of "Swahiliness," residence and kinship were major determinants of an individual's choice of association. One woman joined Banu Saada first, because it was predominant in Mkanyageni, where she was born, and thus more familiar to her; but later she switched to Ibinaal Watan because the woman who raised her was a member of Ibinaal Watan. Defection was frequent. Another woman, who joined Ibinaal Watan because of a family tie with that association, changed to Banu Saada to maintain her self-respect when Ibinaal Watan members sang songs ridiculing a member of her household, a woman who cared for the children. In some cases sisters or cousins were members of rival groups, which in times of intense competition increased family tensions.

Entertainment, status, and mutual aid are among the reasons members themselves cited for their participation in *lelemama* associations. In weddings, *lelemama* constituted one of many days' entertainment, with several hundred women attending, showing off their new clothes, cheering the dancers on, visiting one another, and awaiting the latest rumors and antagonisms to be revealed in song. Especially talented or popular dancers were rewarded by having shilling notes pinned on their clothes or gold jewelry fastened around their necks.

Lelemama was also danced on other special occasions: for *Kibunzi* and *Mwaka*, the celebration of the Swahili solar year around mid-July; for *Mfungo*, the feast before fasting in the month of Ramadan; for *Idd al Fitr* at the end of Ramadan; and for *Idd al Haj* at the end of the month for pilgrimage to Mecca. Besides these communal celebrations, a *lelemama* could be organized whenever the members gathered enough money for a feast— whether as a treat for themselves or as a competitive challenge to their rivals. These dances helped to break up daily routine and to accent important days. The dances must have been exciting

---

* The Christian woman was most probably from the Freretown Mission for freed slaves.

occasions both for poor women, who worked long hours each day, and for elite women, who traditionally left their houses only to attend weddings, funerals, and these gatherings.

Besides entertaining both the dancers and the audience, the associations provided an alternative set of status distinctions and rewards in a society that was very concerned with hierarchy based on descent. Any member who paid the customary fee could demand *heshima* ("rank," "honor," "respect"), not only from the association members but from the rest of the community as well. She had given them their *heshima*, now she deserved hers (as people often explained it, using the term reciprocally). A woman of slave descent could mitigate the stigma of her birth by becoming Queen. Although one should not exaggerate the possibility of social mobility provided by these associations, people of slave origin did found, and hold offices in, *lelemama* organizations. Fatma Mwaita, who founded Ibinaal Watan and Banu Saada, and her mother Sheha wa Mishi, who began Kilungu, were of slave ancestry. The newer organizations had many members from lower social strata; and two of these organizations, Seifu and Land Rova, were founded by an Mnyasa woman of slave ancestry.* Being Queen did not erase social differences between an Mnyasa and an Arab; everyone in the community knew who was freeborn and who was of slave descent. But the *lelemama* ranks offered prestige to women who had few other sources of dignity and honor.

Finally, the women I interviewed stressed the importance of helping fellow members. For example, at a wedding or a funeral, both of which were enormously expensive affairs that lasted for several days, women would contribute money and help prepare food. But reciprocity was demanded: by custom, if a woman was given ten shillings for her daughter's wedding, she had to return twenty shillings at the donor's next celebration.

In addition to these three purposes of entertainment, status attainment, and mutual aid articulated by members themselves, we can deduce such other functions as social control, acquisition of

---

* "Mnyasa" is a person from the Nyasa peoples of central Africa, an area of heavy slave raiding.

skills, expression of rebellion, and promotion of change through competition. The singing of songs about misdeeds reinforced social norms. In an incident that will be described in greater detail below, Ibinaal Watan teased and criticized Banu Saada through songs for contravening the "rules" of dances by allegedly selling rather than eating the cattle that Ibinaal Watan had given them. This use of songs is not limited to *lelemama*, for they had long served as instruments for revenge and criticism, as well as for entertainment, in Swahili society.

The mobilization of people, finances, and equipment for these celebrations trained women in organizational skills and leadership. All members were informed of the time and place of the competitions, which meant notifying several hundred dancers, supporters, and observers. Money was collected for the purchase of anywhere from one to twenty head of cattle, rice, ghee, onions, and other necessities for the feast. The best drummers had to be hired, and on some occasions even microphones and amplifiers were provided in order to outshine the opposition. Banu Saada once arranged for transportation from the island to the celebration site on the mainland by offering all the taxi drivers a free meal there. When Ibinaal Watan tried to find rides to its own dance on the same day, no taxis were available. Last but not least, special seamstresses sewed clothes for all the dancers. At various times Ibinaal Watan and Banu Saada danced in costumes imitating the British Air Force, Army, and Navy, complete with hats, uniforms, bell-bottoms, carved wooden guns, and firecrackers to imitate hand grenades. During World War II, Ibinaal Watan–Banu Saada competitions were a weekly event, and completely new outfits were needed for each occasion. These outfits were designed from magazine pictures and sewn in secret for each dance. If one association learned in advance what the opponent's uniform of the day was to be, they might dress a dog or a cat in the outfit and let it loose at the dance to shame the rival dancers. When the Muslim Women's Institute and the Muslim Women's Cultural Association superseded the *lelemama* groups as the principal women's associations in this part of Mombasa, the Ibinaal Watan and Banu

Saada leaders who joined the newer organizations were able to draw upon their grass-roots organizational experience to good advantage.

There is also an element of rebellion in the activities of the daughters of Kingi and Kilungu. In earlier *lelemama* associations, women of high social status gave financial support, but did not dance in mixed company. However, women of free ancestry of the Ibinaal Watan–Banu Saada generation mounted the bench alongside other performers of lower social status and, without wearing traditional black robes called *buibui*, danced in front of male spectators.* Needless to say, this action caused a considerable stir, particularly among the elite families. At one point the older men of the community threatened to go to the mosque and pray that their daughters drop dead if they continued such behavior (Shamsa Mohamed Muhashamy [IW, MWI], 9.5.73). But the daughters were already married, and if their husbands did not object, they continued dancing. How did it feel to dance before a mixed audience? "We just shut our eyes and did not think about the people, we wanted so strongly to win the competition" (*ibid.*, 10.5.73).

Most functions of *lelemama* associations are straightforward and clear. The enthusiasm with which people recall the competitions and tricks vividly substantiates the pleasure that dances gave to their participants. The pride in the voice of a Queen describing her official position and outfit is evidence of the importance of the rank to her personally. However, the function of the competitiveness of the associations is less easy to understand, since competition brought conflicting results. Stimulated by competition, women adopted new styles and challenged some fundamental values. At other times, though, competition led to periods of bitter antagonism between associations during which the community was torn apart and status differences were reinforced.

No better example of *lelemama ngoma* (dances) can be found than the still disputed competition between Ibinaal Watan and

---

* A *buibui* is a loose black robe worn over other clothing to conceal a woman for the purpose of protecting her modesty and maintaining *heshima* ("respect").

Banu Saada that occurred shortly after World War II. According to one participant, "The Europeans had their war and we had ours!" Hostility between some people continues to this day, and long after the conclusion of the competition each side still claims victory. The following account, by an Ibinaal Watan participant, evokes the spirit of the contest.*

One day while Asha and Khadija (from Banu Saada and Ibinaal Watan, respectively) were talking, they hit upon the idea of having a competition. Each spoke to her club, and the clubs agreed to have a cattle competition like those held by *ngoma* associations in Tanganyika. Ibinaal Watan began by giving Banu Saada five cattle, which were to be eaten at a *lelemama ngoma*. Through an informant in the butchery we discovered that Banu Saada had not slaughtered all five cattle, but had returned some to the market to sell, in order to finance their gift to us. We called a special *ngoma* to shame them, dancing out in the open to attract passersby and singing, "The cattle were sold at the market, so Bwana James says." Banu Saada was very bitter, and after that when rival women passed one another in the street they would fight with sticks.

Then Banu Saada gave Ibinaal Watan ten cattle—by the rules of *ngoma* one must return double the original gift. We went to Changamwe on the mainland on a Saturday. We ate one cow that day, danced *lelemama*, and spent the night there. The next day we slaughtered a second cow, and at 3 P.M. we donned our new costumes, uniforms like those of the British Navy. Each week we had different clothes and more food. We came to Changamwe in our lorries and stepped out into the street. I tell you, in all Mombasa there was not a single person who would stay on the Island. They all came to watch the dance. Those who had cars came in cars, those who had bicycles came on bicycles, those with only legs walked. We did not wear our *buibui*, just our outfits. We stepped out into the street with our trumpets, our songs, and our firecrackers and marched—left, right, left, right. We marched up to the bridge and into the city. Cars followed us, and people—more than for Kenyatta even! We did this each weekend until we had eaten all ten cattle.

We were preparing to offer Banu Saada twenty cattle. Then word leaked that they were not ready to accept twenty because they could not afford to give 40 in return. Without admitting defeat, they wanted five from those that they had given us.† So, we teased them in the streets, singing "They are crying for their cattle." Feelings ran so sour that each weekend we would have *ngoma* to sing abuses at each other. If someone

---

* In translating my anonymous informant's account, I have generally paraphrased and edited. I have also changed personal names at my informant's request.

† Ibinaal Watan gave Banu Saada five cattle; Banu Saada returned ten. Banu Saada wanted to end the competition in a draw, receiving five cattle from Ibinaal Watan.

from Banu Saada had a wedding or funeral, an Ibinaal Watan member would not go, even if it was for her own relative.

We decided to have one last *ngoma* to settle the competition. Chief Ali bin Namaan was asked to select a committee of judges. Each side performed and the judges chose us. We had a bigger audience and more spirit.* That was the second time we beat them, but Banu Saada refused to accept the judgment.

Then the war escalated. One day, coming home from a wedding in Kibokoni, my friend and I met Asha and a friend of hers from Banu Saada. "Stop!" they said. "Aha," I thought to myself, "now we have work to do!" "Why do you abuse my mother when you see her in the street?" "I abuse your mother, so what!" said my friend. The two started tussling, and soon I and the other woman joined in. You know, we were in enemy territory, Kuze, but we fought until those two from Banu Saada ran into a nearby house. Then all kinds of Ibinaal Watan women came running to support us and threw firewood and stones, breaking windows in the house. The police finally came and broke it up; we were allowed to go home.

From that day on Banu Saada was forbidden to pass on our streets, and we on theirs. If we went visiting we stuck to main roads and avoided the narrow paths between houses. Then one day during Ramadan, Banu Saada taunted us by coming right down the main street in our district, dancing as if they were escorting a bridegroom to the bride's house, though actually they were singing abuses at us.

I was sitting outside with a friend, only two of us, but we prepared for war. If they successfully passed down that street, we could never live it down. "Let's go and get them," I said. I took my stick and hid behind a building. My friend wrapped her *leso* tight around herself and held her *rungu*.† They came down the street at us with *panga*, axes, *rungu*, everything. Some assistance arrived, and we successfully defended the street, although we had to take some casualties to the hospital to be stitched.

What could such competition mean? Peter Lienhardt argues that competition is an integrating force. In a small village, "any fragmentary group within the village is drawn to the support of one side or the other, and hence the opposition of the two halves produces solidarity within each of them in place of a much greater number of oppositions between smaller groups" (Lienhardt 1968: 20). However, in a town as large as Mombasa, women had a wider range of alternatives and did not need to join one of the two

---

* In fact, Asha binti Khamis bin Mohamed (IW, then BS), who belonged to Banu Saada at the time of the competition, told me in an interview that the judges called it a draw (22.5.73). This is most likely, given the bitterness surrounding the competition. By committing himself to one side or the other, a judge was bound to lose popularity with the defeated contestants.

† A *rungu* is a stick with a knob on the end; a *panga* is a large machete.

competing associations. Disgruntled members of subgroups could always form new dance associations, and they frequently did. The Ibinaal Watan–Banu Saada competition appears to have solidified neighborhood groupings that were vague boundaries for recruitment into rival associations. But the benefits of such solidarity seem small compared to the drawbacks that the animosity produced during the war.

In the end, rather than integrating society, competition aggravated divisions in Old Town—specifically between people of slave and free ancestry. Some blurring of status differences between the two categories had been achieved within *lelemama* associations by the openness of ranks to both upper- and lower-class women. In encouraging elite women to join the others on the *lelemama* bench and dance in front of crowds, competition further contributed to integration. The same spirit of competition, however, led some of the women of Ibinaal Watan, proud of the greater number of freeborn members in their organization, to jeer at Banu Saada women as *majakazi*, or "female slaves." This action could not help but inflame ethnic tensions.

Uncontrolled competition in effect killed *lelemama* in Mombasa. After the "Battle of Kuze Road," as it might be called, the government banned *lelemama* for a time. No dance permits were issued for weddings or religious celebrations, because the existing bitterness inevitably surfaced in the form of abusive songs. With the cessation of overt hostilities, emotions cooled somewhat. But without competition, interest died out, and the associations lost their strength (Shamsa Mohamed Muhashamy [IW, MWI], 9.5.73). In retrospect, many women now see the *ngoma* as a waste of money. Whether this recognition of misplaced priorities existed 25 years ago and contributed to *lelemama*'s decline is impossible to determine.

The Muslim Women's Institute and the Muslim Women's Cultural Association

Coinciding with the decline of *lelemama* was the emergence of a new consciousness of the condition of coastal Muslim women.

A recognition of Arab backwardness, the example of other Muslim nations (notably Egypt), and the efforts of Arab reformers and colonial officials led some people to question the traditional role of women in Muslim Mombasa.* The pages of the *Mombasa Times* reflected this new consciousness. During the 1950's men's clubs engaged in heated debates about "sex equality" and the propriety of Muslim women attending the cinema. And, male Muslim leaders appealed to the faithful to reduce expenditures on weddings and to allow women to participate in communal prayers in the mosques (we will return to this subject in a later section).

At the same time, it is very difficult to chart the changing consciousness among Muslim women themselves. The *Mombasa Times* does not provide a good index even of male attitudes until 1954, when the fortnightly Arab news summary first appeared. Even after 1954 the opinions of Mombasa women are rarely represented in the letters to the editor because of their high rate of illiteracy, their shyness, and perhaps their lack of interest.

The best indication of the gradually but constantly growing concern about the position of women among Mombasa's Muslims in general, and among its Muslim women in particular, lies in enrollment figures for the government's Arab Girls' School. The Arab Girls' School was established in 1938, when the government absorbed the private coeducational Ghazali Muslim School, which had been founded through the efforts of an Arab reformer named Sheik Mohamed bin Abdulla Ghazali. In the first year, the Arab Girls' School had 114 students; after a decade, in 1947, the number of students was still only 168. The school's enrollment jumped with the arrival of a new principal, Ms. Sylvia Gray, in 1951, and with the construction of a new building in 1952. Ms. Gray's efforts, and her respect for Muslim rules of female seclusion, encouraged many parents to enroll their daughters, so that by 1955 there were 500 students. Muslim women supported the school and appeared in unexpected numbers at the first meeting of the Arab Girls'

---

* Salim 1973: 109–10, describes Arab self-perceptions of backwardness. In an article in the *Mombasa Times* (20.10.54), an Egyptian woman exhorted Mombasa Muslims to educate their girls.

School Parents' Association in May of 1956. Their presence was taken "by the organizers of the association as a sure sign of the changing times and of the interest Arab women [were] taking in the education of their daughters" (*Mombasa Times*, 30.5.56). Thus, without participating in abstract discussions of sex equality, some women were joining male reformers in working to erase a basic educational imbalance in Muslim society.

During the twelve years between the end of World War II and the founding of the first of the new-style organizations of Arab women in 1957, more women in Mombasa became conscious of social and educational problems in the community. And though it is not clear to what extent the decline of *lelemama* was accelerated by this new awareness, several of the leaders of *lelemama* associations were founding members of the Arab Women's Institute (later called the Muslim Women's Institute) and the Arab Women's Cultural Association (later called the Muslim Women's Cultural Association).* Many years after leaving *lelemama*, one of these leaders spoke to me of her dissatisfaction with the *ngoma*: "These [dance] associations were only good for fun. Sometimes they would be called to entertain if a dignitary came. But they had no strength. Because they were not registered, they could not be called upon to help collect money [for a cause]. They could not represent women if the Queen Mother, for example, came. They did not help with social welfare matters" (Shamsa Mohamed Muhashamy [IW, MWI], 9.5.73). Some women understood the need for new kinds of organizational structures to accommodate new community priorities. Nonetheless, as this statement and other contemporary evidence shows, a high priority of the new organizations was to gain prestige within accepted colonial structures.

What is of interest to the historian is not only that new organizations with new goals appeared but also that continuities with

---

* Saada Mohamed Gharib and Kibibi Mohamed Gharib, Omani supporters of Banu Saada, helped start the Arab Women's Cultural Association, according to Fatuma Mohamed (19.5.73). Shamsa Mohamed Muhashamy was active in Ibinaal Watan and was by her own account a founding member of the Arab Women's Institute.

past associations were maintained. In the case of the Muslim Women's Institute and the Muslim Women's Cultural Association, these continuities included leaders experienced in *lelemama* activities; membership reflecting the factional split between Ibinaal Watan and Banu Saada; a lingering, if fading, legacy of competition and bickering; and a concern for prestige. As time passes the latter three factors are becoming less important, but their centrality in the beginnings of the two organizations is apparent.

Just as the adoption by *lelemama* associations of European military titles and dress reflected the colonial milieu in which they functioned, the choices of names and the immediate causes of their formation reveal the impact of a changed, but still colonial, era on these newer associations. During this period, when the British ruled on the coast through Arab representatives, and when being classified as an "Arab" was a step above being labeled an "African," these groups of women chose to identify their constituency as "Arab"—not so much as an ethnic marker as a status claim. This is shown in the definition given by a representative of the Arab Women's Institute in 1960: "Arab" meant *"wanawake wa Kimji* ('women of Old Town') . . . and these included Arabs, Swahilis, and Baluchis" (Fureya Barakat Lemky [MWI], quoted in *Mombasa Times*, 21.4.60). Thus, although the new organizations were identified as "Arab," they drew from the same ethnic population as did *lelemama*.

Competition for prestige within the colonial framework was the immediate cause of the formation of both the Arab Women's Institute and the Arab Women's Cultural Association. Despite an abortive attempt to form an "Arab Women's Association at Mombasa" in 1955 (*Mombasa Times*, 9.2.55), the real impetus for the establishment of a formal group came with the announcement in 1956 that Princess Margaret would visit Mombasa (Fatuma Mohamed [BS, MWCA], 19.5.73). Various women agreed with the suggestion of an Arab member of the Legislative Council that there should be a single organization of women to receive dignitaries on behalf of Mombasa's Arab women. Speaking four years later, in 1960, a representative of the Arab Women's Institute explained the hostility aroused when it was left to the wife of the Liwali, the chief Arab administrator on the coast, to select guests at official receptions: "Since it was not always possible to satisfy everybody, it was only natural that such tasks should carry with them the necessary blames and very little thanks. For instance, when word came from the Government that a list should be prepared in connection with the visit of an important person, some names were left out and some people felt that they were socially as important as the next person and dissatisfaction arose" (Fureya Barakat Lemky [MWI], quoted in *Mombasa Times*, 21.4.60). Though this may seem petty now, it reflects the very real competition for prestige that occurred among individuals and ethnic groups. To prepare for Princess Margaret's visit, a group was formed in which various women were responsible for recruiting among specific districts and ethnic groups. But before a permanent structure could evolve from this beginning, "Bi Uba," the wife of the Liwali and a leader in the nascent organization, died. Her death was a major setback in the effort to establish a new women's organization among Mombasa's Muslims.

A second stimulus for the formation of an Arab women's organization is apparent from an incident described by a founder of the Arab Women's Institute (Shamsa Mohamed Muhashamy [IW, MWI], 6.2.73). Occurring sometime before Princess Margaret's visit, the incident reflects Arab women's sense of inferiority in relation to, and competition with, Asian women, who had formed an Indian Women's Association many years earlier.

Bi Uba and I saw the Indian Women's Association stall at the Mombasa Show, where they were displaying handicraft items. The Vice-President of the Association asked us, "Why don't you people have a stall like this. You are really lagging behind. You are idiots [*wapumbavu*], you can't do anything, you have no display of your handiwork here. You just sit around your houses." I was so bitter that from that day I vowed to organize a women's association.

Though it would be unfair to ignore consciousness of social needs as a reason for the founding of an organization of Arab women, competition for prestige appears as a major element.

The rivalry between ethnic groups, social strata, and individ-

uals all surfaced when Bi Uba's death removed the semblance
of unity that preceded Princess Margaret's visit in 1956. Before
various segments of the temporary group could reunite, 40 women
from the Mjua Kale and Kibokoni neighborhoods of Mombasa
met in December 1957 and formed the Arab Women's Institute,
a "cultural and social organization." The officers and committee
members represented the Omani elite of Mombasa.* Despite its
claim that membership was not restricted to Arabs, a reputation
for exclusiveness plagued the organization from the start. A year
and a half after its inception, a representative of the Arab Women's
Institute proclaimed: "We bear grudge against no one and are
willing to work hand in hand with all, provided the activities do
not conflict with our published aims and objects. We have been
accused at times of discrimination. I deny this vehemently, as the
books of our membership will show" (Fureya Barakat Lemky
[MWI], quoted in *Mombasa Times*, 21.4.60).

Angry at being preempted and excluded by these 40, other
women started the Arab Women's Cultural Association in August
of 1958. Although these women now more openly admit the antagonism of the two organizations at the start, they were scrupu-
lous in denying such ill-feeling at the time. In explaining the purpose of the Arab Women's Cultural Association to the *Mombasa
Times*, the Vice-President stated that the founders wanted "to
bring the women of the community together" and that "there was
no suggestion of rivalry with another women's organization formed

* Shamsa Mohamed Muhashamy (IW, MWI) places the date for the founding of the Institute at August 26, 1957 (interview, 6.2.73). The *Mombasa Times*,
however, stated in its issue of December 19, 1957, that the organizing meeting
had taken place only the Thursday before. The officers as listed in that *Mombasa Times* issue have been identified for me by Fatuma binti Ali Jeneby
(9.4.73): President, Itidal Said Seif (wife of Said bin Seif Busaidi, the nephew
of Sir Ali bin Salim, the former Liwali); Secretary, Fureya Barakat Lemky
(daughter of Mbarak bin Ali Hinawy, then Liwali); Assistant Treasurer, Mrs.
Ashu Sultan bin Brek (daughter of Sir Ali bin Salim); Honorable Secretary,
Mrs. Fathiya Abdalla Soud (granddaughter of Sir Ali bin Salim). Committee
members included Mrs. Fatuma Maamun bin Suleman Mazrui (wife of the
Kadhi), Miss Shariffa Abdalla Salim (daughter of Shariff Abdalla Salim, Arab
member of the Legislative Council), and women from other elite Omani families. Note that the Liwali and the Kadhi were the highest Arab administrative
officers on the coast.

at the beginning of the year" (Fatuma Mohamed [BS, MWCA], quoted in *Mombasa Times*, 7.8.58). Ms. Gray, Principal of the Arab Girls' School, actively helped organize the new association. Because their meetings were held outside Old Town, the Arab Women's Cultural Association attracted women from the newer Majengo areas of Mombasa, including many Hadhrami Arabs. Although it lacked the sprinkling of wives and daughters of Liwalis and Kadhis that was found in the Arab Women's Institute, the Arab Women's Cultural Association included members from various elite Twelve Tribes and Arab families. Consisting of Hadhrami, Baluchi, Punjabi, and Omani Arab women, plus Twelve Tribes women, the officers and committee reflected greater ethnic diversity than was found among the leaders of the Arab Women's Institute.*

Although overt discrimination probably was not practiced by either organization, members tended to join according to criteria of residence, friendship, and membership in former associations. Thus Arab Women's Institute members tended to come from Mjua Kale and Kibokoni districts within Old Town and to be former Ibinaal Watan participants. Similarly, many Arab Women's Cultural Association members from Old Town lived in Kuze and Mkanyageni, the areas of Banu Saada strength, and those who had been in *lelemama* associations earlier included many Banu Saada members. To be sure, whole *lelemama* associations did not transform themselves into the new organizations. Rather, relationships and hostilities that had solidified during the heyday of *lelemama* influenced a woman's choice of organization. Some women with no interest in *lelemama* were strong supporters of the new organizations, and some who had been active in *lelemama* did not move into either the Arab Women's Institute or the Arab Women's Cultural Association.

In the new organizations, a larger proportion of members appear to come from elite families than was the case with *lelemama* associations. The fact that the names of the Institute and the Cul-

* Fatuma Mohamed (BS, MWCA), 20.5.73, identified the members as listed in the *Mombasa Times*, August 7, 1958.

tural Association exist only in English suggests an appeal to relatively more Western-oriented women. This elitism is not surprising, given the goals of the two kinds of groupings. As relatives of the Liwali and other Muslim reformers, elite women could be personally persuaded to take up the causes of girls' education and social welfare. In some families an awareness of the importance of women's education and social reform resulted from the travels of a male relative to Egypt or Europe.* Thus elite women had greater exposure to the new consciousness of community needs. Poorer women not only had less exposure, they were not "socially important" enough—as Fureya Barakat Lemky put it in the quote cited earlier (p. 201)—to participate in the squabbles that contributed to the founding of these organizations of "Arab" women.

The activities of the Arab Women's Institute during its initial years reveal a continuing concern for prestige. For example, in 1957 the Institute invited Seyyid Khalifa, the Sultan of Zanzibar, to visit Mombasa. The importance of the occasion to the women is seen in the following recollection (Shamsa Mohamed Muhashamy [IW, MWI], 6.2.73, 13.2.73).

This was the first really beneficial thing we did, and all women now knew that we had become equals. We invited those very Asian women who had called us fools. We had tea and a reception for Khalifa in a rented building, and we invited everyone. We informed him about the Arab Women's Institute.... Now those Asians could see just how we had "improved."†
... We were the first [women] even to know what a hotel was like. Our organization brought our women into the Oceanic Hotel [to receive Seyyid Khalifa].... Now we were real women. Today we, women of *buibui*, have begun to enter hotels, even marketplaces in the morning [during the busiest time]. But the organization brought us to the hotel. There were Europeans and Indians there. We rented the place and entertained our guests with lectures and speeches in English and Swahili. We saw that now we were equal.

---

* Shamsa Mohamed Muhashamy attributed her father's advanced opinions to his having studied in Egypt. He sent his only daughter to mission school for one year in 1928, but family pressure forced her to quit. She was then tutored at home by European women from the mission. (Interview, 29.11.72.) Alya Namaan (MWCA) was raised by her grandfather, who had traveled in Europe. Her mother had attended school in Zanzibar for a few years. The family ignored public pressure, and Alya was sent to school at age six. (Interview, 11.12.72.)
† She used the English word "improve" in the midst of her Swahili.

The quotation above reaffirms these Arab women's sense of competition with Asian women's standards of achievement. Though their criterion for judging improvement and equality is the acquisition of social skills, one should not demean their efforts. For women raised in *purdah*, mixing at a social gathering with men and women from various ethnic communities was an important first step.*

Further steps have been taken in the past sixteen years to equip these women with skills needed in a broader society. Renamed the Muslim Women's Institute and the Muslim Women's Cultural Association, the organizations emphasize the openness of their membership within the Muslim community, a position that they feel is more consonant with the policies of independent Kenya.

The Muslim Women's Institute has a varied program directed at the needs of women in particular and of society in general. At different times it has offered classes in adult education, religion, child care, and sewing. Beyond this commitment to raising the educational level of Muslim women, the organization supports community projects, aid to mosques, religious classes for children, fund raising for the Coast Institute of Technology, and scholarships for students pursuing university studies abroad. Their long-term project is to build a hall to provide space for adult-education classes, a small library, and fund-raising activities.

Through debate and by personal example, members have tried to change community attitudes on important issues. The Muslim Women's Institute has objected to the custom of holding lavish funerals and weddings, during which neighbors and relatives are fed for several days. Islam, they say, prescribes for funerals a period of quiet prayer and visits by friends. The Institute has also stated that rich and poor alike should make only moderate expenditures for weddings. This campaign has met with limited success; indeed, various Muslim reformers have been advocating such changes since the mid-1930's. The Muslim Women's Institute has debated issues such as the custom of displaying publicly the bridal bedsheet as

* *Purdah* is the practice of segregating men and women from one another.

evidence of the bride's virginity. Younger members object to publicizing what they consider to be a private matter; older members affirm the public confirmation of a community-held value.

Following a different program, the Muslim Women's Cultural Association has concentrated on building and running a private nursery school now called Mbaraki Nursery School. At first, courses were offered in child care, hygiene, reading and writing, religion, sewing, and embroidery. In 1960 these classes were dropped in order to put all energies into raising the 215,000 shillings ($30,700) needed to build the nursery school. After more than ten years of soliciting gifts and holding fund-raising events, the women saw the new building opened by President Kenyatta in 1971. President Kenyatta himself contributed 45,000 shillings to the school, remarking how surprised he was that women in *buibui* had mobilized themselves so effectively (Alya Namaan [MWCA], 11.12.72; Fatuma Mohamed [BS, MWCA], 19.5.73).

While giving credit to the organizations for their efforts to educate and assist both Muslim women and the community as a whole, one must point out some limitations of their approach. Both the Muslim Women's Institute and the Muslim Women's Cultural Association have failed to act on some issues which, to the outside observer, seem of utmost importance to Muslim women.

For example, for several years the Kenya National Assembly has been considering bills that will revise the laws of marriage, divorce, and succession. The Muslim Women's Institute did not lobby for or against passage of any of these bills, but merely replied to a request from the government for reactions to the bills. Following the Koran, the Institute objected to the succession bill's provision that daughters and sons inherit equal portions.* This objection, based

* The succession bill has been passed and provides that in the absence of a will stating otherwise, a Muslim's sons and daughters will inherit equal shares. *Kenya Gazette Supplement* (Nairobi: Government Printer, November 17, 1972), Act 14 of 1972, The Law of Succession Act 1972. By Muslim law each man's share is twice as large as each woman's share. This provision, unlike provisions for divorce, is stated explicitly in the Koran and is thus considered to be unalterably revealed word. Muslim leaders objected to the new succession bill because it forces a Muslim, dying intestate, to break the direct word of Allah (Sheik Mohamed Kassim Mazrui, former Chief Kadhi, 24.11.72).

as it is in religious orthodoxy, is understandable. Less understandable, though, is the failure of either the Institute or the Muslim Women's Cultural Association to support the marriage and divorce bill, which would give women and men the same grounds for divorce: irreparable breakdown of the marriage. Under Shafi'i Muslim law, which prevails on the East African coast, men need give no particular reason for divorcing their wives. However, women's grounds are limited to three: total inability of the husband to consummate the marriage; the repudiation by the wife, upon attaining puberty, of a marriage contracted for her while she was a child; and, in some cases, nonmaintenance. Having proved one of these, a woman may be granted a divorce by the Kadhi (Muslim Judge).* There are no orthodox religious objections to expanding a woman's right to divorce that are based on Koranic injunction, as there are in the case of inheritance. Indeed, male religious leaders support the new bill that expands a woman's grounds for divorce. However, the women's organizations have not rallied to the cause. Since a week's casual conversation in the Muslim community gives ample evidence of marital discontent among women, one cannot argue that there is no need for a new divorce law.

Neither have the women's organizations mounted a campaign to expunge the most obvious examples of male dominance and orientation from religious life, even though these issues have been discussed for years by male reformers. As many as two decades ago (6.10.54), the *Mombasa Times* reported that

Sheik Ali bin Namaan, the Chief of Mombasa, was speaking over the radio against "extravagance of Arab weddings" when he startled his listeners with a sudden and dramatic change of subject—a plea obviously made under stress of emotion, that special arrangements should be made to accommodate women in mosques.

The position now is that although women are not forbidden to enter

---

* The Koran does not stipulate grounds for divorce, which therefore are alterable. Various legal schools, following the interpretation of different legal scholars, have different grounds for which a woman may be granted a divorce by the Kadhi. See Arthur Phillips and Henry F. Morris, *Marriage Law in Africa* (1971), p. 130. In most Muslim countries, liberalization of divorce law has been achieved by adopting legal precedents from the Maliki school of law, which provides the largest number of grounds for women to receive divorces. See N. J. Coulson, *A History of Islamic Law* (1964), Part Three.

the mosque, there is no special place for them where they can pray without being seen by the male votaries, and therefore they have to keep away
and be content with praying at home. "This deplorable situation has gone
on long enough [said Chief Ali]; it amounts, in all, to the exclusion of
women from the House of Worship. As this started well after the Prophet's
time, and would certainly not have had his approval had he been alive,
the practice has by no means any place in Islam. . . ."

"Yes, deprive them of the lavish weddings; but we have no right to
deprive them of the solace of the House of God. I have no doubt that,
after the initial hesitancy and natural indecision following the new opportunity, they will flock to the mosques, responding to the newly won
right as a small plant, withered by the heat, lifts its leaves to the first drop
of rain."

The Sheik's plea has gone unheeded, by men and women alike.
At the opening in 1973 of the newest mosque in Mombasa, some
women grumbled at being excluded after having contributed
money for the construction. However, during the planning for the
mosque, no women's organization pressed for the inclusion of a
separate women's section.*

Why have these issues of direct importance to women not received the attention of the Muslim Women's Institute and the
Muslim Women's Cultural Association? The explanation lies, I
believe, in the underlying philosophy of the two organizations. At
various times leaders have expressed the need to organize in order
to improve the situation of women. But the fact remains that both
groups have developed as self-help and community-oriented, rather
than as feminist, organizations.†

Yet Mombasa had at least one feminist. A woman speaking at an
early, abortive attempt to form a sort of women's organization in
1955 stated clearly that women should organize themselves *for*
themselves. "A women's association should be formed," she said,
"and should be entrusted with the task of devising ways and means
to raise funds among ourselves so that we, too, could have what
we need in the way of maternities, nursing homes, and a nursery

* This fact was reported to me by Dorothea Driever, who attended the Majengo Mosque opening on February 24, 1973.
† I use the term "feminist" to describe an ideology that gives top priority
to women's issues and women's rights.

school for our daughters—even if it takes us a generation to achieve our aims" (Mrs. Mohamed Ali Moses, quoted in *Mombasa Times*, 9.2.55). The 300 women assembled heard a remarkable emphasis on women's independence. The money was to come from "among ourselves" and the benefits were to go to women and their daughters alone. The organization—perhaps because of its ideology—never took hold.

Contrast the above statement with the stated goals of the Arab Women's Institute at its inception. As reported in the *Mombasa Times* (19.12.57), the main speaker at the first meeting "explained that the purpose of the meeting was to form a ladies club in Mombasa. She went on to say that such an organization would bring some benefit not only to the women but also to their families and the community. 'As mothers, we have a responsibility to our children, families, and the community as a whole. Upon us will depend progress.'" The emphasis was not solely on women's needs but rather on community service; in fact, the former is justified by the latter. This is the basis for the program of the Muslim Women's Institute, including women's classes, aid to refugees, and scholarships. Separate instruction is given to women in religion, reading and writing, and first aid, because rules of modesty forbid the mixing of men and women. But scholarships are allocated to young men and women both, evidence that the organization does not perceive any special need to support girls. Their emphasis on women stems from *purdah* rather than feminist ideology.

Similarly, the Muslim Women's Cultural Association began with classes in reading and writing, health, and handicrafts for women. After a short time, a delegation of women approached the President of the Association and suggested that a nursery school for their children was of more use and importance to them than adult education for themselves. Given limitations of finance and energy, the leaders have decided to suspend all other activities until the school is running efficiently. The Muslim Women's Cultural Association thus has concentrated its interest on the welfare of the children rather than of the women in the community.

Neither the Muslim Women's Institute nor the Muslim Women's Cultural Association has developed as a women's pressure group, although the members occasionally have been politically active. The women's issues that they have supported generally have been linked to ethnicity. Seen in the context of the intense rivalry between Asians and Arabs during the colonial period, the campaign to enfranchise Arab women described at the beginning of this article appears to have resulted as much from ethnic pride as from a desire for equal rights. A similar mixture of ethnic and feminist sentiment is evident in the protest by female Muslim leaders against forced marriages of young Asian women to members of Zanzibar's Revolutionary Council. The leaders claimed that their objections were "not a matter of race."* Nevertheless, issues devoid of ethnic overtones—for example, divorce reform—have not found widespread support among women in either the Institute or the Cultural Association.

Ethnic politics, on the other hand, has engaged the members even where the organizations themselves have taken no stand and where no explicit appeal has been made to women. Because of their Arab identification, many women in the Institute and the Cultural Association supported the Coast People's Party during the *mwambao* struggle in the late 1950's and early 1960's.† With the failure of this movement to affiliate the Muslim coast with Zanzibar under the Sultan, these Arabs and their allies have felt discredited and vulnerable under the new African government. To protect their interests as a minority group, some of Mombasa's Muslim women have demonstrated in the streets in support of their community's legislative representatives.‡

* The protest was made jointly by leaders of the Mombasa Women's Association (predominantly an Asian group), Maendeleo ya Wanawake (the national women's organization), the YWCA, the Muslim Women's Institute, and the Muslim Women's Cultural Association. *East African Standard* [Nairobi], Oct. 10, 1970.

† See Salim 1973: 233–43, regarding this movement urging coastal autonomy from up-country Kenya.

‡ The August 7, 1975, demonstration sparked a vigorous exchange of opinion in editorials and letters printed in subsequent issues of the *Daily Nation* [Nairobi].

This, then, is the final continuity between the Muslim Women's Institute and the Muslim Women's Cultural Association and their predecessors, the *lelemama* associations. All have met certain personal and community needs, whether for entertainment, prestige, mutual aid, or self-improvement. However, until their priorities are rearranged, they will remain organizations *of*, rather than specifically *for*, women.

Protestant Women's Associations in Freetown, Sierra Leone

FILOMINA CHIOMA STEADY

SIERRA LEONE, one of Africa's newest and smallest republics, with a population of approximately three million, is situated on the west coast of Africa. Its capital city, Freetown, the setting of this article, has some of the most picturesque natural attributes of any place in West Africa. In addition to its evergreen mountains, some of which are found very near the coastline, a generous allotment of white, sandy beaches lapped by the Atlantic Ocean contributes to a natural scenic beauty that is still largely undisturbed. What has become the modern state of Sierra Leone started in 1787 as a settlement at Freetown for freed slaves from Britain, the Caribbean, North America, and other parts of West Africa. The settlement expanded in time, and by 1808 a British Crown Colony was established that included the Sierra Leone peninsula, on which Freetown is located, and a few nearby islands—an area of 256 square miles. The country's interior, over 27,000 square miles, came under British control as a Protectorate in 1896.*

The descendants of the various groups that settled in and around Freetown collectively became known as Creoles [Krios]. For the most part they were Christian and literate, and had no

* Data for this article were collected during a period of field research on women's associations in Freetown, Sierra Leone, from July 1970 to September 1971. I wish to thank the Wenner-Gren Foundation for Anthropological Research for their financial support. My gratitude also goes to Peter Marris for his valuable comments on an early draft of this article. A shorter version of this article was first presented at a conference on "Christianity in Independent Africa" sponsored by the School of Oriental and African Studies, University of London, and by the University of Ibadan, which was held at the University of Ibadan, Jos Campus, Jos, Nigeria, in September 1975.

strong corporate ethnic identity. The majority became clerks and artisans, and some entered commerce and the professions. In many instances, Creoles served as assistants to, or co-administrators with, the British colonial officers. Consequently they became identified with the ruling group. Some Creoles became highly successful in commerce; others became missionaries and teachers, and subsequently worked in Sierra Leone and other parts of West Africa.

During the second decade of the twentieth century, large numbers of immigrants from the Protectorate, who were adherents of Islam or traditional African religions, began arriving in Freetown in search of jobs, educational opportunities, and the "bright lights" of the city. This influx of immigrants greatly changed the character of the city from fairly homogeneous and predominantly Christian to heterogeneous and religiously diversified.

Certain socioeconomic and political changes that followed were soon to affect the Creole position of dominance. The spread of education to the interior, as well as the migration of young people to Freetown for schooling, resulted in the creation of a larger educated group that was not of a single ethnic composition. In addition, Syrian and Lebanese traders, who had been arriving in Freetown since the beginning of the twentieth century, gradually replaced the Creoles as the dominant group in commerce by using more ruthless trading methods. Moreover, friction between the Creoles and the peoples from the Protectorate took on political dimensions over the years and coincided with constitutional changes destined to reduce Creole political power. In 1951, the Sierra Leone Constitution was revised, and the Colony and the Protectorate were henceforth jointly represented in an enlarged Legislative Council with an elected unofficial African majority and party rule. Since the peoples of the Protectorate greatly outnumbered the Creoles, they rapidly gained political supremacy. Under the unified Sierra Leone administration, the former Protectorate became collectively the Provinces, and the former Colony was restyled the Western Area. Sierra Leone became an independent state within the Commonwealth of Nations in 1961, and ten years later declared itself a republic.

Today Freetown has become a cultural mosaic. Although it is the home of the Creoles it is no longer a predominantly Christian or Creole city. Regardless of this heterogeneity, and despite the physical proximity of diverse groups, people still act essentially within their own social spheres. The present article examines some of the patterns of social action in one of these spheres.

Introduction

In keeping with the emphasis on processes of social change found throughout the literature, studies of urban formal associations in Africa have tended to focus on those joined by immigrants from rural areas (see, for example, Little 1965). This continued stress on the new relationships stemming from population movement from rural to urban areas has tended to submerge the importance of formal associations among settled urban populations.* A similar methodological orientation can be noted in studies of Christianity in Africa. The primary interest has been the impact of Christian religions and their colonial associations on traditional African religious systems. Investigations have focused on the adjustments the African has had to make in turning from his or her traditional religion to a new religion with its associated Western ethics and culture. Where the result of this transition has led to the formation of schismatic religious movements, these have received much attention because of their political significance as protest movements.†

The emphasis on change and adjustment has tended to eclipse the importance of Christianity for a group of Africans for whom Christianity and Western culture are as old as their very existence

* Floyd Dotson, in his 1951 paper "Patterns of Voluntary Associations Among Working-Class Families," notes that degrees of urbanization and demographic stability are important variables in studies of voluntary associations.

† Edouard Bustin, in "Government Policy Toward African Cult Movements: The Case of Katanga" (1975), examines "the relations between secular authorities and religious nonconformists under colonial rule and after independence in Katanga" and makes the suggestion that "the relationship is characterized not so much by mutual suspicion as by lack of a common base of reference. This hampers the process of communication, and so long as it does, a certain amount of misunderstanding is bound to continue between church and state" (p. 135).

as a group. For the Creoles of Freetown, Sierra Leone, Christianity
is the traditional religion, and Western ethics and culture form
part of their multifaceted life-style and ideology.* Observing that
Christianity in its Western forms has been a part of Creole society
and culture for well over a century and a half, a Creole clergyman
has declared: "If both the leaders who decide the policy of the
churches and the members of the churches are Africans, it is . . .
absurd to suggest that the Freetown churches are not native
churches. Even so-called Western services have a distinctive quality
of their own, which is not imported from Europe!" (Fashole-Luke
1968: 132). This article seeks, first, to examine the role played by
the women of a settled, urban, and African community in foster-
ing certain Christian values in their religious associations and,
second, to determine the extent to which some of the functions
of these associations tend to promote a conservative ideology that
inhibits the full emancipation of women within the church. Finally, it suggests that attempts at unification of Christian women
of all denominations and from different ethnic groups might lead
to a new female consciousness oriented to change.

Freetown Creole Society

The theoretical importance of the Creoles of Freetown for African studies was pointed out a quarter of a century ago (Little
1950), but anthropological field research in Sierra Leone has
largely ignored them.† Even when noteworthy field studies have
been conducted in Freetown, the main focus has been on "tribal"
immigrant life in the city.‡ Scholars have tended to see the Creoles primarily in terms of their relations with other ethnic groups.
Consequently, the theoretical interest has been in minority- and

---

* In Sierra Leone, the term "Creole" (or "Krio") is used to denote descendants of the various groups of freed slaves who settled in and around Freetown
from the late eighteenth century on. The people call themselves "Krios."

† One notable exception is Arthur Porter's *Creoledom: A Study of the Development of Freetown Society*, an excellent study that is sociological as well as
historical.

‡ See for example Michael Banton's *West African City: A Study of Tribal
Life in Freetown*.

ethnic-group studies within an urban setting.* The neglect of the study of Creole institutions is a serious oversight, since the Creoles represent an excellent example of cultural synthesis on the African continent.

Freetown did not become a city—it was planned that way. The various groups of repatriated former slaves that settled in Freetown between 1787 and 1863 came from very different places—England, Nova Scotia, Jamaica, and Africa, especially Nigeria. These people were for the most part already exposed to urban and Western patterns of behavior.

The early settlers were Christians—predominantly Wesleyans, Baptists, and members of the Countess of Huntingdon's Connexion.† The Church Missionary Society, an Anglican body that received material and moral support from the British colonial government, was active in promoting Christianity among subsequent groups arriving at Freetown, as were missions of other denominations. For the Creoles, a group whose members were of diverse backgrounds, Christianity—especially the Protestant Christianity adopted by the majority—became a vital integrative catalyst. Moreover, Protestantism was consistent with urban values since it encouraged such concepts as individualism, thrift, and industry. Furthermore, Creole Protestantism emphasized self-improvement. This was ultimately linked with the Calvinist doctrine of salvation, for much of this self-improvement was aided by what Creole society regards as "blessing." The person who has blessing can only prove this by advancing himself or herself in society; but more important is the fact that if a person has blessing he or she is bound to advance in society. This is usually possible as a result

* There are fifteen ethnic groups in Sierra Leone, all of which are represented in Freetown. Of Freetown's population of 128,000, Creoles constitute about 25 percent. They are the second-largest ethnic group in Freetown (*1963 Population Census of Sierra Leone*, vol. 2, p. 13).

† "Selina Hastings, Countess of Huntingdon (1707–91), was the central figure in the evangelical revival of the eighteenth century in England and founder of the Countess of Huntingdon's Connexion.... 'Countess of Huntingdon' churches were founded in Sierra Leone by Negroes from Nova Scotia who landed at Freetown in 1792 after being granted freedom following the American Revolutionary war" (*Encyclopedia Britannica* [1973], p. 897).

not only of divine predestination but also of the opportunities for
achievement and innovation through individual effort in urban
Creole society. Much of this self-improvement is made possible
through education, which is a supreme value in Creole society
(see Sumner 1963 and Harding 1968). To be a good Creole one
has to have attended school regularly. Consequently, virtually all
Creole women have received formal schooling, and some have distinguished themselves by attaining high positions within their
chosen professions. One of the subsidiary but widespread functions
of many women's associations in Freetown is to raise funds for
secondary-school scholarships for girls, since all schools in Sierra
Leone have fees (see Steady 1973). The Annie Walsh Memorial
School was founded in 1849 by the Church Missionary Society,
succeeding the Female Institution established two years earlier.
Many Creole women educators have themselves founded schools
and some were pioneers in providing an alternative curriculum to
the domestic science orientation of the earlier missionary schools
for girls. Mrs. Hannah Benka-Coker became a legend through
her contributions to female education in Sierra Leone, and a statue
was erected to her memory at the Freetown Secondary School for
Girls, which she helped bring into being. Many Creole women
have played prominent roles in public life: to mention just one,
Mrs. Constance Cummings-John became Mayor of Freetown in
1966.

Another important feature of Creole Protestantism is that it
supports Weber's controversial thesis that there is a compatibility
between Protestantism and the development of capitalism (see
Weber 1930, Marris 1968, Marris and Somerset 1972, and Karp
1975a).* Thus commerce, which became the basis of the city's economy, was consistent with Protestant Christianity. Both Protestant-

* The study by Marris and Somerset of entrepreneurs in Africa suggests that
the processes involved in the development of capitalism are extremely complex
and depend to some extent on coincidental combinations of factors such as
frustration and opportunity. Karp points out that "though Moslems, the Mourids [of Senegal] exhibit in all essential respects the same 'ethic' that Max
Weber ascribed to the Calvinists and their Anglo-Saxon counterparts, the
Puritans" (p. 197).

ism and commerce aided the development of institutions and attitudes (such as class consciousness)* that are mainly urban and that have been in existence for over a century (Fyfe 1968: 6):

The values of the Creole bourgeoisie who emerged in the mid-nineteenth century were . . . urban values rooted in a city from which they derived their wealth. Their orderly, respectable, law-abiding, church-going way of life fitted a city laid out on a regular plan, where the majority of public buildings were churches. Their enterprises and thrift found outlet in trade and property investment. Their lives were divided between their homes, their shops, and their churches. In their homes they found the privacy characteristic of urban living. In their shops they showed an urban readiness to adapt to change. Their sophistication they displayed in their churches . . . and also outside their churches in the Sunday church parade. So Freetown formed its citizens in an urban pattern. It also acted as a modernizing agent, mediating new ideas and techniques to its citizens and to the inhabitants of the surrounding countries.

Freetown Creole society has marked Christian and English characteristics that are apparent in its religious and educational institutions. It must be added, however, that there are also important retentions of African and Caribbean influences. A significant but not exclusively African feature is the Creoles' strong identity with their ancestors, expressed in after-death rituals such as *awujoh* and graveside libations (see Sawyerr 1964 and 1965, Fashole-Luke 1968, and Peterson 1968). Most *rites de passage* have strong African elements, as does the complex bilateral kinship structure. Caribbean and African influences are apparent in Creole architecture and music (*gumbe*), in the traditional dish *fufu*, and in female ethnic dress—*print en enkintcha*, or its forerunner, *kabaslot en kotoku*.† That Creole culture represents a blend is readily apparent from its language, Krio. This language is derived largely from English but contains many words from various West African languages and a few words from other European languages, notably

* Porter (1963: Part Two) analyzes the historical development of social stratification in Creole society. The most well known Marxist from Sierra Leone was a Creole—the late I. T. A. Wallace-Johnson.
† In a 1950 article, "The Significance of the West African Creole for Africanist and Afro-American Studies," Kenneth Little discusses some similarities between Creole and Caribbean music; Porter (1963: 104) discusses the origin of the dish *fufu*.

French. Krio is the lingua franca of Sierra Leone, but Mende and Temne are also widely spoken.

Christianity, the most important feature of Creole society, enabled the early settlers to withstand the vicissitudes of political and economic life (including attacks from other ethnic groups*) and has enabled their descendants to survive their subsequent decline from political and economic dominance in Freetown.† The Christian religion also provided a common identity and a basis of solidarity. It engendered a system of beliefs, outlined a code of morality, served as a means of social control, and encouraged self-improvement and philanthropy. All of these ideals were considered worthy of inculcation and preservation. Hence communities developed around churches. The church provided the inspiration to practice these ideals in everyday life and served as a potential link for all the members of the parish. In short, Christianity became a way of life. Associational recruitment on the basis of religion was therefore highly desirable, since this would strengthen ties based on common beliefs and purposes and would help to preserve Christian ideals.

Religious Associations

In the study of formal associations in Creole society, one must look for interpretations other than the conventional ones that view urban institutions as necessarily involved in processes of

* In a series of uprisings in 1898 known as The Hut Tax War, many European, American, and Creole missionaries, plus some Creole traders, were killed (Porter 1963: 60).

† Christopher Fyfe's *A History of Sierra Leone* is a monumental work that gives a detailed history of the Freetown settlement and the difficulties encountered in establishing it. John Peterson's *Province of Freedom* examines the resilience of the settlers in the face of some of these difficulties. Arthur Porter's *Creoledom* analyzes Creole attainment to and subsequent loss of a position of dominance in Freetown on account of political and economic changes. Michael Banton's *West African City* discusses tribal life in Freetown and comments on the nature of intergroup tensions. Martin Kilson's *Political Change in a West African State* is an authoritative work on the political history of Sierra Leone and gives an insight into the politics of ethnicity there, though John Cartwright's *Politics in Sierra Leone* examines the ethnic dimension more closely. Leo Spitzer's *The Creoles of Sierra Leone* is a study of Creole responses to colonialism.

social transition. Much of what is sociologically relevant to other African societies in terms of processes of social change has already become a way of life for the Creoles of Freetown—not in the sense of the caricatures of Black Englishmen flippantly portrayed in some travelogues,* but in a pertinent and meaningful way. What is modern in some other contexts is traditional to the Freetown Creoles; what is a process elsewhere is a norm here (see Fyfe & Jones 1968: 199–201). The study of formal associations among Protestant Creole women in Freetown is a case in point. The significance of these associations lies in their functions as institutions promoting pattern maintenance rather than social change.

Because of the prevailing influence of Christianity in the way of life and identity of the Creoles, religion has often taken on a formal meaning that pertains directly to church organization and worship. Associations that are classified as religious in this article are those attached to churches (see Table 1). In Freetown society it is important to behave in a religious manner. For women, religious piety is extended through participation in one or more of the women's associations attached to the church. The really pious woman not only knows the whole order of service and most of the hymns by heart, she also belongs to several religious associations. Most of the Christian associations in Freetown are women's associations.

It has been estimated that there are 50,000 Muslims and 40,000 Christians in Freetown (Fashole-Luke 1968: 127). The fact that the Muslims outnumbered the Christians, according to this estimate, deserves comment. In general, Muslim women in Freetown, especially those belonging to the orthodox sects, are subject to more restrictions than Creole women. According to Bassir (1954), only the more prosperous Okus (Muslims of Yoruba ancestry) gave their daughters equal opportunities with their sons. Muslim men's attitudes toward their women have not affected Creole men's attitudes. This is partly owing to the fact that Muslims and Christians operate under independent belief systems. It is also because of the

* See for example Mary Kingsley's *Travels in West Africa* and Graham Greene's *Journey Without Maps*.

TABLE 1
Women's Religious Associations Studied by the Author

I. *Anglican Associations at the Diocesan Level*
Mothers' Union
Women's Volunteers

II. *Anglican Associations at the Local Level*
Mothers' Union
Women's Volunteers
Dorcas Association
Committee for Ladies
Ladies Working Band
Women's Guild

Ad Hoc and Quasi Associations
Harvest Committee
Prayer Groups
Women's Class Meetings

III. *Methodist Associations at the Level of the Synod*
District Women's Work Committee

IV. *Methodist Associations at the Local Level*
District Women's Work Committee
Dorcas Association
Ladies' Guild
Sisterhood
Ladies Industrial
Silent Worker
Ladies Auxiliary
Ladies Union

Quasi Associations
Prayer Bands
Women's Class Meetings

V. *Semireligious Catholic Associations*
Sierra Leone Catholic Nurses Guild

VI. *Evangelical United Brethren Associations*
Women's Society for World Service

VII. *"Revivalist" Women's Associations*
Martha Davies Confidential Benevolent Association
Mrs. Pinkney's Spiritualist Association
Emmanuel Association

VIII. *United Christian Women's Association*
United Church Women (Sierra Leone)

tendency to regard Creoles as the reference group, since their early education enabled them to acquire the skills necessary for advancement in modern society. The impetus for change in Muslim women's status has come in part from Muslim women themselves. An increasing number of them have been through secondary school, and some have obtained university degrees. Many Muslim women's associations in Freetown—such as the All-Muslim Women's Association, the Amalgamated Muslim Women's Movement, and Tariku Fil Islam—in addition to giving religious instruction to their members and mutual-aid services, raise funds to provide secondary-school scholarships for promising Muslim girls. To some extent, it may be true to say that the educational achievements of Creole women have been catalytic in this regard; but the fact that many Muslim women in Freetown have always had a great deal of mobility and earning power as traders may have contributed to an independent outlook and a desire to secure modern education for their daughters, if not for themselves. A few Muslim women have distinguished themselves in public life. Among the most well known is Hajah Iyesha Rahman, who exposed a financial racket among organizers of the annual pilgrimage to Mecca. This led to a government inquiry, and she was herself subsequently appointed as the first woman to lead a group of pilgrims to Mecca. The pilgrimage to Mecca is very important for Muslim women since it gives them a higher social and religious status, allows them to wear distinctive attire for ceremonial occasions, and confers on them the title "Hajah."

The associations considered in this study are Protestant associations, mainly because the majority of Creoles are Protestants. Of the 65 churches in Freetown, only three are Roman Catholic (Fashole-Luke 1968). In general, Creoles who are Catholics have been converted to Catholicism from Protestantism as a result of having attended a Roman Catholic school or as a result of marriage. Though very few Creoles are Catholics, much of this discussion of Protestant associations has relevance for Catholic women. In Freetown society, Catholic women are regarded as being less emancipated within their church than their Protestant counterparts on account of the highly specialized roles of the Roman Catholic priests and other religious functionaries. Of the several Protestant denominations, the most prestigious is the Anglican. St. George's Cathedral, the Diocesan seat of the Anglican Church, situated in the center of Freetown, is the largest and most highly esteemed, and has in its membership some of the more affluent of Freetown's citizens. Porter (1963: Part Two) analyzes the historical development of social stratification in Creole society. In an earlier article he noted the tendency for social mobility to be expressed in terms of church affiliation. "Case histories of families demonstrate this tendency to move, as the economic position improves, from the smaller to the larger churches, from the Methodist to the Anglican and, finally, to the Cathedral" (Porter 1953: 12–13). Other Anglican churches that have increased in prestige over the years are Holy Trinity in the East End of Freetown and Christ Church in the West End. Yet in his 1963 study, Porter indicates that church affiliation as an indicator of class position is on the decline (p. 87).

In theory no church sets out to have a single ethnic composition. However, there are churches that carry an ethnic designation and whose services are conducted in that language. Such churches are characteristic of American denominations (e.g., the Assemblies of God and the Evangelical United Brethren), which are of late arrival in Freetown. Their membership is drawn mainly from recent immigrants to Freetown. One reason offered for the establishment of these churches is "the need for the various tribal groups to worship separately in their own language, so that they may more readily understand the services and offer their worship intelligently" (Fashole-Luke 1968: 130).

Not all Creole women join religious associations, and the number of active participants is usually smaller than the enrolled membership. In addition, the most active participants tend to be in their middle years (45 to 60). But the concern of this article is with institutional structure and function and not so much with degree of participation or statistical variables. It is significant enough that some women are active.

These associations, variously styled as bands, committees, groups, guilds, unions, or societies, are autonomous bodies within each church. However, some—such as the Mothers' Union and the Women's Volunteers (Anglican), and the District Women's Work Committee (Methodist)—operate at national and local levels. This is also true of the Women's Society for World Service of the Evangelical United Brethren denomination, which is multiethnic. Each association has its distinctive uniform (usually a white dress, a sash, and a straw hat with the association ribbon) and membership badges. Despite the autonomous nature of these associations, there is a similarity in their functions—a factor underlying the points being discussed.

The main functions of these associations can be discussed under three headings, two of which clearly indicate the associations' conservative nature. First, these associations support the church. Second, they contribute to the maintenance of the male-dominated clergy (the status quo) by providing alternative avenues for the development of female religious leadership. Third, they help maintain a double standard of morality, which has a very pragmatic basis in that it ensures the present structure of marriage as a legal entity with economic obligation of the husband. The last two functions are most significant in terms of female emancipation within the church.

Supporting the Church

Since the church symbolizes Christian values, one of the main functions of these associations is to ensure that this religious edifice is preserved in a physical and material sense. This is done primarily through fund-raising activities such as luncheon sales, bazaars, fetes, and thanksgiving services. The proceeds go toward the general maintenance and renovation of the church, or toward the purchase of some particular item, e.g., a silver chalice or a stained glass window. In some cases associations such as Women's Guilds and Women's Volunteers have been formed for a special fund-raising project—to purchase a pipe organ or to help the church clear some of its debts. Once the equipment has been purchased or the debt cleared, they may cease to function. Some associations are seasonal—for example, Harvest Committees, which are active

only during the period of the harvest festival. As a result there is
much proliferation of short-term women's religious associations,
which consequently constitute the largest type of women's associations.

A number of religious associations guarantee the general upkeep of the church by setting aside a maintenance fund for minor
repairs and renovations. One association, the Ladies Working
Band, is found in all Anglican churches (except for St. George's
Cathedral), and functions in a direct caretaking capacity. The
members of each Band regularly clean the church premises, and
they decorate it on ceremonial occasions. In the Methodist churches, associations with the names Ladies' Guild, Silent Worker, Ladies Union, Ladies Industrial, and Ladies Auxiliary usually perform similar functions. Members of a number of other associations
act as sideswomen (ushers) during services. However, not all fund-
raising and caretaking efforts are directed toward the church. In
keeping with Christian teachings on philanthropy, and with the
tendency in Creole society to link generosity with kindness and
goodness (quite apart from implication of status and reciprocity),
a portion of the funds collected are donated to charitable organizations. In addition, association members visit hospitals, orphan-
ages, and homes for the handicapped at Christmas to sing carols
and to present gifts to the inmates. Members of the Dorcas Association formerly made clothes and purchased food and religious
books for others less fortunate than themselves.

Providing Alternative Avenues for the Development of
Female Religious Leadership

Needless to say, the record of Christianity in terms of the development of female clerical leadership is a poor one. Historically,
women have been the scapegoats of Christian asceticism and have
been viewed as the contaminating force of sin, especially for the
male clergy. Reflecting the strongly patriarchal family law of the
Old Testament, canon law institutionalized male dominance.
This legacy is still reflected in the suspicion of the all-male clergy
toward female emancipation in the church. A function of religious
associations therefore is to provide avenues for the development

of religious leadership among women who hold no formal position in the clerical hierarchy in Freetown.

Women's desire for religious leadership is legitimate, since Christian doctrine promises equal spiritual dignity to all; and women's need to express this dignity through leadership is logical. Meetings usually have periods devoted to the reading of passages from the Scriptures, to Bible study, to prayers, and to hymn singing. Most women enjoy this devotional aspect of meetings because of the pleasure they derive from "feeding the soul" through religious songs, studying the Scriptures, and praying. Some of the associations, such as the Martha Davies Confidential Benevolent Association and Mrs. Pinkney's Spiritualist Association—named by their founders—are essentially prayer groups that have become formalized. These two groups offer a revival type of worship, faith healing, and extemporaneous prayer—popular kinds of devotional expression among some Freetown women. Whereas in many cases in Africa this sort of worship results from a complete break with the orthodox church and the development of separatist churches, which in some cases have women priests (Jules-Rosette, ed., forthcoming), in Freetown members of these prayer groups have not severed links with the traditional churches.* They still retain active membership in their "orthodox" churches. This may be because "orthodox" Christianity is already a meaningful religion whose values have become internalized to such an extent that they are an integral part of Creole everyday life. Those desiring a less formalized type of worship in the churches have tended to become affiliated with one or more of the American evangelical churches in Freetown.

In Creole society prayer is often regarded as a powerful force in solving problems and assuaging anxieties; the prayers offered by prayer groups can be seen as an extension of this view. Though

* D. B. Barrett, in *Schism and Renewal in Africa*, credits Freetown with the first ecclesiastical schism south of the Sahara (p. 18). This occurred in 1819, when settlers seceded from the Wesleyan mission. Despite this early start, separatist bodies have not developed much in Sierra Leone. Fashole-Luke (1968) gives some reasons for this. The separatist groups that do exist were imported from Nigeria, and the most successful of these is the Church of the Lord (Aladura), which forms the subject of Harold Turner's *History of an African Independent Church*.

Creole belief systems accommodate other forms of metaphysical power, such as those derived from the ancestors, and though some Creoles occasionally consult the occult power of the sorcerer, prayer is generally regarded as the more continuous and sustaining force. Prayer provides women with a weapon in the fight against hardship. Creole women often "take their troubles to God" and rely heavily on His justice, saying *lef gi God* ("let God decide"). They believe that their faith and reliance on God gives them the strength to withstand the "trials and tribulations" of life. Creole society prescribes that troubles should be borne bravely if one is to remain alive and sane, for hardship is seen as part of life. As Mrs. Etta McEwen put it in 1970, "It is not trouble that kills you, but how you take it." There is a tendency to identify with stories of suffering and persecution in the Bible because life in Freetown has been difficult for many. Women in particular believe that their lot is a hard one and that the burden of maintaining the health, happiness, and unity of the family falls heavily on them. Although high morale and levity are often apparent, women live with the constant threat of family illness,* death, burglary, and economic hardship. For many, the only consolation is their religion, which promises salvation and offers comfort. Religious associations offer women an opportunity to enjoy devotional fellowship with others who share similar problems. Reliance on prayer is learned early in childhood through the institution of family prayers. The parlor in Creole homes is traditionally an important religious sanctuary where the family Bible and other religious books are kept on the center table. The room is symbolic of the paramount importance of religion in the life of the family and serves as the site of worship. In many families prayers are said every Sunday morning, and in the more devout families every day or even twice daily. Prayers also mark significant occasions in the lives of family members and figure in the opening of a new house or in the welcoming of a student who has returned home after years of study abroad. Such prayers are often led by a minister

* Malaria and various infectious diseases are common in Freetown, and the high population density also contributes to the persistent hazards to health.

who is a relative or a close friend of the family. Although women often lead a family group in prayer and, by virtue of their role in the family, often are responsible for the religious instruction of the young, only very old women lead others in prayer at these ritual gatherings or during formal religious devotion.

There is evidence from historical sources that in the early days of settlement Creole women often had experience in church leadership. According to Fyfe (1962: 102) "they preached and testified in the Nova Scotian churches." One woman had her own congregation in her house in Water Street. However, the development of such female leadership was not encouraged by the Church Missionary Society or by the Methodist missionaries. Nor did the African clergy that later assumed the leadership of the missions allow the development of female leaders.*

Religious leadership tends to command a large measure of automatic respect even outside the church hierarchy, and this accounts for its importance to men and women alike. It was apparent at most business meetings of religious associations that the Chairman or President had very strong administrative and decision-making powers in addition to ceremonial leadership. For example, the President, instead of inviting motions from the members to resolve formal debates, often issued directives that were willingly accepted and even expected.

Association leadership not only makes a woman an "exceptionally good Christian" but also adds to her status in the community. Moreover, it secures for her the ultimate glory of a grand funeral. The greatest honor a Creole can receive after death is to be laid out in church and to have a well-attended funeral spilling over into the churchyard and adjacent streets. A cortege of association members in uniform marching at a woman's funeral procession is testimony to a life well lived as a Christian. Only very active church women (usually leaders of religious associations) receive this great honor.

* The African Methodist Episcopal (A.M.E.) Church was an exception. One woman, Jane C. Bloomer, rose to the rank of Deacon (minister) and was pastor of a church.

Preserving a Double Standard of Morality

A third function of these religious associations is that of preserving a system of morality based on Christian marriage. In keeping with Christian doctrine and statute law, Creole marriage is monogamous. This may provide another explanation for the relative absence of separatist churches among the Creoles. Oosthuizen (1968: 180–82) observed that polygamy is a significant feature of these churches. An explanation offered by Hodgkin (1957: 130) is that monogamy is frequently regarded not as a Christian institution so much as a specifically European one, lacking spiritual sanction.

The archetypal example of an association preserving what has come to be regarded as Christian marriage is the Mothers' Union, a worldwide body that sets itself up as the guardian of Christian marriage and morality. The Mothers' Union of Sierra Leone is organized on two levels—diocesan and local. Each branch, headed by the "enrolling member," is attached to a church; and at the local level each branch functions separately. However, all branches meet together once a year in October to mark the opening of the Mothers' Union year. At this annual meeting, members reinforce their commitment to uphold the sanctity of Christian marriage and family life, which carry a great amount of prestige in Freetown society. It is possible that these women guard not morality but their economic security by acting in some respects like a "women's trade union."* Maintaining monogamous marriage as an ideal is important as long as family security and continuity depend on the husband playing the role of breadwinner.

During the early days of settlement, women had a great deal of economic independence through trade; in fact, some of the best properties in early-nineteenth-century Freetown were owned by women (Fyfe 1962: 102). Today many Creole women own property that they either acquired independently or inherited. Several women have independent incomes from trade and salaried em-

* I am grateful to Peter Marris for suggesting this apt phrase.

ployment. However, with the exception of a few highly successful women entrepreneurs, career women, and women from well-to-do families, a woman's income is generally regarded as supplementary to that of her husband.

The Household Survey of 1966–68 estimated the contribution of wives to total household income at 8 percent (Household Survey 1968: 17). Bearing in mind that this figure pertains to all ethnic groups in Freetown and not just to Creoles, one may assume that the major contribution to the household income is made by the husband. However, since it is customary for women engaged in commercial activities to be very discreet about disclosing their incomes, one must view this figure of 8 percent with a certain amount of caution.* Be that as it may, women's contribution to the household budget is an important supplement since the cost of urban housing, school fees, and transportation impose tremendous strains on the husband's income, and a working wife (self-employed or salaried) is often regarded as an economic asset. Indeed, I would suggest that as the cost of urban living rises, the earning potential of a woman will increasingly become as important a criterion of desirability in mate selection as family influence, good looks, breeding, and romantic love. In recent times there has been some improvement in employment opportunities for women, but the allocation of family resources still follows the traditional pattern. Thus women's earnings are seen essentially as supplementary, and women largely seek economic security in marriage even though an increasingly dominant aim is to be self-supporting.

According to its secretary, the Mothers' Union is open to married women but also wishes to expand its membership to "reach as many women as possible, to bring them into the moral fold, and to offer them moral uplift and spiritual guidance for family life." She was certain that if the rules pertaining to Christian marriage and family life were applied too rigidly, i.e., if membership were

---

* The Household Survey (1968: 56) gives the proportion of women salesworkers as 63.8 percent. Since, according to the Survey, most of the salesworkers are self-employed, the most likely interpretation is that the majority of employed women in Freetown are traders.

restricted to married women, half of the present members would
be ineligible, for divorced and separated women have been accepted as members. Some women are defaulters in Christian marriage through no fault of their own, and, as the secretary noted,
a large number of them are "tormented with problems of family
life in a rapidly changing city where nearly every conventional
mode of conduct is being challenged and threatened." The Mothers' Union therefore fills the need for moral support and advice
when marriage and family life seem threatened. The following is
part of a prayer sometimes offered:

> O Lord Jesus Christ
> Who has taught us that if the house will stand
> It must be built upon a rock
> For otherwise it falls,
> Grant us in the Mothers' Union
> To stand firm on the rock of Thy word—
> That those whom God hath joined
> May not by man be put asunder,
> That love must never fail;
> Grant us in our inward faith and outward witness
> To bring encouragement and hope
> To those who falter
> Through ignorance, or weakness, or despair. . . .

In addition, marriage counseling is usually provided through the
Mothers' Union Workers and the "enrolling members." These
women are dedicated to the ideals of Christian marriage and family
life, and are seen as having invaluable wisdom in helping to resolve
marital problems. In addition to holding individual consultations,
they frequently address branch meetings on various topics concerning the home and family.

In Freetown society, as elsewhere, Christian monogamy in its
truest form (marital fidelity) is only an ideal and not the norm.
Oosthuizen (1968: 182) has observed that "the great danger in
Africa . . . is the impression that is often given that monogamous
marriage is automatically good—in spite of immoral developments
within it in modern urban society." In Freetown, several forms of
unorthodox sexual liaison among Christians exist, the two most
customary being (1) faithful concubinage of single people and (2)

the keeping of long-standing mistresses, with or without children, by some men before and after marriage. This latter form is called *om na trit*, keeping an "outside home." From interviews with married men it would appear that prostitution—defined here as "an *on the spot* exchange of sexual services for money"—has never played as significant a role in providing a "safety valve" for the shortcomings of monogamy as it has in the West. Alternatives to prostitution are provided by a category of women occasionally referred to as "surplus women"—usually mature spinsters, women who are divorced or separated, or widows—who may enter into a liaison with a married man. There may be very strong economic reasons for this, especially among widows with no independent financial resources. In the absence of welfare-state benefits and the institution of the levirate, an *om na trit* relationship may be the only alternative to destitution. Other sociological reasons for the institution of *om na trit* among the Creoles have been discussed elsewhere (Steady 1976).

Affairs in the Western sense of "temporary flights into fantasy" were rare in the past, but are increasingly becoming fashionable among young professional men, who do not appear to want the additional economic burden of supporting an outside home. Apparently their desire for a higher standard of living and their more receptive attitude toward modern contraceptive methods help to ensure that these affairs remain transitory. Very often these transitory extramarital liaisons progress to more stable relationships and may threaten the stability of the legal home; for the more permanent they are, the greater the risk of family disintegration. Although divorce is rare, separations are not uncommon. Divorce tends to occur among the highly educated, especially those who have been abroad (Fashole-Luke 1968: 137). Young married women with good careers feel less dependent on a spouse and can therefore initiate a divorce and free themselves of an unreliable husband.

The tensions that some of these deviations create are brought out from time to time in the deliberations of the Mothers' Union. The dilemma of the Mothers' Union is the impossibility of recon-

0234   FILOMINA C. STEADY

ciling ideals and practices. The ideals, dictated by the church, are
supported chiefly by women. But the practice is dictated by men,
whose behavior in the majority of cases does not conform to the
Christian ideals of family life and marriage (Fashole-Luke 1968:
136–37). The paradox of the Mothers' Union is that it is a wom-
en's association seeking to uphold the sanctity of an institution
that involves both men and women. In its attitude toward sexuality, the Mothers' Union follows traditional Creole views. Chastity before marriage and fidelity after marriage have always ranked
higher in the system of merit for women than for men. Formerly,
a bride had to be proved a virgin on her wedding night—the prestige of her family depended on it. A married woman who commits
adultery is severely reproached by her husband and by Creole society—the severest criticism coming from other women. Indeed, a
married woman can easily fall from grace among members of her
own sex if she is even alleged to have committed adultery, or if she
is seen flirting with another man. But Creole mores do not demand
or expect such fidelity from men. It is clear then that a double
standard exists for men and women, and that the Mothers' Union
promotes it—for the onus of maintaining sexual "chastity" before
and after marriage in practice falls on women alone.

By manipulating each other to conform to the moral code, Creole women hope to preserve the moral integrity of their own domestic group; but more important is the fact that this also protects
their economic interests. Those women who do not conform are
seen as belonging in fact to the other side, "the male side," which
in Creole women's sexual categorization stands for "the wild."*
Women on the wrong side either are treated as social deviants who
should be brought back to the "moral fold" or are abandoned as
"lost souls" if they resist conformity.

Conclusion

The Protestant associations we have examined are not transitional institutions but extensions of institutions that are already

* See Edwin Ardener, "Belief and the Problem of Women," in J. S. La Fontaine, ed., *The Interpretation of Ritual,* for an interesting analysis of the categorization of "the wild" among the Bakweri of Cameroon.

part of Creole social organization. Thus, to a great extent they preserve and promote Christian values already entrenched in Creole society.

It may be argued that some of these associations are imported from Europe. In a study of associations in Mexico, Dotson (1953: 386) observed that "acculturation will loom large as a complicating factor in cross-cultural studies." But acculturation is not the relevant concern in the Creole context. Religious associations here must be seen not as results of acculturation but as consequences of a cultural synthesis that has become a way of life. The important point is not that they are imported, but that they have become adopted by and have acquired intense relevance for Creole society.

The fact that these are *women's* associations may have relevance on a psychosocial level. In their attempt to preserve and promote standards and values considered "good" in Creole society, these associations develop solidarity among their members. This group consciousness takes on symbolic manifestations on ceremonial occasions through the custom of dressing identically. The Creole custom—originally a Yoruba one—of wearing the *ashuobi* (dresses of identical fabric and design) at weddings as a means of identifying a group of women who are usually, but not necessarily, related by kinship ties has often been extended to celebrations of other kinds. These uniforms emphasize the fact that each woman is working toward a goal shared by other women. This leads in turn to the development of a collective system of ideas (a kind of female ideology). Through this ideology women manipulate each other to conserve, promote, and conform to society's values and standards. The fact that these values may be inconsistent with social reality or may endorse institutions that do not recognize women's needs or potentials is often overlooked.

Recent developments, however, are likely to lead to some changes. An attempt at uniting all Christian women's associations is being made by the United Church Women, which maintains close cooperation with the Sierra Leone United Christian Council, a nondenominational body. The United Church Women aims at encouraging women to come together in a spirit of fellowship "to study, speak, and act on issues in the country and in the world that involve moral, ethical, and spiritual principles inherent in the Christian gospel" (to quote the Draft Constitution). This exercise could lead to a more critical evaluation of women's position in the church. Since this unity seems to be creating a new awareness among Christian women, it is possible that Creole women will achieve more power within the church. The activities of this association seem to suggest that it is gaining importance in Creole society and that it is setting a precedent in many areas of church life. For its 1975 Thanksgiving Service, the United Church Women chose a woman as a lay preacher. Prior to this, in most churches women's participation in the liturgical aspect of such services had not extended beyond the reading of the Scripture Lessons. Cooperation between Protestant and Catholic women in this association seems to have led Catholic women to take a more active role in associational activity and committee work within their own churches. Furthermore, an attempt is being made to incorporate Christian women from the ethnic churches in Freetown, many of which do not have women's associations. In an interview, the organizing secretary of the United Church Women emphasized the need to incorporate in the association's programs women from the various ethnic churches in Freetown so as to achieve true unity of all Christian women. This need was felt particularly after attempts at extending the work of the United Church Women into the Provinces proved impossible on account of difficulties in communication and transportation, as well as a lack of funds. Although this is a Christian association, it hopes to establish communication links between Christian and Muslim women through informal meetings and discussions.

At the time of my research, the United Church Women was in the early stages of formation. However, it was already evident that the development of a nondenominational multiethnic women's religious association on a national level would be helpful in leading to the development of a female consciousness oriented toward change. I would submit—based on my study of women's political associations in Sierra Leone (Steady 1975) and of women's associations in general (Steady 1973)—that the more diverse the ethnic composition of a women's association the more inclined it is toward developing a female consciousness and agitating for the improvement of the status of women. I suggest that the same is likely to be true of the United Church Women in a few years' time. It is possible that this association will begin to concern itself with issues relating to women in general—such as problems of Christian morality and the position of women within the family and in society. The question of female leadership within the church is likely to become an issue in the near future. This association could develop into a strong ecumenical pressure group, advocating the recognition of women's needs and potentials within the church and in society at large, and still could have the sanctity of a religious association.

Nonetheless, unless vocational opportunities for women expand, much of these efforts will be wasted; for the paradox of some of the functions of these associations is their particular claim to economic support. The importance of women's religious associations as "women's trade unions" is likely to decrease as women become more independent economically. Active members of these associations tend to be women in their middle years whose financial security, in many cases, depends on the present economic structure of the family. Younger women are gaining increasing access to careers, are relying on their own efforts for advancement, and thus are tending to look for economic security outside marriage. They are therefore less tolerant of the double standard of morality and may not hesitate to initiate divorce. As women take a fuller place in the economic fabric of society, many of these religious associations will become less important as "women's trade unions" and may indeed cease to function. Alternatively, they could develop along entirely new lines and expand their membership to include men.

Women and Economic Change in Africa

LEITH MULLINGS

THIS PAPER considers the status of African women in village communities, colonial and postcolonial class-stratified societies, and liberation movements, using the materialist perspective first developed by Engels and Marx.* The nature of the argument and the availability of data mean that many of the propositions will be both general and provisional, and subject to modification and refinement through further research.

Some of the most provocative, although general, anthropological approaches to the study of contemporary sex-role differentiation are those that include a historical perspective. Two such formulations have been elaborated by Eleanor Leacock (1972) and Kathleen Gough (1971). Both follow the general outlines of Engels's method as presented in *The Origin of the Family, Private Property, and the State*, in that they analyze the position of women in the context of the basic social relations prevailing within society at any given epoch. Differences in the perspectives of Leacock and Gough have been cited by Webster and Newton (1972). Leacock asserts that in hunting and gathering and early horticultural societies, relations between the sexes were equal. This equality—expressed in the communal household, the reciprocal division of labor, the independence of the wife and children, and the decision-making powers of the woman—deteriorated with the advent of class society. Gough, on the other hand, claims that as a result of prehuman division of

* An earlier version of this paper was presented at the UCLA African Studies Center Colloquium on Women and Change in Africa, May 1974.

labor between male defense and female child care, women have always been in some sense subordinate to men. However, she proceeds to point out that in hunting and gathering and early horticultural societies this subordination is a result of the division of labor conditioned by the needs of survival and occurs in a context where the woman has control over the products of her labor, and where she has dignity, freedom, and mutual respect. With the growth of private property these conditions disappear; male dominance and female subordination increase.

The focus of disagreement revolves around the question of whether any societies have existed in which women were "completely equal" (Gough 1971: 761) to men. However, the complementarity of these positions may be clarified by distinguishing between the categories "equality" and "symmetry." From Engels's perspective, "equality" derives from all the members of society having the same relationship to the resources of society, particularly the means of production. Inequality, in this context, occurs when such resources are appropriated by particular strata as private property. At this historical point, women are excluded from social production and thus from full participation in society. I will use "inequality," then, to refer to differential access and rights to the means of production or resources of society. I differentiate this from "asymmetry," where access to the means of production may be equal, but where men and women may not have access to the same roles and statuses; in some cases, sex roles may be differentially evaluated. This distinction provides the framework for examining societies in which the relationship between men and women may be equal but asymmetrical: the distribution of resources may be egalitarian, with surplus redistributed rather than used for personal ends, but a group of males may retain formal control over the distribution; males and females may not have access to the same roles and statuses, and there may be differing cultural evaluations of these roles. Asymmetry may, under certain circumstances, constitute the basis for the development of inequality.*

* The category of asymmetry is implicit in Engels's discussion of the division of labor; however, asymmetry may also refer to ideational evaluations of male and female roles in the division of labor.

According to my formulation of these categories, Gough's description of the relations between the sexes in classless societies can be characterized as asymmetrical rather than unequal.

However, the general paradigm presented by Engels, Leacock, and Gough is one that contrasts the status of women in societies where there is an absence of private property with the status of women in class societies. It suggests that the position of women, relative to that of men, deteriorates and becomes unequal with the advent of class society.

Africa is a good geographical area in which to examine this problem. Of the range of societies contained in Africa, a relatively high proportion can be categorized as having been village communities until recent times. By village community I mean a form of society based on agricultural production by small independent farmers.* The degree of commercialization of agriculture is slight; technology and tools are relatively simple. It is essentially a system without classes: the major means of production, land, is collectively owned, and tools are easily made and readily available.† Allocation and distribution of land are accomplished through the lineage structure; units of production and consumption include some level of the extended family. This type of society, prevalent in West Africa at one time, has been degenerating and no longer exists in its original form. Although it is being rapidly replaced by class-stratified societies, some aspects of its structure remain; thus it is possible to draw some tentative conclusions about the position of women in this type of society.

Anthropologists have tended to underestimate the importance of female productive labor (aside from child-bearing and child-rearing) and consequently have obscured the significance of the female role in the functioning of the total society. The relationship

---

* This type of society does not correspond directly to the primitive communalism in which Engels asserts that women were truly equal to men. Most of these African societies would probably fall into the category of "middle and upper barbarism," in which the process of male domination over the means of production had begun to evolve.

† Essential equality with respect to the means of production does not preclude all forms of social differentiation, particularly those of age and sex.

between women's participation in social production (public as opposed to private labor) and their status in society was foreseen by Engels. The extent to which women's labor is public is seen to correspond with stages of society: the absence of private property makes men's work and women's work of equal significance.

In African hunting and gathering societies and village communities, the female contribution to labor for the production of subsistence is significant. A brief examination of hunting and gathering societies indicates that both males and females contribute to subsistence: men do the largest proportion of game hunting and women predominate in the gathering of vegetable products. Although the early anthropological literature tended to focus on the hunt,* in most of the world's hunting and gathering populations (with the exception of those in arctic and subarctic areas) hunting appears to provide only 20 to 40 percent of the diet. The diet of the !Kung, for example, is 80 percent vegetarian (Steward 1972: 323).

As early as 1928, Baumann (1928: 289) documented women's predominance in hoe agriculture in African village communities, linking it to their connection with gathering. Irrespective of whether there is a causal connection with gathering, women's predominance in hoe agriculture is now amply documented, inspiring Boserup (1970:16) to refer to Africa as "the region of female farming *par excellence*." Utilizing the *Ethnographic Atlas*, Goody and Buckley (1973: 108) note that women presently play a major part in cultivation in 53 percent of the societies of sub-Saharan Africa.

Having clarified the extent to which African women contribute to subsistence, we turn to the problem of the relationship between women's participation in production and their status in society. Despite the division of labor in hunting and gathering populations, ownership of resources appears to be communal and distribution is egalitarian. The position of women appears to be compar-

---

* Further research may modify the traditional anthropological perspective concerning the dominance of the hunting motif. Leacock (1972: 39), for example, suggests that the awe surrounding childbirth should be reassessed and compared with the mystique that is said to surround hunting.

able to that of men in many respects. Gough (1971: 768) notes that women in such societies are "less subordinate" than women in other types of societies with respect to men's ability to command or exploit their labor or to control their produce, as well as in several other areas of life. Sacks examines the status of women among the Mbuti, a hunting and gathering society of Zaire— noting in particular women's status in society and the family, their organization of productive activities, and their property owner-ship—and concludes that among the Mbuti, women are essentially the equals of men (1974: 214). Sanday's study verifies the fact that women's contribution in horticultural societies was substantial (1973: 1692) and makes the point that "many African women have wielded considerable economic, and sometimes political, power" (*ibid.*: 1682). She concludes, however, that there is no direct corre-lation between the contribution of women to subsistence and their status. The female "contribution to production is a *necessary* but not *sufficient* condition for the development of female status" (emphases hers; *ibid.*: 1695). She cites other factors—such as the duration of participation and the development of solidarity groups —that must also occur. However, Sanday does not elaborate on the context in which Engels's distinction between private and public labor becomes significant—the extent to which products can be controlled by individuals or strata for personal ends, rather than for distribution or redistribution—although she does allude to the importance of that distinction in her discussion of the re-lationship between female power and female production of valued goods.

Several anthropologists have hypothesized that in societies where men and women are engaged in the production of the same kinds of socially necessary goods, and where widespread private property (and therefore class structure) has not developed, women's par-ticipation in production gives them access to and control over the products of their labor, as well as considerable freedom and inde-pendence (Leacock 1972, Boserup 1970, Gough 1971). While suffi-cient data for verification are lacking, Sacks's (1974) study suggests that the hypothesis correlating the development of private prop-

erty and the subordinate status of women is supportable.* She
examines four African societies prior to European domination: the
Mbuti of Zaire, the Lovedu and the Pondo of South Africa, and
the Ganda of Uganda. Using a variety of indices to measure the
economic, social, and domestic status of women, she concludes
that, in most respects, in the egalitarian Mbuti and Lovedu societies, women are the equals of men; among the class-stratified
Ganda, women are very subordinate; and among the Pondo, whose
society falls between egalitarian and class-stratified, women occupy
a fairly subordinate position.

There is, then, some evidence to indicate that in village communities where private property had not developed, women participated in the production of the primary resources of the society
and had equal access to the products of their labor.† Yet available
evidence also suggests that relationships were asymmetrical, with
men predominating in formal political offices.‡ However, the degree to which relations were asymmetrical, and the extent to which
asymmetry resulted in relations of domination and subordination,

* She elaborates on this thesis by suggesting that in class societies it is the
dichotomization of family and society—where women are responsible for the
production of private use value and men are responsible for the production of
exchange value—that is the basis of male supremacy.

† Bridget O'Laughlin's excellent article (1974) on the relationship between
symbolic expressions of sexual asymmetry as manifested in food prohibitions
and male control of the forces of production appears to contradict this line of
reasoning. She contends that among the Mbum of Tchad egalitarian rules of
property assignment in the jural superstructure do not reflect the real relationships of production, which are characterized by sexual and generational inequality. There are two points that must be clarified, however, before we can
accept this as a contradictory case. First, although she has demonstrated that
access to appropriation of surplus labor is vested in male elders, she has not
demonstrated that the surplus is turned toward personal ends rather than redistributed. In fact, in discussing the authority of the head of the granary
group, she states, "The head of a granary group . . . distributes equal shares of
grain to the wives of the group for consumption and allocates millet for special
purposes . . ." (p. 306). The second point of interest here is whether the advent
of cash-cropping had some effect in stratifying the relationships between males
and females. She notes that in cotton cultivation, a man controls the cash
revenues of his wives and unmarried sons (p. 306). If cotton cultivation is of
fairly recent origin, it is interesting to note the claim of the elders that in their
youth men engaged in food prohibitions similar to those of women (p. 302).

‡ In village communities, political offices often emerged from defense roles.

has yet to be ascertained. Recent studies suggest (1) that women exercised political power more frequently than was formerly assumed (see Lebeuf 1963; Hoffer 1972, 1974); and (2) that although the symbolic expressions of women's power differed from those of men's, women were not necessarily considered to be less powerful (see Lebeuf 1963, Calame-Griaule 1962, and the papers by Van Allen and Okonjo in this volume).

It is clear, however, that with the beginning of animal husbandry, which is often the form of the first private property, male dominance appears. Engels (1972: 118) noted that the domestication of animals and the breeding of herds created entirely new social relations. Because they were a source of wealth that could reproduce themselves, livestock represented goods or resources with productive potential. Engels's formulation is not unlike Barth's (1972: 11) concerning the "inherent growth capacity" of the "pastoral enterprise." In surveying African societies, Amin (1964: 11) noted, "But even where the ownership of the land has remained really collective, the ownership of livestock is already individualized and very unevenly shared."* Goody (1973: 1076) notes that almost everywhere in Africa the animal-drawn plow, husbandry, and hunting became the male province (see also Brown 1970: 1076, and Dupire 1963: 75). Brown (1970) has suggested that the demands of child care were probably the basis for the initial lack of female participation in animal husbandry. Clearly the manner in which this division of labor is transformed into unequal relations as livestock ownership develops into private property warrants further investigation. It appears that asymmetry provided the basis under these conditions for the growth of inequality.†

Perhaps the most feasible way to approach the change in women's status is by examining the processes from the other direction—

---

* However, among the Nuer of East Africa, cattle had not yet fully developed into a commodity; although men "owned" the cattle, only women, girls, and uninitiated boys were permitted to milk them.

† It is interesting to note here that in Sanday's sample (1973: 1696) one of the African societies where women contribute significantly to subsistence (45 percent) but have least access to status is the Somali, where certain livestock

to analyze how the status of women has changed as society has become increasingly stratified.* Although forms of stratification were developing in Africa before colonialism (and of course many state systems existed), the European intrusion, through slave trade† and colonialism, accelerated the division of the population into classes (Kilson 1958: 371). Thus it might be productive to examine the effects of colonialism on the status of African women.

Leacock (1972: 39), Rodney (1972: 248), and Boserup (1970: 53) have categorically asserted that colonialism resulted in the deterioration of the status of women relative to that of men. Several investigators have cited particular areas in which independent female participation has deteriorated as a result of colonial influence: e.g., the decline in significance of the stool of the Ashanti queen mother (Christian 1959: 58); the limitation on women's freedom of choice of a husband as a result of inflated bridewealth (Suret-Canale 1971: 424); and the disequilibrium resulting from the modification of traditional marriage by colonial laws (Dobkin 1968: 396).

Van Allen contributes one of the best documented examples of the process of the decline of political power among the Igbo women of southeastern Nigeria. She attributes this decline to the fact that the British colonialists, as a result of their "Victorian

---

have exchange value: "Women were forced, under threat of physical violence from their husbands, to perform all the menial and heavy work and were allowed to tend sheep and goats. Somali men considered it beneath their dignity to tend anything but camels, cattle, and ponies—the most valuable economic assets of the Somali."

* A number of factors make it difficult to draw definitive conclusions about the status of women in village communities. Owing to what has been termed the "male bias" in anthropological literature, there is frequently a lack of data about the role of women in many areas of social life. In addition, most of the African village communities for which we have data are societies in which there has been some development of stratification and private property, often hastened by European influence; thus reconstruction of earlier periods presents methodological difficulties.

† Although I will not discuss the effects of the Atlantic slave "trade" in this paper, it must have significantly modified the status of women. In societies where the relationship between men and women may have been characterized by a division of labor in which weapons were the domain of men, the conditions imposed by slave trade must have produced a situation of extreme dependency for those who did not have access to weapons.

view of women," saw politics as a man's concern (see Van Allen 1972). Like Wipper's assertion (1972: 12) that "In their struggle for equality, African women have had to contend with a kind of coalition between Western and African men about what their roles should be," Van Allen's view does not deal adequately with the underlying structural processes of colonialism. It might be more useful to understand the deterioration of the status of African women as bound to the disruption of African society as a whole through colonialism's imposition of a social structure based on stratification by class and sex. Colonialism often resulted in the differentiation of social and domestic labor, the introduction of large-scale production for exchange, and the transformation of productive resources into private property—processes that significantly altered the status of women.

Almost everywhere, the introduction of widespread production for exchange disrupted whatever reciprocal division of labor existed. We have demonstrated that in village communities women made a major contribution to the production of foodstuffs and appeared to have had access to the products of their labor. But in areas where cash-cropping was introduced, the production of cash crops often became the domain of men.* Boserup (1970: 53–56) cites numerous instances in which colonial personnel excluded women from cash-crop cultivation, taught men modern techniques, and gave men access to machinery that could raise the level of production. As cash-cropping developed and the commodity economy became widespread, women's labor (the continued cultivation of food crops) became inferior and private: it did not produce the cash needed to enter the money economy and its function was now limited to the domestic group.

In the colonial relationship, land often became a commodity that could be acquired by the colonial power. In many areas land was in fact communally owned and utilized; however, in a ritual or supervisory sense it was often vested in a chief or a group of male elders. Through "indirect rule," traditional offices were often

---

* Igbo women of eastern Nigeria, who cultivated cassava, are a well-known exception.

modified to facilitate the acquisition of land by the colonialists; those who possessed supervisory rights were sometimes able to assume "ownership" in the sense of private property and to sell the formerly unalienable land. Because women (along with the majority of men) were not usually in the category of formal "owner-ship," they often fell into the lower strata as stratification based on land ownership developed. In addition, Boserup (1970: 59–61) documents cases in Rhodesia and the Union of South Africa where European "reform" has resulted in the transfer of women's land to men (see also Simons 1968).

In general, men were usually able to enter the money sector of the economy more easily than women were. Men predominated in cash-cropping; recruitment of labor to the plantations was often restricted to men (Boserup 1970: 76); and men had the advantage in obtaining whatever education was available to the indigenous population (see Little 1973: 30). Thus women, in addition to having to support themselves and their children when compulsory labor took the men away from home, found themselves in a money economy where the products of their labor were inferior and found that they no longer had access to the resources of the society. (For an example of such a situation, see Margaret Hay's paper on the women of Kowe in this volume.)

Investigators who maintain that women's status improved as a result of European contact often link sex-role differentiation to trading opportunities that were expanded by European contact (Ottenberg 1959; McCall 1961; Christensen 1961). Mintz (1971: 251) notes, however, that regardless of whether European contact appears to have expanded or diminished the internal market, "What seems likely is that the percentage of total economic activity represented by marketplace trade is declining in these societies, even while marketplaces themselves continue to grow. . . . [T]hen it is conceivable that the expansion of economic opportunities within the internal market system can occur in ways and at rates that lag far behind the growth of other economic opportunities in the same society." If this is the case in societies where the female role is associated with trade, he asks, what are the implications for the future role of women in the context of "Westernization"? He notes that although a few market women in Senegal appear to have gained in wealth and influence, cassava trading among Igbo women does not serve as a means of capital accumulation; moreover, those market women who "reinvest" in the education of their children generally are only able to educate them to lower-status jobs, and Nigerian female trading appears to be threatened by male commercial activities. He suggests, then, that "while the economic growth advanced by Westernization has doubtless increased opportunities for (at least some) female traders, it may also and simultaneously limit the range of their activities, as economic changes outside the internal market system continue to multiply" (*ibid.*: 265).

Other investigators have substantiated Mintz's hypotheses. Little (1973: 45) points out that although there are individual cases of very successful market women, the great majority of West African market women are petty traders. Boserup (1970) found that products sold by women are primarily agricultural (p. 91); that the bazaar represents an intermediate step between agriculture and modern occupations and eventually "will begin to feel competition not only from imports but also from a growing modern sector" (p. 179); that market women, on the whole, have few opportunities to enter other sectors; and that "particularly in Africa, the participation of women in modern trade is held down by their low level of literacy and by the general tendency to give priority to men in employment and recruitment to the modern sector" (p. 99).

Since women have been virtually excluded from the industrial labor force (Little 1973: 30, Boserup 1970: 109), few alternatives to marketing exist in the urbanizing and industrializing sectors. Women, then, find themselves in a commodity economy where their traditional productive role has been devalued and where they have limited access to the new means of production. Clearly this is not to suggest that all males, or even the majority of males, are in a structurally dominant position. With the development of class stratification, a group of male wage laborers who do not *own* the means of production develops. But the essential difference here is that, to the extent that they are involved in social production of the resources of the society, their work is social, rather than private. The exclusion of women from access to the major means of production, in the context of stratification, means that they are unequal to the men of their class.

Having examined the generalizations, I will now turn to a particular case. My own research in Labadi, a Ga town of about 25,000 in southeastern Ghana, supported the thesis that the acceleration of class stratification under colonialism resulted in the deterioration of the position of women relative to that of men.

Land in Labadi, originally a community of farmers and fishermen, was owned communally in precolonial times by lineage groups. Relations of production can be said to have been essentially egalitarian in that every individual had, directly or indirectly, right of access to the land. The residence system was based on the principle of separation by sex: in general, men lived in male compounds with patrilineally related men, and women lived in female compounds with matrilineally related women. Several investigators have commented on the freedom of movement and solidarity among women fostered by the traditional residence system (Field 1940: 7–8; Mills-Odoi 1967: 34).

The fact that the Ga were situated on the coast meant that they were directly affected by European penetration and colonialism. Available evidence indicates that before European domination the town was a theocracy governed by priests who represented the lineage groups. When the British instituted indirect rule, the *mantse* ("father of the town") was transformed from a "medicine," thought to bring victory to the warriors, to the British conception of a chief in order to facilitate the acquisition of land (now a commodity) by the colonial regime. The British acquired land—through sale, lease, and grant—from the town elders and officers in whom it had been symbolically vested often by utilizing fraudulent methods of persuasion and manipulation. The archival records are replete with suits Ga people brought against various chiefs and elders for selling land (usually to the colonial government) for their "personal enrichment," "without the consent of the people."*

One result of the alienation of the land, the development of a money economy, and such measures as taxation and compulsory labor was to stratify the formerly equal cultivators. No doubt a small stratum profited from the sale of land and from participation in long-distance trade, but the most numerous lower strata were more or less pushed off the land and into the work force. Land had never been formally vested in women in precolonial times, and they do not appear to be represented in this small stratum that was able to benefit from the sale of land. Under these conditions, then, the asymmetry characteristic of the village community again becomes the basis for stratification by class.

Labadi women took up petty trading enthusiastically. The census of 1901 describes the inhabitants of Labadi as mainly involved in farming and fishing, "with a small amount [involved in] petty trading, which is on the rise." By the time of the 1960 census, 74 percent of the employed women were reported as being in commerce (mainly petty trading) and 70 percent of the men were employed in mining and quarrying, manufacture, construction, commerce, transport, storage, and communications.

As the market economy first developed, marketing was probably a form of division of labor between husband and wife. However, an independent relationship emerged that was fostered by the traditional residence system and accelerated by the developing economy. As the small farmers were pushed off the land, their wives, being in the money sector, were often better able to survive. Farmers and fishermen reported having to borrow money from their wives in lean seasons. Where wives marketed their husbands' products, the husbands universally complained that the wives retained a larger portion of the money from the sale of the products than they agreed to. Since husbands had no way of knowing the selling price of their products, they had to be content with whatever portion of the price the wives decided to turn over to them. The women claimed that whatever they made at marketing, especially

* For a fuller discussion of this, see my dissertation "Social Change, Religion and Healing in Southeastern Ghana" (University of Chicago, 1975).

if the capital was their own, was their business and that it was not necessary to tell the husbands the size of their profits. One market woman said, "At times, men are troublesome. If we tell them that the marketing is improving and then I ask him for some money, he will not give it to me because he knows that I am marketing and have money. So sometimes we don't tell them the truth. If I happen to make two cedies at the market today, I will tell my husband that I didn't make anything." The women's profits from marketing are generally applied to care of themselves and their children.

These circumstances have led to the general impression that women have profited from the development of the market economy and are now in better positions than their husbands. This perspective, shared by the farmers themselves, is also prevalent among researchers: "In the matter of money, there are no people on earth whose women are in as enviable position as are the Ga" (Field 1940: 55–56); or "All the same, the wives tend to make more than their husbands" (Mills-Odoi 1967: 123). Upon closer examination of the emerging trends, however, we may find that appearances belie a developing reality.

The market women operate in the traditional sphere of the money economy in that they mainly sell agricultural produce, cloth, and canned goods. A market woman who sells agricultural produce may buy from any of the farms in the area and may sell in any of the markets between Labadi and Accra. In "good" periods it is sometimes possible to buy the products for half of the price for which they will later be sold; at other times the margin of profit will be much less. The market woman must also pay transportation costs (40 pesewas per basket from the outlying areas to Accra*) and rent her stall at the market (at the Accra market a stall is 80 pesewas per month). A product's selling price depends on the season, the supply, and the demand. In the dry season, from December to June, one large tomato may sell for 10 pesewas, whereas from June to December six tomatoes may sell for 5 pesewas.

Petty marketing is extremely precarious and time-consuming. Market women often work six days a week and 12 hours a day; they

* In 1971, one pesewa = one U.S. cent, and one new cedie = one U.S. dollar.

carry their infant children on their backs, and take their older children with them, too, if they have no female relative to leave them with. Profits vary: sometimes it is possible to make 10 new cedies a week or more; at other times even the capital is lost and the woman is plunged into debt. The petty trader is at the mercy of the vagaries of the market economy. Therefore, while a minority of petty traders are very successful, the majority appear to subsist marginally.

Thus although it appears that the position of market women relative to that of men has improved, if Mintz's hypotheses are correct the position of women may not be as secure as it seems. We have noted that petty trading is precarious by nature; when we examine the statistics, we find that women are generally confined to the traditional sectors of the economy. It appears that they have much less access to the high- or even the low-status jobs that are in the sectors that would expand through industrialization. We find that women are significantly less represented in all of the non-traditional sectors. Of the total Labadians employed in sales, primarily petty trading, approximately 91 percent are female and 9 percent are male. However, in professional, technical, and other related occupations only 26 percent are female; in clerical work 11 percent are female; in transport and commerce 3 percent are female; and of craftsmen, production process workers, and laborers only 14 percent are female.*

The growth of the nuclear family was a component of industrialization, urbanization, and stratification in Labadi. Although many women find monogamous marriage and nuclear-family relationships preferable in many ways, these new arrangements curb independence—especially when they occur without the development of alternative methods of sharing domestic responsibilities and child care. Traditional kinship patterns were such that a woman and child were less dependent upon a particular man: responsibility for individuals was vested in the lineage and was manifested in lineage responsibility for ownership of land, for debts

* These figures are computed from the 1960 Population Census of Ghana, Special Report "A" (Statistics of Towns) (Accra, 1964).

incurred by individuals, and for care of children in cases of death of the father. Field (1940: 60) reported that the rotation of cooking and sexual responsibilities characteristic of polygynous arrangements allowed women much freedom for trading and other activities. The residential system, based on compounds of matrilineal kin, meant that there were several women who could cook for a woman's husband and look after a woman's children if necessary (*ibid.*: 68).

Social change has resulted in important modifications of this pattern. Mills-Odoi (1967: 188), comparing a "modern" quarter with a "traditional" one in Labadi, noted that in the former there were some men who did not allow their wives to work at all, and that the wives of such men became economically dependent on their husbands. The monogamous union and nuclear-family residence gave one woman full responsibility for such household tasks as preparation of the food and care of the children. Mills-Odoi concluded that this personal responsibility significantly curtailed the woman's freedom of movement and her ability to engage in independent economic activities.

Colonialism also appears to have brought about a decline of women's power in traditional politics. We have seen that land, the major form of wealth in precolonial times, was owned communally in Labadi. Political power, too, was fairly diffuse, divided as it was among priests, elders, and male and female captains representing the lineage groupings. In Labadi, a *manyei* ("mother of the town") represented the women.* I was told that her office rotated among certain lineages and that she regularly met with the female captains to make decisions on any matters related to women. Though the office of *mantse* was transformed into a "chieftainship" and strengthened by colonialism, the office of *manyei* appears to be moving toward oblivion. When I did my research, I was told by the chief that there was no *manyei* because he had set certain edu-

---

* Field (1940: 52) refers to the post "Head of Stool-Washers or Stool Mother" but does not give the Ga name or discuss its function except to point out that unlike the Ashanti "queen mother" the holder of this post is not the mother of the heir.

cational qualifications for the office that had not been met. When I asked what the *manyei*'s sphere of influence had been, the answer was vague. He indicated that she "had control over all the women in the town" and that the women made decisions in areas concerned with everyday life, such as the cost of funeral obligations and "the attitudes of the men toward the women." However, decisions about such things as the sale of land are now made by the traditional council, on which women are not formally represented.

In Labadi, then, colonialism accelerated the dissolution of the village community and the development of class society. In the population as a whole there was a general loss of access to the means of production as the structure of society changed from one based on communal ownership of land and essentially egalitarian relationships to one based on private property, wage labor, and stratification. As land became a commodity, political power, formerly diffuse, became concentrated in the hands of the colonialists and, to a lesser extent, the chief and a few elders. This development had particularly negative results for women, especially since it appears to have been accompanied by the decline of their vehicles of traditional power.* Although women's access to the marketplace gives the appearance of improved status (especially where the majority of men are farmers and fishermen), I suggest that this improvement in status is illusory. As long as women's access to all nontraditional sectors of the economy remains limited, their transitional hegemony is doomed to ultimate deterioration as industrialized stratified society replaces the traditional village community.

It appears, then, that the development of stratification by class, particularly as accelerated by colonial relationships, has resulted in the decline of women's status relative to that of men. Although the development of industrialization produces conditions that have the potential for making the status of women increasingly

* One traditional area in which women continue, or have possibly increased, their political influence is in their role as spirit mediums; a medium who is known for efficacy can command a large income and an influential clientele. See the paper by Iris Berger in this volume.

equal and symmetrical,* this potential does not appear to have been realized in the context of class stratification. The reciprocal relationships of the village community have deteriorated, and women now have unequal access to the means of production. Clearly, the relationships between men and women are asymmetrical in that women do not have access to the same positions and statuses as men.

Although I have described the ways in which colonialism has worsened the position of women, I am by no means suggesting that African women reacted with apathy or inertia. Indeed, African women have struggled against colonialism, just as men have—from the "Women's War" in Nigeria to the poll-tax and pass-law demonstrations in South Africa. This participation was particularly evident in the liberation movements against the remaining colonial regimes of the former Portuguese colonies in Africa, where African women are moving toward qualitatively new roles, based on the achievement of equal and symmetrical relationships between males and females.

Some of the most significant transformations in the status of women have occurred in Mozambique and Guinea-Bissau,† where the liberation of women was declared a major and necessary step in the process of social revolution. The struggle for liberation in these areas differed from those elsewhere in Africa in that the liberation movements confronted a colonial power—ruled by a

* Increased development of technology eliminates the need for certain forms of division of labor that may have been necessary at one time (such as the feeding of children).

† On September 4, 1973, after more than a decade of armed struggle, the National Assembly of Guinea-Bissau proclaimed the Republic of Guinea-Bissau; it was recognized by the United Nations General Assembly on November 2, 1973, and by the Portuguese government on September 10, 1974, following the overthrow of the Caetano dictatorship. On June 25, 1975, Mozambique became independent. Angola achieved its independence on November 11, 1975. Women participated in the struggle in Angola through the MPLA (Popular Movement for the Liberation of Angola). Since independence, the Organization of Angolan Women (OMA) has organized a campaign to develop the contribution and consciousness of women. Although there is little documentation of their role, available evidence indicates that developments are similar to those in Mozambique and Guinea-Bissau.

fascist dictatorship and buttressed by arms and equipment from NATO—that refused to end its political hegemony. The liberation movements that emerged in these areas were not simply nationalist in character; they were also committed to the total transformation of social relations, based on the principle of equal access to the means of production. It was in this context of conscious construction of a new society that the status of women was markedly altered: women have assumed a variety of roles, including those of warriors* and political functionaries, over and above their role as producers of subsistence. In the remainder of this paper I shall discuss the emerging status of women in these societies.†

The Mozambique Liberation Front (Frelimo) came into existence in exile in 1962 from the merger of three smaller groups. Eduardo Mondlane headed the movement in its early years, until he was assassinated in Dar es Salaam by a letter bomb in 1969. Other important leaders included Samora Machel, now President of the People's Republic of Mozambique, and Marcelino dos Santos, now Machel's vice president. From its earliest days, Frelimo declared that the emancipation of women in Mozambique was one of its central concerns, and clearly related the achievement of this goal to the transformation of the social order. Samora Machel expressed this stand as follows (Machel 1975).

The emancipation of women is not an act of charity, it does not result from a humanitarian position or act of compassion. The liberation of woman is a fundamental necessity of the Revolution, a guaranty of its continuity, a condition for its triumph. The Revolution has as its essential objective the destruction of the system of exploitation and the construction of a new liberated society where the potential of every human being is reconciled with work and nature. The equality of women is set within this context.

. . .

We have seen that the basis of the domination of women lies in the system of economic organization of society, private ownership of the means of production, which necessarily leads to the exploitation of man by man.

---

* This development is especially interesting in light of Sanday's assertion that male predominance in defense and warfare gives them an initial advantage.

† I would like to thank Nancy Hafkin for allowing me to make use of data she gathered during a trip to Mozambique in August and September of 1975 and for assisting me in writing the section of this paper on women in Mozambique.

That this commitment to equality for women was not simply ideological is clear both from the period of the armed struggle (1964–74) and from the brief postindependence period (since 1975).

Soon after guerrilla warfare began in 1964, Frelimo decided that women would participate fully at all levels of the struggle—not only in food production and the transportation of war materials, but also in combat and defense. In 1966 a Women's Detachment (*Destacamento Feminino*) of the army was formed, and by January 1967 women were receiving the political and military training necessary "to carry out all the tasks of the revolution."* Many women chose active combat roles, although most were assigned to militia units guarding villages in the "liberated" zones of northern Mozambique from Portuguese attack. The Women's Detachment was also assigned to political education, recruitment, and mobilization of the population for guerrilla warfare—despite the fact that these were closely allied to traditional male roles. But members of the Women's Detachment asserted that for men to see armed women was an act of political education in itself that would help eradicate stereotypes limiting women to domestic tasks. Communal child-rearing centers were created, where both men and women cared for the children, to facilitate the participation of members of the Women's Detachment.

Frelimo declared that women were to become the equals of men and were to participate fully in former male realms, especially politics. To this end, the movement stressed that women should have access to education and should study the same subjects as men. As Machel wrote (1973):

In capitalist society, men maintain a monopoly over scientific fields of study and keep women from discovering the possibility of modifying the social order.

If half of the exploited, oppressed people [in Mozambique] are women, how can they be left at the margins of the struggle? ... If the revolution is going to be pursued by new generations, how can we assure the new revolutionary generations of *continuadores* if the mother, the first educator, is left outside the revolutionary process?

---

* "O Papel Da Mulher na Revolução," *Movimento das Forças Armadas Boletim*, June 24, 1975, p. 7.

For woman to be emancipated it is necessary that she have a politically engaged consciousness. She should become a practicing revolutionary, dedicated to the destruction of an exploitative society; she should take part in the liberation struggle; she must be engaged in production. She must have scientific and cultural education. Thus women will come to full levels of responsibility in all institutions in society.

How this ideological stand has been put into practice is evident in the political sphere. Women held positions on the Central Committee of Frelimo during the period of armed struggle, and since independence have filled positions of high responsibility in the new government; there are now three women members of the Central Committee of Frelimo. It is especially significant, in view of the goals enunciated by Machel, that a woman is the Minister of Education and Culture.

After impressive gains during the period of armed struggle, the revolution now faces the task of bringing the progress made in the closely regulated liberated zones in the north* to the cities of the south and making the gains of the revolution permanent. This will require the integration of women from all parts of the country; moreover since the government has declared a multiracial Mozambique to be its goal, reeducation of large numbers of Portuguese women will be necessary. Since the Women's Detachment was thought to be an inappropriate institution for accomplishing these new tasks, the responsibility for women was shifted to the *Organização das Mulheres Mocambicanas* (Organization of Mozambique Women). Headed by Deolinda Guismane, a member of the Frelimo Central Committee, the OMM is incorporated into the Frelimo structure. An OMM member functions as part of each of the decentralized *grupos dinimizadores* ("dynamizing groups") established to promote political education at work places and residences in former colonialist areas. In order to ensure full par-

* During the decade of guerrilla warfare, Frelimo's activities were concentrated in northern and central Mozambique. By the fall of 1974, the new regime in Portugal had negotiated a cease-fire with the Mozambican guerrillas and a transitional government with a Frelimo majority came to power in the former colony. Frelimo consequently transferred its center of operations from the liberated zones—where extensive political education had been going on for a decade—to Lourenço Marques, the capital city in southern Mozambique, which had been under Portuguese political control.

ticipation of women workers, the OMM representatives in each "dynamizing group" have been establishing day-care facilities for children of women workers at places of employment. The OMM has also engaged in campaigns to eliminate prostitution, which was seen as one of the legacies of colonialism most degrading to women, by setting up work camps for the recuperation and political education of prostitutes.*

Although many of these changes in women's status are still in the formative stages, the foregoing discussion indicates that the new government has committed itself to the process of transforming the roles of women in the new society. Although it has grounded the question of women's liberation in "equality," based on the elimination of private property and equal access to the means of production,† the leadership of independent Mozambique has also concerned itself with the problem of role symmetry—the ability of women to participate at all levels of the society, ensuring that women become full partners in social production. In this context, Frelimo has given attention to the distribution of domestic roles, urging men to enter the domestic realm. According to Machel, "Men will be in all realms, also—in housework, schools, child care, and hospitals" (1975). Minister of Education Graça Simbine repeated this theme at a women's conference held in Lourenço Marques in 1975. She stressed that for women's equality to be realized, "it is necessary to begin in our homes," for "to free women is also to free men" (O Tempo, March 16, 1975). The popular press in Mozambique has also taken up the theme of sex-role symmetry. An article appearing in the Lourenço Marques weekly magazine O Tempo stated: "It is not true that the place of women is in the kitchen. The mato [countryside] is also her place in the struggle. It is not true that women do well only at cooking. They also do well in camouflage in surprising the enemy. Men will not be excused

* For accounts of the campaign against prostitution in Mozambique, see "Vamos Acabar Com a Prostituição," O Tempo, April 20, 1975; and "Para Onde Foram As Prostitutas," O Tempo, August 31, 1975.
† The recent establishment of cooperative farms and nationalization of land represent steps in this direction.

from washing dishes or sweeping the house on the grounds that it shows lack of virility to do domestic work" (Calane da Silva 1975).

However, Machel (1975) warns against placing priority on the concept of symmetry, thus emphasizing "mechanical equality":

There are those who see emancipation as mechanical equality between men and women. This vulgar concept is often seen among us. Here emancipation means that women and men do exactly the same tasks, mechanically dividing their household duties. If I wash the dishes today you must wash them tomorrow, whether or not you are busy and have the time. . . . As we can see from the example of capitalist countries, this mechanically conceived emancipation leads to complaints and attitudes which utterly distort the meaning of women's emancipation.

The continuing process of transformation of the status of women was seen to require conscious ideological struggle geared toward attitudinal change. This included analysis of traditional practices thought to be detrimental to women, and political education for adults and children specifically directed toward eradicating stereotyped conceptions of male and female roles that would preclude the achievement of full human potential. One symbolic manifestation of this is the abandonment of the former terms of address *Senhor* and *Senhora* in favor of *Camarada* for both sexes.

Similar transformations in women's status have been occurring in Guinea-Bissau. During the struggle for liberation, the African Party for the Independence of Guinea-Bissau and Cape Verde (PAIGC) clearly charted a socialist direction for the country. Several journalists and scholars have commented on the relatively extensive development of free social services, "people's stores," and agricultural cooperatives (see, for example, Urdang 1974; Cornwall 1972; Davidson 1969; and Pelissier 1975). This direction was formalized in Chapter 1, Article 8, of the Constitution of the Republic of Guinea-Bissau: "The State plays a fundamental role in the planning of the national economy, and the property of the colonialist state will be transformed into national property." Recently, concrete steps have been taken to move the country in this direction. In May 1975, the People's National Assembly approved a law to facilitate the nationalization of all land, urban and rural.

Even before independence, Stephanie Urdang (1974) documented significant transformations in the role of women in the new society: the participation of women in all areas of work; the conscious integration of women into all levels of political leadership;
the eradication of oppressive marriage and divorce traditions; and
the increase in educational opportunities for women. As areas
were liberated during the armed struggle, village councils were
elected in each village to supervise the organization of the village
and act as liaison between the population and PAIGC. In order to
ensure that women would be brought into leadership on the village level, PAIGC insisted that at least two of the five members of
each council be women. In order to overcome opposition of both
male and female villagers to female participation on the village
council, female members were initially assigned to be responsible
for food production, which was originally considered to be a female
role. Over time, women began to function as vice presidents and
presidents of village councils and assumed responsibilities beyond
the village level. In this case, PAIGC was able to utilize the traditional division of labor to initiate modification of traditional roles.
Urdang noted that "The number of women in all fields of work
has been growing steadily. They receive strong encouragement by
the party to take on more and more responsibility, and in turn are
demanding this themselves. There are women nurses (and heads
of hospitals), political commissars, regional health responsibles,
teachers (and directors of schools), radio communications tech-
nicians, and women involved in political work among the population, in villages and beyond" (1974: 8).

These admittedly sketchy data suggest tentative conclusions. It
appears that in these societies, which are in the process of recon-
structing themselves on the basis of equality of access to the means
of production, women are being propelled into participation at
all levels. This is a conscious development that is occurring in conditions that differ from those that obtained in precolonial village
communities. Technological developments now provide the material conditions for transforming such areas as food production
and child care in ways that will allow liberation from the confines

of the traditional division of labor, upon which asymmetrical relations were based.

In this paper I have attempted to examine some of the effects of the class stratification accelerated by colonialism on the status of women in African societies. In order to place the development of class stratification in perspective, I have compared the status of women in contemporary class-stratified societies (1) with what we know of their status in precolonial village communities and hunting and gathering societies, and (2) with the goals and emerging trends in postcolonial societies committed to the eradication of class stratification. I have used the concepts "equality" and "symmetry" and "inequality" and "asymmetry" to clarify my argument. Although the data are fragmentary and inconclusive, indications of convincing correlations between stratification by class and the status of women should justify further research into these areas.

I have suggested that there is evidence to indicate that hunting and gathering societies and village communities were characterized by equality of access to the means of production. Since there was, however, a division of labor, with women predominating in some areas and men in others, we can say that relationships between the sexes were *equal* but *asymmetrical* in that men and women did not participate in the same roles. However, the data suggest that the equality of access to the means of production limited the extent to which the asymmetry of roles produced relations of dominance and subordination.

With the advent of private property and the emergence of classes —which had been taking place in some parts of Africa before the arrival of the Europeans, but which were accelerated by colonial domination—relations between the sexes became both asymmetrical and unequal. It appears that the existence of asymmetry often provided the basis for the development of inequality under changed conditions. Now, however, in the societies recently liberated from Portuguese colonial domination, there is evidence to indicate that private property is being abolished and that women are gaining access to roles on all levels of society. Although it will be some time before conclusive evidence is available, it appears that the societies of Mozambique and Guinea-Bissau are attempting to establish relations between men and women that are both equal and symmetrical. Equality seems to be a precondition for symmetry; for although equality may appear without symmetry, it is unlikely that symmetry will exist without equality.

Less Than Second-Class:
Women in Rural Settlement Schemes
in Tanzania

JAMES L. BRAIN

IN 1965–66 I spent fifteen months in Tanzania as a member of a Syracuse University research team that was reporting on a village settlement program mounted by the Tanzanian government.* My fieldwork took place in a village in eastern Tanzania called Bwakira Chini, and it involved the Luguru and Kutu, two of the matrilineal peoples of that region among whom I had spent several years during the twelve years I served in Tanzania. In April of 1966 I presented a paper on the status of women at the University of Dar es Salaam during a week-long seminar on settlement.

The conclusion I reached at that time—that the women were far worse off on the settlement scheme than in their traditional societies—has subsequently been reinforced by other studies on African women during the last few years showing that the impact of colonialism on them has been far from favorable. The paper that follows includes the material I originally presented and the response it evoked from Tanzanian faculty members and senior civil servants.

Bwakira Chini is situated in Ukutu, a very fertile area in the plains at the foot of the eastern face of the Uluguru Mountains, which rise to peaks of 8,000 feet. Because of their locations, the Kutu and Luguru peoples have had different exposures to the outside world: the Luguru in their mountains have remained relatively undisturbed, whereas the Kutu have been in continuous

* For a short factual account of this program, see *Tanzania Today* (Nairobi, 1968), pp. 150–54.

contact with outsiders since the First World War. In Uluguru
the climate is pleasant and healthy, and it is possible to irrigate
small gardens even in the dry season so that no one goes hungry.
However, land is very scarce and can be obtained usually only
through inheritance. Most unusually for this part of Africa, women
possess similar rights in land to those of men. As one would expect,
land is inherited from the maternal uncle; one is also often able to
obtain land from one's father. This in no sense involves a system
of bilineal descent; rather, one has expectations from the matrilineal descent group to which one is complementarily filiated. In
the main, land in Uluguru is used solely for food crops, but small
amounts of cash crops are raised (chiefly vegetables) and are sold
outside the immediate area. In Ukutu, land is available in unlimit-
ed amounts to anyone with the energy to develop it, and thus inheritance of land is of little consequence. Both women and men
have their own fields, and it is common for women to produce
crops not only for the family food but also for cash, often hiring
laborers to do so. Thus, among both the Kutu and the Luguru,
women had a greater degree of economic independence than is
found among most of the peoples of Tanzania, where women are
usually dependent on their husband's agnatic descent group to
supply them with land that is theirs by privilege rather than right.
In most Tanzanian societies descent is patrilineal, residence is
patrilocal, and women own little beyond personal movable property; in the event of divorce, children are retained by the husband's
group. Among the Luguru and Kutu, by contrast, a woman keeps
her children after a divorce. This fact, coupled with women's economic independence, contributes to a high rate of divorce among
both peoples (see Brain 1969).

   Another unusual feature of Luguru society is that the women
choose the leader (male) of the basic, autonomous political and
landholding group, the subclan, whose claim to a particular tract
of land is validated in a mystical way by the presence on it of the
ancestral graves. Not only do the women choose the leader, they
may also depose him should they be dissatisfied with him. Though
cases of deposition are extremely rare, the fact that it is possible

is an important check on the power of the subclan head in this acephalous and relatively egalitarian society. The Kutu traditionally had an acephalous political organization similar to that of the Luguru, but because of the plentitude of land in Ukutu and the consequent options in residence, the political leaders there were of little importance compared to the subclan heads in Uluguru. Kutu women do not seem to have been involved in the choice of political leaders; on the other hand, the ready availability of land gave them a high degree of potential economic independence. Though virtually all girls are married at puberty, divorce is easy and it is not uncommon to find unattached women living alone.

One might think that the security in rights to both offspring and land, together with the choice of the political leader, would give the women a position of dominance in society. Though it is true that Luguru and Kutu women display a degree of outspokenness unusual among women in Tanzania, at the same time they are in no sense dominant. It seems probable that a tendency toward potential dominance is effectively curbed at puberty by one of the longest rites of passage in the world. At her first menstruation a girl was incarcerated in a darkened hut, where she was kept until her coming-out ceremony, which was usually concomitant with her marriage. In the 1930's the period of seclusion could last as long as six years; more recently it has been reduced to two or three. There is a vague, though unsubstantiated, notion current that the independent government has banned the custom, but it was still taking place in the mid-1960's. Two years of solitary confinement in the dark and a subsequent ritual simulated rebirth of *man* rather than woman can hardly fail to ensure a traumatic feeling of subservience toward men.

Shortly after Tanzania achieved independence in December 1961, the new government decided to embark on a program of establishing villages throughout the country. It might be thought odd that Tanzania should plan to have villages; surely people already lived in villages? In fact this was not so. Most rural Tanzanians lived on small homesteads organized around the extended family or the lineage group. President Nyerere felt that the village was the minimum level of social organization necessary before the benefits of modern development could be brought to the people. Until Tanzanians begin to live in villages, he said, "We shall not be able to use tractors; we shall not be able to build hospitals, or have clean drinking water; it will be quite impossible to start small village industries; and instead we shall have to go on depending on the town for all our requirements, and even if we had a plentiful supply of electric power we should never be able to connect it up to each isolated homestead" (Nyerere 1962). Nyerere's aim was to develop *Ujamaa*, which has been translated as "African Socialism" but which means something more akin to "familyness." Yet the specific goals he announced in the 1962 speech to Parliament just cited reflect the thinking of the expatriate advisers on whom Tanzania was then heavily dependent. The Village Settlement Agency, in particular, was staffed almost entirely by former British colonial civil servants. These men were honest, hardworking, and sympathetic to Tanzania's development, but because of their background, they were totally incapable of grasping what Nyerere had in mind. Today Nyerere and other Tanzanian leaders have visited China and have come to realize that large-scale capital investment in tractors and other heavy equipment is not necessary to effect rural transformation. In 1965, however, expatriate planners from the West were still highly influential, and the settlement schemes reflected their ideas.

Observers outside Tanzania often express surprise at the disparity between Nyerere's publicly expressed ideas and the reality of rural life. This view seems to me curiously naive. President Nyerere is not a dictator and can only introduce change by persuasion and legislation achieved through democratic processes. Even legislation can be interpreted and acted upon in very different ways.

The settlement scheme at Bwakira Chini was founded in 1965 (three years after independence) and was located on a former German freehold farm purchased from the widow of the previous owner by the government. Owing to the limited size of the farm only 80 families were to be settled in contrast to the 250 customary on the other schemes. The expatriate planners were committed to a layout of the housing in the villages on a grid with each house occupying a one-acre lot, the houses lying at some distance from the actual farm area. The rationale for this, based on no sociological foundation, was that the settlers would feel that they had a real stake in the scheme. In reality the result was more like a Long Island suburb. All the villages launched in the early years of independence were pilot projects; the ultimate aim was for all Tanzanians to live in villages. Part of the reason for establishing Bwakira Chini was to tempt some of the Luguru down from their overcrowded mountains, which was something the colonial government had tried to do, without success, for several decades (see Young & Fosbrooke 1960). In the event, after some months of recruiting, only 38 Luguru men could be found who were willing to leave the pleasant climate, agricultural security, and mystical protection of the ancestors in the mountains in exchange for the potential future profits of the hot plains village and the more immediate baits of free food, pocket money, and plowing by tractors. Many of the less successful Kutu, on the other hand, begged to be allowed to join the scheme, hoping to obtain a life of relatively profitable indigence. The government, anxious to get the village under way before another season was lost, allowed these Kutu men to take the other 42 places. The ultimate result of the recruitment was that most of the Luguru were very hard workers who hoped that by joining the scheme they would avoid the constraints and shared poverty of the overcrowded mountains. Some of the Kutu were feckless and lazy; a few were good workers.

I have noted that most Tanzanians did not live in villages. They did not, however, live in isolated single houses either, so that the new village was totally alien to the Luguru. By a curious irony, the Kutu were one of the very few Tanzanian peoples who *did* live in villages, very much like European ones, with perhaps a hundred or more houses clustered along a main street with a marketplace, shops, and a mosque at the center. None of the planners ever considered developing one of these indigenous and viable villages. The spread-out nature of the planned village made communication extremely difficult, was unfamiliar alike to Kutu and Luguru, and made any form of discipline almost impossible, particularly any system based on the sanction of shame. It was also obvious, and reported to the planning office, that at least one-third of the houses would be in a swamp during the rains. This proved to be the case and they had to be evacuated.

Each village in the government's settlement program was to be run by a manager and his staff—some sixteen in all—and there was a vague notion that somehow, like the Marxian state, these people would wither away after some indefinite period of time and leave the settlers responsible for their own future. The entire capital cost of the scheme, including the salaries of all the staff members, was to be charged to the settlers, who it was hoped would be able to pay it off over the following twenty years. In the mean-time, the staff adopted a totally different life-style from that of the settlers. They received high salaries (monthly rates in excess of what was hoped for as an annual income for settlers), and elaborate housing was planned for them. As a result a rigid social stratifica-tion rapidly developed, to the extent that at one scheme near Lake Victoria the settlers called the staff the *Wakoloni*, "the co-lonialists," and at Bwakira Chini the area inhabited by the staff was known as *Uzunguni*, "the European area," though in both cases the staff was entirely African.

The original plans for the villages had envisioned that work would be done collectively. Because of recruitment problems every-where similar to those at Bwakira Chini, most settlers tended to be the least effective farmers in the country. (In Kenya the situation was completely different, since thousands of Africans were land-less; Tanzania in general has no shortage of land, though particu-larly favorable areas of soil and climate have some problems.) It seemed that only the hope of individual profit would provide adequate motivation to carry out all the tasks still needed when only the initial cultivation is done by tractor. Tractors are one of the great illusions of the developing countries. Unless they are used intensively every day for every task, the huge capital invest-ment is not justified. And if they are used intensively perhaps 80 to 90 percent of the people have nothing to do. They could, as in the West, move to the cities and work in factories, but Africa in general has neither cities nor factories.

At Bwakira Chini a compromise between collective and individual work was adopted. The 80 male settlers and their wives were divided into sixteen teams (five men and their wives in each). Where these teams reflected existing bonds of kinship or affinity, this solution worked fairly well; where there were no such bonds, tension developed over differing degrees of commitment to attendance and hard work. Ultimately feeling became so strong that a secret ballot was held over the division of work and profits. Teams of the former type remained as units; those of the latter type broke up. All settlers joining the scheme were supposed to have been selected from among the best farmers of their home areas by local chairmen of the nationalist party, membership of the party being a precondition for joining. In fact, no good farmer, in the plains anyway, wanted to leave his farm. Any person can join the party, but an entry fee deters many. It was found that most of the settlers had joined the party to be eligible for the scheme rather than because of political enthusiasm; indeed, one survey showed that their ignorance of the political structure of the country and of national figures other than Nyerere was almost total.

Plans for the women on the settlement scheme were nil. Each man who was chosen as a settler could only come if accompanied by a wife, rather as though a wife were a necessary piece of equipment. Fearing that they might lose their rights to land in the hills if they ceased using it, some of the Luguru men left their legal wives behind and picked up partners among the many divorcees living in Ukutu. In Uluguru there are always some unattached women around because of the frequency of divorce; in Ukutu, for various reasons, there are many more. Some of the women, too, like some of the Kutu men settlers, were more attracted by the idea of tractor cultivation and free food than by any great ideological commitment to village settlement *per se*, and therefore were not potentially the best material for a new venture. It was found that 23 of the 80 male settlers had brought common-law wives. Not all these women were just parasites along for the ride; many worked hard and were fine people.

The legal position of these women was what first alerted me to the generally poor position of women on the scheme. By traditional Kutu and Luguru law, when a couple divorced, the proceeds from any crops they had grown together were divided between them; where a couple were simply living together, no such guarantee protected the woman. On the schemes it was presumed that whatever local law and custom prescribed would be followed. It was quite possible for the settlers to pass a rule affecting the settlement scheme (providing it did not infringe territorial law), but such rules would have to be ratified by the Village Settlement Agency, the department of government that planned and supervised the schemes.

My awareness of the poor status of the women at Bwakira Chini was dramatically heightened when in early 1966 I was asked by the agency to visit another scheme in southern Tanzania that had been running for three years; called Kingurungundwa, this was one of the first of the pilot schemes. I went with an agricultural expert from the agency; he was to report on the farming, I on the social situation. Alarming reports had reached the agency that the women on the scheme were in a state of revolt. The problem had been diagnosed by the local agricultural extension officer, a Chagga (the Chagga are a strongly patrilineal people), as resulting from inadequate male control over women in a matrilineal area (Yao, Makonde, Mwera, Makua). My report to the government suggested that had I been a woman on this scheme I would have been leading the revolt. The women were bitterly disgruntled to find that they were incomparably worse off than they had been before they joined the scheme, when they had their own cashew nut orchards and other crops apart from those raised jointly with their husbands. Elsewhere in Tanzania, and in Africa as a whole, even where women have no direct rights in land, they do "hold small amounts of personal and domestic property in their own right," as Beattie observes (1964: 109), and this often allows them to obtain a certain amount of private pocket money. This parallels the situation in the American farm family, where the wife often keeps the cash obtained from the sale of eggs or other small items as her personal perquisite. For East African women the personal pocket money has come most often from the sale of eggs, vegetables, roots for medicines, or bananas. Even where women have rights in land (as in Uluguru and Ukutu), they still carry on this personal commerce. (For a further discussion of East African women as traders in a traditional economy, see Margaret Hay's paper on the Luo women of Kowe elsewhere in this volume.) The conclusion Gideon Sjoberg draws in his book *The Preindustrial City*—that women in the traditional rural society "have and had greater freedom and less differentiation by sex than [women] in the town" (1960: 170)— can be extended, albeit cautiously, to the village settlement schemes we are discussing. Though some of the problems of adjustment rural women face in cities are very different from those they face in such settlements as Bwakira Chini, the lack of opportunities to make personal pocket money is felt in both (see Southall 1961: 50, and McCall 1961: 286).

My experience at the Kingurungundwa scheme led me to look more closely at the women's situation at Bwakira Chini. Encouraged by the research team coordinator (the late Carol Fisher), I prepared a paper for presentation at a week-long seminar on settlement in East Africa held at the University of Dar es Salaam in April 1966, and jointly sponsored by that institution and Syracuse University (see Brain 1966). The meeting, officially opened by Tanzania's Vice President, was attended not only by faculty members but by many senior African civil servants. Since the University of Dar es Salaam is under the aegis of the government (all tuition is free and students are directed to jobs on graduation), the faculty members and civil servants together represented, as a group, the new ruling elite. The discussant for my paper was the then Commissioner for Community Development, but he was unable to attend and sent a set of prepared remarks that were read by his deputy, who clearly endorsed their sentiments, as did the audience—with two exceptions. (The exceptions were representatives of the Ruvuma Development Association, about which I shall speak below.) When considering the discomfort occasioned by the views I expressed, it is worth recalling that most of the audience (including the absent Commissioner) were old friends and colleagues.

The paper was read without interruption, as were the Commissioner's comments, and afterwards there was an acrimonious discussion. For my present purpose I shall take each point and the response to it. I hope to show that the sentiments of the relatively uneducated and unsophisticated male settlers were far more in accord with the views of President Nyerere regarding justice for women than were those of the ruling elite, who in rejecting colonial rule have nevertheless retained attitudes about appropriate sex roles not very different from those found in bourgeois Victorian England.

The question of the common-law wives was discussed with the settlers, who saw the injustice and suggested that a rule might be instituted compelling a man to share the proceeds of the harvest with his partner if they separated. On the one hand, the Commissioner responded that no rule was needed since most people would behave decently and split the proceeds anyway (though the settlers thought not); on the other hand, he took a puritanical stand about the morals of the unmarried spouses, noting that "only legal wives should accompany their settler husbands. Those not legally married accompany men at their own risk, and I see no reason why such women should claim part of the man's income." The audience evidently sympathized with this harsh view and remarks were passed about "good-time girls" (a phenomenon common enough in the city and publicly deplored while privately exploited by many of the elite). Whatever the original motivation may have been for some of these women, the element of "good time" involved in a settlement scheme of this nature was thin indeed, but I found it impossible to get this point across. It is necessary to realize that few if any of the audience had at that time ever visited any settlement scheme; certainly no one ever visited Bwakira Chini. To get there required a drive of seven to nine hours (two hours for 100 miles of paved road and five to seven for 65 miles of an appalling dirt road), and the climate and disease factor make it an area from which most people try to stay away (see Burton 1860: 127, 156).

It seemed to me that legal wives, too, were clearly worse off in a settlement than they had been in traditional Luguru and Kutu society: we have seen the considerable rights in land women held in Uluguru and Ukutu; by contrast, they had no rights whatsoever in the settlements. All rights in land were vested in the husband, and, as a corollary, all proceeds were handed over to him. It would have been theoretically possible for a woman to retain her rights in land outside the scheme, but for most Luguru women, in particular, this would have been difficult. Luguru custom dictates that a person must cultivate his or her land or forfeit it; moreover, a person cannot hire labor to work the land in his or her absence, for the Luguru do not sanction the hiring of kinsmen, and virtually everyone in a particular area of Uluguru is related in some fashion. Some Kutu women might have been able to retain their rights to land because the hiring of labor has become common in Ukutu. Also, Bwakira Chini is located in Ukutu, so that Kutu women could supervise their land if it was not too distant. With the promulgation of the Arusha Declaration (a statement of Tanzania's socialist ideology) the following year, such hiring would have become illegal.

I had discussed this question and that of the lack of opportunity to obtain even pocket money with the older and most responsible settlers at Bwakira Chini. It seemed to me that the women there, like those at Kingurungundwa, might well revolt against the imposed condition of virtual serfdom once a year or so had passed and their condition become apparent to them. Struggling with my inclinations, I had not discussed it with the women. The men rapidly recognized the injustice and proposed a number of solutions. After a week had passed I carried out a survey of opinions among the men. Fifty-seven of the 75 men I polled felt that each woman should statutorily receive at least 10 percent of any profits made as her personal property. Three men felt that the women of the settlement should have a field to cultivate collectively, though they were unable to say how the women would find time to work such a field. Five men suggested that a (small) part of each settler's holding should be apportioned to his wife. Two simply felt that the government should issue some order on the subject. Only eight men believed that there was no need for any special arrangement in this matter, and they based their opinions on the Christian principle that because a man and his wife are one flesh, a man is bound to give his wife a fair share.

The fact that 89 percent of the settlers recognized that a problem existed, and that a large majority opted for a statutory amount to be given to women, was in marked contrast to the views of the elite audience at the meeting. The Commissioner wrote: "Might not some new rules set up by the authorities cause discontent among the people because they bring to the forefront problems which they would not have thought so important? Women may demand their new rights, and this would disrupt the relationship between husbands and wives." Many of the comments of the audience implied that even bringing the issue to the attention of the settlers constituted what in other contexts might be termed "dangerous agitation." The notion that any women should be legally entitled to a share of any income appeared to be particularly threatening to the audience.

Another aspect of the women's role on the settlement schemes was raised in the seminar with totally negative results. This was the question of the relative availability of men and women for work. In all the planning for the village settlements, it was assumed that a man and his wife equaled two working units for farm labor. One might question why this should not be so, since traditionally African women performed the majority of the farm work. What this position ignores is that there is a vast difference between carrying out the necessary tasks merely for subsistence and growing not only the food but also large quantities of crops for cash sale. Whereas the men were only expected to carry out farm work, the women were also expected to cook, keep the house and its surroundings clean, care for the children, pound corn for an hour or two daily, fetch water from the creek (which ran about a quarter of a mile from the nearest houses and almost a mile from the farthest), and cut and fetch firewood from the bush at least once a week. The audience, like the planners, knowing that African women were the traditional field workers, could not see why the women were unable to carry out an eight-hour working day in the fields. One logical way to make women and men equal in farm tasks is seen on an Israeli kibbutz, where all the burden of cooking and child rearing is removed from the mother; but such a solution would have been too radical in the circumstances of Bwakira Chini. I did suggest introducing day-care centers to relieve settlement women of part of their burden, and further suggested that they might well be run by the wives of the staff members, who were then living in a style only comparable to that of the colonial wives. (It said a lot for the humility of the settlers' wives that one rarely heard from them any overt criticism of the position of the staff members' wives—probably because they did not yet realize that they were supporting these superior mortals.) In fact, I pointed out that a settlement scheme bore a marked resemblance to a feudal manor, with the manager acting as the lord, his staff as the gentry (not soiling their hands with manual toil), the wives of the staff as the noble ladies (idling away the hours in gossip), and the settlers as the ignorant peasants in the fields.

My comments were ill received. The feelings were well represented by the Commissioner's comments. "Why limit the development of a group of people who have risen a bit above the others? Should everyone stay along with everyone else without trying to better herself? Is it improper to take care of oneself, individually, first? This in turn will help the community." This attitude is in curious contrast to the views of Nyerere expressed the following year in his essay on socialism and rural development. Writing of villages under a socialist system, he notes that "the essential element in them would be equality of all members of the community, and the members' self-government in all matters which concerned only their own affairs. For a really socialist village would elect its own officials and they would remain equal members with the others, subject always to the wishes of the people" (Nyerere 1967: 18).

Another feature of the settlement schemes that showed a dis-

regard for the rights of women involved the question of inheritance. Though in most Tanzanian societies women rarely had
rights in heritable land, even in patrilineal societies women were
allocated land to use by their husbands' groups. (Land is rarely
owned by individuals; it is controlled by a descent group and allocated to its male members, who retain rights in it while they continue to use it, and who may pass it on to their male heirs.) A
woman whose husband died could take advantage of the levirate—
by which one of her deceased husband's brothers would take her as
one of his wives—and continue to use the same land, or she could
return to her own people (though if she did this the bridewealth
payment would have to be returned). If she returned to her people
she might marry again; alternatively, she might stay with her own
people and work land allocated to her by her father's group.
Among the Luguru and Kutu, as we have seen, women actually
have rights in land unaffected by marriage, so that if a woman
divorces her husband or if he dies, her position is little changed in
an economic sense. The government scheme, presumably based on
the patrilineal notion that women are given land by their husbands, made no provision at all in the event of the husband's death.
Under the legislation establishing the village settlement program,
a man had to nominate an heir to his land. Precisely who this
would be was rather fuzzy, but it was generally presumed that it
would be the settler's son or sons. The actual nomination of heirs
had not taken place at the time I was there, but I conducted a survey among the male settlers that revealed great confusion, some
saying the sister's son, some the son. No provision, however, was
made for the wife. In traditional society, as we have seen, the death
of a husband would not have been a matter of great crisis; in the
settlements it might well be, for many women would have lost their
traditional rights to land in their areas of origin. This would be
particularly true for the Luguru women since land is very scarce.
Another related problem that could have occurred (though one
year was not long enough to test this) affected the Luguru. As I
have shown elsewhere (Brain 1969), it is common for a couple to
separate when their son has married; after he has produced an heir

for his wife's group, he is allowed to exercise the "delayed right of bride removal," whereby he takes his wife to live at his maternal uncle's hamlet. At this point his mother, now an honored grandmother, moves to the same place, so that she and her brother are once more together, as well as her brother's heir—her son. No one had worked out how this system could possibly operate were everyone living on a settlement scheme based on patrilineal descent. During the year I spent at Bwakira Chini two settlers died—both young men, both of tetanus, unnecessarily and agonizingly—and in neither case was there a son old enough to take over. It was assumed in each case that the woman would leave the scheme and go home. The idea that she might work the land alone, or, even more radically, recruit a man as the men were expected to recruit women, was not entertained. In fact, in the second case, the woman was allowed to remain because a brother of her deceased husband took over both the land and her. Yet it is quite easy to imagine a situation where a widow pushed off a settlement and sent back to her home area might find it difficult to sustain a claim to land because of her long absence.

The reaction of the Commissioner to this section of my paper—a reaction heartily endorsed by the audience—was this: "Why does a woman on a Settlement need any more safeguards than her counterpart who is not on a Settlement? . . . Are there safeguards for wives of farmers in other countries? If women consider that they are not getting their full rights, they, themselves, will quickly demand them, as the suffragettes demanded the vote in England." I hope that it has been made clear that the situation of the wives on the settlement scheme was in no way comparable to that of the wives of farmers. Moreover, when at Kingurungundwa the women had demanded their rights, the response of the government had hardly been encouraging and the scheme was closed shortly afterwards.

As a contrast to the situation on the government schemes, in July 1966 I spent two weeks at a village in southern Tanzania that was one of a group of eleven based entirely on local initiative and receiving no financial or supervisory assistance. They were known as the Ruvuma Development Association. To join one of these villages a person had to undergo a probationary period of six months. The villages were recognizable as such: a main street with neatly constructed houses under shade trees, a community center, and an office. The people involved were the patrilineal Ngoni. For generations their family life had been disrupted by a pattern of migrant labor for the men, and they had determined to build a better life at home. Here was found exactly what Nyerere had always envisaged and what he later described in his writings. There was a close resemblance to the early kibbutzim, and the spirit was much the same as I saw on a kibbutz I visited in 1946. The results in productivity and general atmosphere were startlingly different from those in the staff-managed and heavily capitalized government settlements. In spite of the fact that the Ngoni were a patrilineal people who traditionally demanded a high degree of subservience from their women, in these new villages every effort was made to involve the women in decision-making, all profits were to be divided exactly equally between all the settlers regardless of age or sex, and, most surprising of all, women were allowed to go to the fields at eight and return at noon. Men went at seven and returned at three or four. The point was that domestic work was understood to be just as much work as field work, and just as important to the effective running of a village. All offices were filled by election and could only be held for a year at a time. On the government schemes only youthful men were permitted to join; here one found even old men and women and one or two cripples. Each person did what he or she was capable of doing.

On my return from this visit a seminar was organized at Kivukoni College, the training center for political leaders operated by the nationalist party, TANU (Tanzania African National Union), at which I read a report on these villages. This audience of young, radical men and women was extremely receptive to my report, and interested and in agreement with the contrasts I made with the government-sponsored villages. I was told that President Nyerere was very pleased with the report, as he had taken a personal interest in the villages since their inception. I was unable to interest any of the previous audience at the university in the villages; their attitude to them was one of skepticism and even derision. That their attitude was totally at variance with the perceptions of Nyerere is clear from the following quote from his *Socialism and Rural Development*, published the next year. He writes of the inferior position assigned to women in traditional society and notes that "It is impossible to deny that the women did, and still do, more than their fair share of the work in the fields and in the homes. . . . If we want our country to make full and quick progress now, it is essential that our women live in terms of full equality with their fellow citizens who are men" (Nyerere 1967: 3). Some three years later it was distressing to hear that the cooperative association that was formed from these villages had been declared a subversive organization and ordered to disband. It is known that Nyerere tried to intervene personally, but could not overcome the opposition of the local party officials, who perceived the villages as a threat to their authority. The threat is very hard to see; could it have been that women were accorded equality with men? ·

In 1967 Tanzania committed itself to a fully socialist economy in the Arusha Declaration. One of the new policies concerned villages. It was now proposed to abandon completely the original village settlement plans, partially at least as a result of the reports of the Syracuse research team (see Richards 1969). Instead it was planned that encouragement should everywhere be given to people to form their own villages without expert supervision and without capital input. The idea and ideal was to establish villages, rather like the ones described above, that would be called *Ujamaa* villages. *Ujamaa*, it will be recalled, is the term used to translate "African Socialism."

It has been very hard to obtain accurate information about the *Ujamaa* villages. The government discourages outside visitors. The Political Science Department at the University of Dar es Salaam produced a small booklet about the villages containing various essays, some adulatory but most critical of details of organization. A 1973 report in *Africa Digest* claimed that since 1967 over two million people have moved into the villages, and subsequent reports have stated that it is the aim of the government to have everyone living in a *Ujamaa* village by 1976. The reports I have read speak of agriculture, schools, clean water, and so on, but so far nothing whatever has been said about women and their status.

It will be interesting to see whether the ideas of Nyerere, which are acceptable to the ordinary villagers, can overcome the resistance of his own ruling elite.

Reference Matter

References Cited

Hafkin and Bay: Introduction

Afigbo, A. E. 1972. The Warrant Chiefs: Indirect Rule in South-Eastern Nigeria, 1891–1929. London.

Boserup, Ester. 1970. Woman's Role in Economic Development. New York.

Brown, Beverly Bolser. 1975. Review of Kenneth Little, African Women in Towns, in *ASA Review of Books*, 1, no. 1.

Clignet, Remi. 1970. Many Wives, Many Powers. Evanston, Ill.

Diner, Helen. 1963. Mothers and Amazons. New York.

Elam, Yitzchak. 1973. The Social and Sexual Roles of Hima Women. Manchester, Eng.

Evans-Pritchard, E. E. 1965. The Position of Women in Primitive Societies and Other Essays in Social Anthropology. London.

———. 1974. Man and Woman Among the Azande. New York.

Forbes, Frederick E. 1966. Dahomey and the Dahomans. London. Originally published in 1851.

Hardy, Georges. 1939. "Préface," in Marie-André du Sacré-Coeur, La Femme noire en Afrique occidentale. Paris.

Hoffer, Carol. 1974. "Madam Yoko: Ruler of the Kpa Mende Confederacy," in M. Z. Rosaldo and Louise Lamphere, eds., Woman, Culture, and Society. Stanford, Calif.

Kenyatta, Jomo. 1938. Facing Mount Kenya. London.

Krige, E. J., and J. D. Krige. 1943. The Realm of a Rain-Queen. Oxford.

Lebeuf, Annie M. D. 1963. "The Role of Women in the Political Organization of African Societies," in Denise Paulme, ed., Women of Tropical Africa. Berkeley, Calif.

Little, Kenneth. 1973. African Women in Towns. London.

Ngugi, James. 1967. A Grain of Wheat. New York.

Paulme, Denise, ed. 1960. Femmes d'Afrique noire. Paris.

———. 1963. Women of Tropical Africa. Berkeley, Calif.

Rattray, R. S. 1923. Ashanti. Kumasi, Ghana.

Rogers, J. A. 1972. Great Men of Color. Vol. 1. New York.

286 *References Cited*

Rosaldo, M. Z. 1974. "Woman, Culture, and Society: A Theoretical Overview," in M. Z. Rosaldo and Louise Lamphere, eds., Woman, Culture, and Society. Stanford, Calif.

Brooks: Signares of Saint-Louis and Gorée

Ames, D. W. 1956. "The Selection of Mates, Courtship, and Marriage among the Wolof," *Bulletin d'Institut Français d'Afrique Noire*, 18, nos. 1–2.
Angrand, Armand-Pierre. 1946. Les Lébous de la presque'île du Cap-Vert. Dakar, Senegal.
Bennett, Norman R., and George E. Brooks, Jr., eds. 1965. New England Merchants in Africa. Boston.
Bird, Charles S. 1971. "Oral Art in the Mande," in Carleton T. Hodge, ed., Papers on the Manding. New York.
Brooks, George E., Jr. 1970. "Enoch Richmond Ware, African Trader: 1839–1850, Years of Apprenticeship," *The American Neptune*, 30, nos. 3–4.
Cariou, Pierre. n.d. "Promenade à Gorée." Unpublished manuscript.
———. 1950. "La Rivale inconnue de Madame de Sabran dans l'Ile de Gorée," *Notes Africaines*, 45.
———. 1952. "Costumes d'autrefois à Gorée," *France Outre-Mer*, 270.
Delcourt, André. 1952. La France et les établissements français au Sénégal entre 1713 et 1963. Dakar, Senegal.
Demanet, Abbé. 1767. Nouvelle histoire de l'Afrique Française. Paris.
Dodwell, H. 1916. "Le Sénégal sous la domination anglaise," *Revue de l'Histoire des Colonies Françaises*, 4.
Galloway, Winifred F. 1974. "A History of Wuli from the Fourteenth to the Nineteenth Century." Unpublished Ph.D. dissertation, Indiana University.
Gamble, David P. 1967. The Wolof of Senegambia. London.
Hargreaves, John D., ed. 1969. France and West Africa: An Anthology of Historical Documents. London.
Knight-Baylac, Marie-Hélène. 1970a. "Gorée et 'La Petite Côte': Origines et développement; Les relations commerciales avec les pays du sud (jusqu'au Rio Grande), 1677–1789." Unpublished *mémoire*, Université de Paris-Sorbonne, Centre d'Etudes Africains.
———. 1970b. "La Vie à Gorée de 1677 à 1789," *Revue Française d'Histoire d'Outre-Mer*, 57.
Labarthe, Pierre. 1802. Voyage au Sénégal, pendant les années 1784–1785, d'après les mémoires de Lajaille. Paris.
Lamiral, Dominique Harcourt. 1789. L'Affrique et le peuple Affriquain. Paris.
Lindsay, John. 1759. A Voyage to the Coast of Africa in 1758. London.
Machat, J. 1906. Documents sur les etablissements français de l'Afrique Occidentale au xviiie siècle. Paris.

Martin, Eveline C. 1927. The British West African Settlements, 1750–1821. London.

Nardin, Jean-Claude. 1966. "Recherches sur les 'gourmets' d'Afrique Occidentale," *Revue de l'Histoire des Colonies Françaises*, 53.

Pelletan, [?]. 1800. Mémoire sur la colonie française du Sénégal. Paris.

Prélong, [?]. 1793. "Mémoire sur les Iles de Gorée et du Sénégal," *Annales de Chimie*, 18.

Pruneau de Pommegorge, Antoine Edmé. 1789. Description de la Négritie. Amsterdam.

Rodney, Walter. 1970. A History of the Upper Guinea Coast, 1545 to 1800. London.

Villeneuve, René Claude Geoffroy de. 1814. L'Afrique, ou histoire, moeurs, usages, et coutumes des Africains. Paris.

Okonjo: Igbo Women and Community Politics

Afigbo, A. E. 1972. The Warrant Chiefs: Indirect Rule in South-Eastern Nigeria, 1891–1929. London.

———. 1974. "Women in Nigerian History." Unpublished paper.

Basden, G. T. 1966. Niger Ibos. London.

Biobaku, S. O. 1960. "Madam Tinubu," in Prominent Nigerians of the Nineteenth Century. Cambridge, Eng.

Egharevba, Jacob. 1960. A Short History of Benin. Ibadan, Nigeria.

Green, Margaret M. 1964. Igbo Village Affairs. London.

Henderson, Richard N. 1972. The King in Every Man. Evolutionary Trends in Onitsha Ibo Society and Culture. New Haven, Conn.

Lebeuf, Annie. 1963. "The Role of Women in the Political Organization of African Societies," in Denise Paulme, ed., Women of Tropical Africa. Berkeley, Calif.

Leith-Ross, Sylvia. 1939; 2d ed., 1965. African Women: A Study of the Ibo of Nigeria. London.

Okonjo, Kamene. 1974. "Political Systems with Bisexual Functional Roles —The Case of Women's Participation in Politics in Nigeria." Paper presented at the Annual Meeting of the American Political Science Association, Chicago.

———. 1975. "The Institution of *Omu* Among the Igbos of Southeastern Nigeria Living West of the River Niger." Paper presented at the Canadian African Studies Association Conference, Toronto.

Paulme, Denise, ed. 1963. Women of Tropical Africa. Berkeley, Calif.

Thomas, Northcote W. 1914. Anthropological Report on the Ibo-Speaking Peoples of Nigeria. London.

Van Allen: 'Aba Riots' or Igbo 'Women's War'?

Adler, Renate. 1969. "Letter from Biafra," *The New Yorker*, Oct. 4.

Afigbo, A. E. 1972. The Warrant Chiefs: Indirect Rule in South-Eastern Nigeria, 1891–1929. London.

Ajayi, J. F. Ade. 1965. Christian Missions in Nigeria, 1841–1891: The Making of a New Elite. Evanston, Ill.

Akpan, Ntieyong U. 1971. The Struggle for Secession, 1966–1970. London.

Anene, J. C. 1967. Southern Nigeria in Transition, 1885–1906. New York.

Basden, G. T. 1927. Edith Warner of the Niger. London.

Boserup, Ester. 1970. Woman's Role in Economic Development. New York.

Bretton, Henry L. 1966. "Political Influence in Southern Nigeria," in Herbert J. Spiro, ed., Africa: The Primacy of Politics. New York.

Bulifant, Josephine C. 1950. Forty Years in the African Bush. Grand Rapids, Mich.

Crocker, W. R. 1936. Nigeria: A Critique of British Colonial Administration. London.

Dike, K. Onwuka. 1956. Trade and Politics in the Niger Delta, 1830–1885. London.

Esike, S. O. 1965. "The Aba Riots of 1929," *African Historian* (Ibadan), 1, no. 3.

Fallers, Lloyd Ashton. 1963. "Political Sociology and the Anthropological Study of African Politics," *Archives Européennes de Sociologie*.

Forde, Daryll, and G. I. Jones. 1950. The Ibo- and Ibibio-Speaking Peoples of South-Eastern Nigeria. London.

Gailey, Harry A. 1970. The Road to Aba, New York.

Green, M. M. 1947. Igbo Village Affairs. London.

Gwynn, Stephen. 1932. The Life of Mary Kingsley. London.

Harris, J. S. 1940. "The Position of Women in a Nigerian Society," *Transactions of the New York Academy of Sciences*. New York.

Jones, G. I. 1963. The Trading States of the Oil Rivers. London.

Kingsley, Mary H. 1897. Travels in West Africa. London.

Leith-Ross, Sylvia. 1939. African Women: A Study of the Ibo of Nigeria. London.

Little, Kenneth. 1973. African Women in Towns. London.

Livingstone, W. P. n.d. Mary Slessor of Calabar. New York.

MacIntosh, John P., ed. 1966. Nigerian Government and Politics. London.

Maxwell, J. Lowry. 1926. Nigeria: The Land, the People and Christian Progress. London.

Meek, C. K. 1957. Law and Authority in a Nigerian Tribe. London.

Mintz, Sidney W. 1971. "Men, Women, and Trade," *Comparative Studies in Society and History*, 13.

Nwoga, D. I. 1971. "The Concept and Practice of Satire among the Igbo," *Conch*, 3, no. 2.

Nzirimo, Ikenna. 1972. Studies in Ibo Political Systems: Chieftaincy and Politics in Four Niger States. Berkeley, Calif.

Ojukwu, C. Odumegwu. 1969. Biafra. New York.

Okonjo, Kamene, 1974. "Political Systems with Bisexual Functional Roles—The Case of Women's Participation in Politics in Nigeria."

Paper presented at the Annual Meeting of the American Political Science Association, Chicago.

Olisa, Michael S. O. 1971. "Political Culture and Political Stability in Traditional Igbo Society," *Conch*, 3, no. 2.

Onwuteaka, J. C. 1965. "The Aba Riot of 1929 and Its Relation to the System of 'Indirect Rule,' " *The Nigerian Journal of Economic and Social Studies*, November.

Ottenberg, Phoebe V. 1959. "The Changing Economic Position of Women Among the Afikpo Ibo," in W. R. Bascom and M. J. Herskovits, eds., Continuity and Change in African Cultures. Chicago.

———. 1965. "The Afikpo Ibo of Eastern Nigeria," in James L. Gibbs, Jr., ed., Peoples of Africa. New York.

Ottenberg, Simon. 1959. "Ibo Receptivity to Change," in W. R. Bascom and M. J. Herskovits, eds., Continuity and Change in African Cultures. Chicago.

Perham, Margery. 1937. Native Administration in Nigeria. London.

———. 1960. Lugard: The Years of Authority, 1898–1945. London.

Peters, Helen. 1971. "Reflections on the Preservation of Igbo Folk Literature," *Conch*, 3, no. 2.

Pool, Janet E. 1972. "A Cross-Comparative Study of Aspects of Conjugal Behavior Among Women of Three West African Countries," *Canadian Journal of African Studies*, 6, no. 2.

Sanday, Peggy R. 1973. "Toward a Theory of the Status of Women," *American Anthropologist*, 75, no. 5.

Schaar, John H. 1970. "Legitimacy in the Modern State," in Philip Green and Sanford Levinson, eds., Power and Community. New York.

Sklar, Richard. 1963. Nigerian Political Parties. Princeton, N.J.

Uchendu, Victor C. 1965. The Igbo of Southeast Nigeria. New York.

United Nations Economic and Social Council (UNESCO). 1968. "Problems of Plan Implementation: Development Planning and Economic Integration in Africa."

Uzoma, Chinwe. 1974. "The Role of Women in the Nigerian/Biafran Civil War as Seen Through My Experiences Then." Unpublished personal communication to Judith Van Allen.

Van Allen, Judith. 1972. " 'Sitting on a Man': Colonialism and the Lost Political Institutions of Igbo Women," *Canadian Journal of African Studies*, 6, no. 2.

———. 1974a. "African Women—Modernizing into Dependence?" Paper presented at the conference on "Social and Political Change: The Role of Women," sponsored by the University of California, Santa Barbara, and the Center for the Study of Democratic Institutions.

———. 1974b. "From Aba to Biafra: Women's Associations and Political Power in Eastern Nigeria." Paper presented at the UCLA African Studies Center Colloquium on Women and Change in Africa, 1870–1970.

———. 1974c. "*Memsahib, Militante, Femme Libre*: Political and Apolitical Styles of African Women," in Jane Jaquette, ed., Women in Politics. New York.

Wood, A. H. St. John. 1960. "Nigeria: Fifty Years of Political Development among the Ibos," in Raymond Apthorpe, ed., From Tribal Rule to Modern Government. Lusaka, Northern Rhodesia.

Hay: Luo Women and Economic Change

Brett, E. A. 1973. Colonialism and Underdevelopment in East Africa. London.
Douglas, Mary. 1966. Purity and Danger. London.
Hay, Margaret Jean. 1972. "Economic Change in Luoland: Kowe, 1890–1945." Ph.D. dissertation, University of Wisconsin.
Hopkins, A. G. 1974. "Toward a Theory of Innovation in a Colonial Context: African Entrepreneurs in Lagos, 1851–1921." Paper presented to the 1974 summer workshop in African economic history at Madison, Wisc.
Leys, Colin. 1975. Underdevelopment in Kenya. Berkeley, Calif.
Mboya, Paul. 1938. Luo Kitgi gi Timbegi. Nairobi, Kenya.
Ogot, Bethwell A. 1967. A History of the Southern Luo Peoples, 1500–1900. Vol. 1. Nairobi, Kenya.
O'Laughlin, Bridget. 1974. "Mediating Contradiction: Why Mbum Women Do Not Eat Chicken," in M. Z. Rosaldo and Louise Lamphere, eds., Woman, Culture, and Society. Stanford, Calif.
Richards, C. G. 1956. Fifty Years in Nyanza—The Story of the C.M.S. Maseno, Kenya.
Whisson, Michael. 1961. "The Rise of Asembo and the Curse of Kakia," East African Institute of Social Research Conference Paper. Kampala, Uganda.
Wolff, Richard. 1974. The Economics of Colonialism: Britain and Kenya, 1870–1930. New Haven, Conn.
Wrigley, C. C. 1965. "Kenya: The Patterns of Economic Life, 1902–45," in Vincent Harlow and E. M. Chilver, eds., History of East Africa, vol. 2. Oxford.

Robertson: Ga Women and Socioeconomic Change

Acquah, Ione. 1958. Accra Survey. London.
Amoah, F. E. K. 1964. "Accra: A Study of the Development of a West African City." M.A. thesis, Institute of African Studies, University of Ghana.
Azu, G. A. M. 1966. "The Impact of the Modern Fishing Industry on the Ga Traditional Fishing Industry." M.A. thesis, Institute of African Studies, University of Ghana.
Boserup, Ester. 1970. Woman's Role in Economic Development. London.
Caldwell, John C. 1968. Population Growth and Family Change in Africa. Canberra, Australia.
Cruickshank, Brodie. 1853. Eighteen Years on the Gold Coast of Africa. London.
Daniell, W. F. 1856. "On the Ethnography of Akkrah and Adampe Gold Coast, West Africa," Journal of the Ethnological Society of London, 4.

Debrunner, H. n.d. "The Church of Christ at Accra Before 1917," unpublished manuscript, Basel Mission Papers. Ghana National Archives, EC 7/19, 2, 6.

De Marees, Peter. 1600. "A Description and Historical Declaration of the Golden Kingdome of Guinea," in Hakluytus Posthumus or Purchas his Pilgrims, ed. S. Purchas, trans. G. A. Dantisc. New York, 1965.

Dickson, Kwamina. 1969. A Historical Geography of Ghana. London.

Field, M. J. 1940. The Social Organization of the Ga People. London.

Hajnal, J. 1965. "European Marriage Patterns in Perspective," in D. Glass and D. E. C. Eversley, eds., Population in History. London.

Kilson, Marion. 1966. "Urban Tribesmen: Social Continuity and Change Among the Ga in Accra, Ghana." Ph.D. dissertation, Harvard University.

Little, Kenneth. 1973. African Women in Towns. London.

Manoukian, Madeline. 1950. Akan and Ga-Adangme Peoples, in D. Forde, ed., Ethnographic Survey of Africa, West Africa, Part I. London.

McCall, Daniel. 1962. "The Koforidua Market," in P. Bohannan and G. Dalton, eds., Markets in Africa. Evanston, Ill.

Mills-Odoi, D. G. 1967. "The La Family and Social Change." M.A. thesis, Institute of African Studies, University of Ghana.

Nypan, Astrid. 1960. Market Trade: A Sample Survey of Market Traders in Accra. Accra, Ghana.

Ozanne, Paul. 1962. "Notes on the Early Historic Archaeology of Accra," Transactions of the Historical Society of Ghana, 6.

Robertson, Claire. 1974. "Economic Woman in Africa: Profit-Making Techniques of Ga Market Women," Journal of Modern African Studies, 12, no. 4.

——. "The Impact of Education on Ga Women," Africa, forthcoming.

Sai, F. A. 1971. "The Market Woman in the Economy of Ghana." Unpublished M.S. thesis, Cornell University, Ithaca, N.Y.

Wolfson, F. 1958. Pageant of Ghana. London.

Lewis: The Market Women of Abidjan

Ardener, Shirley. 1964. "A Comparative Study of Rotating Credit Associations," Journal of the Royal Anthropological Institute, 94, no. 2 (July–Dec.).

Geertz, Clifford. 1966. "The Rotating Credit Association: A 'Middle Rung' in Development," in I. M. Wallerstein, ed., Social Change: The Colonial Situation. New York.

Lewis, Barbara C. 1971. "The Dioula in the Ivory Coast," in Carleton T. Hodge, ed., Papers on the Manding. Bloomington, Ind.

Olsen, Mancur. 1968. The Logic of Collective Action. New York.

Wolin, Sheldon. 1960. The Politics of Vision. Boston.

Berger: Rebels or Status-Seekers?

Albert, Ethel M. 1963. "Women of Burundi: A Study of Social Values," in Denise Paulme, ed., Women of Tropical Africa. Berkeley, Calif.

Ardener, Edwin. 1972. "Belief and the Problem of Women," in J. S. La Fontaine, ed., The Interpretation of Ritual: Essays in Honour of A. I. Richards. London.

Arnoux, Alex. 1912. "Le Culte de la société secrète des Imandwa au Rwanda," *Anthropos*, 7.

Bamunoba, Y. K. 1965. "Diviners for the Abagabe," *Uganda Journal*, 29, no. 1.

————, and F. B. Welbourne. 1965. "Emandwa Initiation in Ankole," *Uganda Journal*, 29, no. 1.

Beattie, John. 1957. "Initiation into the Cwezi Spirit Possession Cult in Bunyoro," *African Studies*, 16, no. 3.

————. 1961. "Group Aspects of the Nyoro Spirit Mediumship Cult," *Human Problems in British Central Africa*, 30.

————. 1964. "The Ghost Cult in Bunyoro," *Ethnology*, 3, no. 2.

————. 1969. "Spirit Mediumship in Bunyoro," in Beattie and Middleton, eds.

————, and J. Middleton, eds. 1969. Spirit Mediumship and Society. London.

Berger, Iris. 1973. "The *Kubandwa* Religious Complex of Interlacustrine East Africa: An Historical Study, ca. 1500–1800." Unpublished Ph.D. dissertation, University of Wisconsin.

Bessell, M. J. 1938. "Nyabingi," *Uganda Journal*, 6, no. 2.

Bösch, Fridolin. 1930. Les Banyamwezi. Münster, Germany.

Colle, P. 1937. "Essai de Monographie des Bashi." Mimeo. Kivu, Belgian Congo.

Cory, H. 1955. "The Buswezi," *American Anthropologist*, 57, no. 5.

Coupez, A. 1956. "Deux textes rwanda: initiation au culte de Ryangombe," *Kongo-Overzee*, 22, nos. 2–3.

Curley, Richard T. 1973. Elders, Shades, and Women. Berkeley, Calif.

Des Forges, Alison. 1972. "Defeat is the Only Bad News." Unpublished Ph.D. dissertation, Yale University.

Edel, May M. 1957. The Chiga of Western Uganda. London.

Elam, Yitzchak. 1973. The Social and Sexual Roles of Hima Women. Manchester, Eng.

Firth, Raymond. 1950. "Problem and Assumption in an Anthropological Study of Religion," *Journal of the Royal Anthropological Institute*, 89, no. 2.

Gorju, Julien, et al. 1938. Face au royaume hamite du Ruanda: le royaume frère de l'Urundi. Brussels.

Grant, James. 1864. A Walk Across Africa. London.

Gray, J. M. 1960. "A History of Ibanda, Saza of Mitoma, Ankole," *Uganda Journal*, 24, no. 2.

Horton, Robin. 1969. "Types of Spirit Possession in Kalabari Region," in Beattie and Middleton, eds.

Kagame, A. 1967. "Description du culte rendu aux trépassés du Rwanda," from the *Bulletin des Séances* of the Académie Royale des Sciences d'Outre Mer (Belgium).

Lee, S. G. 1969. "Spirit Possession Among the Zulu," in Beattie and Middleton, eds.

Lewin, H. B. 1908. "Mount Mubende, Bwekula," *Uganda Notes*, 9, no. 6.

Lewis, I. M. 1971. Ecstatic Religion: An Anthropological Study of Spirit Possession and Shamanism. Harmondsworth, Eng.

Lubogo, Y. K. 1960. A History of Busoga. Kampala, Uganda.

Millroth, Berta. 1965. Lyuba: Traditional Religion of the Sukuma. Uppsala, Sweden.

Nyakatura, J. W. 1970. "The Customs of Kitara in the Old Days." Trans. J. D. Besisira. Unpublished handwritten manuscript. Kampala, Uganda.

Roberts, Andrew. 1970. "Nyamwezi Trade," in Richard Gray and David Birmingham, eds., Pre-Colonial African Trade. London.

Rodegem, F. M. 1970. Dictionnaire Rundi-Français. Tervuren, Belgium.

———. 1971. "La Motivation du culte initiatique au Burundi," *Anthropos*, 66.

Rwandusya, Zakayo. 1972. "The Origin and Settlement of People of Bufumbira," in Donald Denoon, ed., A History of Kigezi in Southwest Uganda. Kampala, Uganda.

Scherer, J. H. 1959. "The Ha of Tanganyika," *Anthropos*, 54, nos. 5–6.

Schweinfurth, G., et al. 1888. Emin Pasha in Central Africa: Being a Collection of His Letters and Journals. London.

Southall, Aidan. 1969. "Spirit Possession and Mediumship Among the Alur," in Beattie and Middleton, eds.

Speke, John. 1863. Journal of the Discovery of the Sources of the Nile. Edinburgh.

Stenning, Derrick. 1959. "Ecology and Social Structure." Paper presented at the Annual Meeting of the Association of Social Anthropologists.

Taylor, Brian K. 1957. "The Social Structure of the Batoro." Unpublished M.A. thesis, University of London.

Turner, Victor W. 1969. The Ritual Process. Harmondsworth, Eng.

Van Sambeek, J. 1949. "Croyances et coutumes des Baha." Mimeo. Kabanga, Belgian Congo.

Viaene, L. 1952. "La Religion des Bahunde (Kivu)," *Kongo-Overzee*, 18, no. 4.

Williams, Lukyn. 1937. "The Inauguration of the Omugabe of Ankole to Office," *Uganda Journal*, 4, no. 4.

Wilson, Peter J. 1967. "Status Ambiguity and Spirit Possession," *Man*, n.s. 2, no. 3: 366–78.

Zuure, Bernard. 1929. Croyances et pratiques religieuses des Barundi. Brussels.

Strobel: From Lelemama to Lobbying

Berg, F. J. 1968a. "The Coast from the Portuguese Invasion to the Rise of the Zanzibar Sultanate," in B. A. Ogot and J. A. Kiernan, eds., Zamani. Nairobi, Kenya.

―――. 1968b. "The Swahili Community of Mombasa, Kenya, 1500–1900," *Journal of African History*, 9, no. 1.

―――. 1971. "Mombasa Under the Busaidi Sultanate: The City and Its Hinterland." Unpublished Ph.D. dissertation, University of Wisconsin.

―――, and B. J. Walter. 1968. "Mosques, Population, and Urban Development in Mombasa," *Hadith*, vol. 1.

Cooper, Frederick. 1974. "Plantation Slavery on the East Coast of Africa in the Nineteenth Century." Unpublished Ph.D. dissertation, Yale University.

Coulson, N. J. 1964. A History of Islamic Law. Edinburgh.

Knappert, Jan. 1970. Myths and Legends of the Swahili. London.

Lienhardt, Peter. 1966. "A Controversy over Islamic Custom in Kilwa Kivinje, Tanzania," in I. M. Lewis, ed., Islam in Tropical Africa. London.

―――. 1968. "Introduction," in Hasani bin Ismail, The Medicine Man, Swifa ya Nguvumali. London.

Phillips, Arthur, and Henry F. Morris. 1971. Marriage Law in Africa. London.

Prins, A. H. J. 1952. The Coastal Tribes of the North-Eastern Bantu. Ethnographic Survey of Africa, Part III. London.

―――. 1965. Sailing from Lamu. Assen, The Netherlands.

―――. 1967. The Swahili-Speaking Peoples of Zanzibar and the East African Coast. Ethnographic Survey of Africa, Part XII. London.

Ranger, T. O. 1975. Dance and Society in Eastern Africa, 1890–1970: The Beni Ngoma. Berkeley, Calif.

Salim, A. I. 1973. The Swahili-Speaking Peoples of Kenya's Coast, 1895–1965. Nairobi, Kenya.

Strobel, Margaret. 1975. "Muslim Women in Mombasa, Kenya, 1890–1973." Unpublished Ph.D. dissertation, University of California.

Trimingham, J. Spencer. 1964. Islam in East Africa. London.

Steady: Protestant Women's Associations

Ardener, Edwin. 1972. "Belief and the Problem of Women," in J. S. La Fontaine, ed.

Banton, Michael. 1957. West African City: A Study of Tribal Life in Freetown. London.

Barrett, David B. 1968. Schism and Renewal in Africa: An Analysis of Six Thousand Contemporary Religious Movements. Oxford.

Bassir, Olumbe. 1954. "Marriage Rites among the Aku (Yoruba) of Freetown," *Africa*, 24.

Bustin, Edouard. 1975. "Government Policy Toward African Cult Movements: The Case of Katanga," in Karp, ed.

Cartwright, John R. 1970. Politics in Sierra Leone, 1947–1967. Toronto.

Dotson, Floyd. 1951. "Patterns of Voluntary Associations Among Working-Class Families," *American Sociological Review*, 16.

————. 1953. " A Note on Participation in Voluntary Associations in a Mexican City," *American Sociological Review*, 18.

Fashole-Luke, Edward. 1968. "Religion in Freetown," in Fyfe and Jones, eds.

Fyfe, Christopher. 1962. A History of Sierra Leone. London.

————. 1968. "The Foundation of Freetown," in Fyfe and Jones, eds.

————, and Eldred Jones, eds. 1968. Freetown: A Symposium. Freetown, Sierra Leone.

Greene, Graham. 1936. Journey Without Maps. London.

Harding, Gladys. 1968. "Education in Freetown," in Fyfe and Jones, eds.

Hodgkin, Thomas L. 1957. Nationalism in Colonial Africa. London.

Jules-Rosette, Bennetta, ed. The New Religions of Africa: Priests and Priestesses in African Cults and Churches. Ithaca, N.Y., forthcoming.

Karp, Mark. 1975a. "The Protestant Ethic of the Mourids of Senegal," in Karp, ed.

————, ed. 1975b. African Dimensions: Essays in Honor of William O. Brown. Boston.

Kilson, Martin. 1966. Political Change in a West African State: A Study of the Modernization Process in Sierra Leone. Cambridge, Mass.

Kingsley, Mary. 1898. Travels in West Africa. London. Reprinted 1965.

La Fontaine, Jean S., ed. 1972. The Interpretation of Ritual: Essays in Honour of A. I. Richards. London.

Little, Kenneth. 1950. "The Significance of the West African Creole for Africanist and Afro-American Studies," *African Affairs*, 49.

————. 1965. West African Urbanization: A Study of Voluntary Associations in Social Change. London.

Marris, Peter. 1968. "The Social Barriers to African Entrepreneurship," *The Journal of Development Studies*, 5.

————, and Anthony Somerset. 1972. The African Entrepreneur: A Study of Entrepreneurship and Development in Kenya. New York.

Oosthuizen, G. C. 1968. Post-Christianiʤy in Africa: A Theological and Anthropological Study. Grand Rapids, Mich.

Peterson, John. 1968. "The Sierra Leone Creoles: A Reappraisal," in Fyfe and Jones, eds.

————. 1969. Province of Freedom. London.

Porter, Arthur T. 1953. "Religious Affiliation in Freetown, Sierra Leone," *Africa*, 23.

————. 1963. Creoledom: A Study of the Development of Freetown Society. London.

Sawyerr, Harry. 1964. "Ancestor Worship—The Mechanisms," *Sierra Leone Bulletin of Religion*, 6.

————. 1965. "Graveside Libations in and near Freetown," *Sierra Leone Bulletin of Religion*, 7.

Sierra Leone Government. 1965. 1963 Population Census of Sierra Leone. Freetown.

————. 1968. Household Survey of Western Area: Final Report. Freetown.

Spitzer, Leo. 1974. The Creoles of Sierra Leone: Responses to Colonialism, 1870–1945. Madison, Wisc.

Steady, Filomina C. 1973. "The Structure and Function of Women's Voluntary Associations in an African City: A Study of the Associative Process Among Women in Freetown." D. Phil. dissertation, Oxford University.

———. 1975. Female Power in African Politics: The National Congress of Sierra Leone. Pasadena, Calif.

———. 1976. "Male Roles in Fertility: The Moving Target." Paper presented at the International Sociological Conference, Lomé, Togo.

Sumner, Doyle L. 1963. Education in Sierra Leone. Freetown.

Turner, Harold W. 1967. History of an African Independent Church. London.

Weber, Max. 1930. The Protestant Ethic and the Spirit of Capitalism. New York.

Mullings: Women and Economic Change

Amin, Samir. 1964. "The Class Struggle in Africa," Africa Research Group Reprints, 2.

Barth, Fredrik. 1972. "A General Perspective on Nomad-Sedentary Relations in the Middle East." Unpublished paper.

Baumann, H. 1928. "The Division of Work According to Sex in African Hoe Culture," *Africa*, 2.

Boserup, Ester. 1970. Woman's Role in Economic Development. New York.

Brown, J. K. 1970. "A Note on the Division of Labor by Sex," *American Anthropologist*, 72.

Calame-Griaule, G. 1962. "The Spiritual and Social Role of Women in Traditional Sudanese Society," *Diogenes*, 37.

Christian, Angela. 1959. "The Place of Women in Ghana Society," *African Women*, 3.

Christensen, J. B. 1961. "Marketing and Change in a West African Tribe," *Southwestern Journal of Anthropology*, 17.

Cornwall, Barbara. 1972. The Bush Rebels. New York.

da Silva, Calane. 1975. "As moçambicanas em Luta," *O Tempo*, Mar. 16.

Davidson, Basil. 1969. The Liberation of Guine. Baltimore, Md.

Dobkin, Marlene. 1968. "Colonisation and the Legal Status of Women in Francophone Africa," *Cahiers d'Etudes Africaines*, 8.

Dupire, Marguerite. 1963. "The Position of Women in a Pastoral Society," in D. Paulme, ed., Women of Tropical Africa, Berkeley, Calif.

Engels, Frederick. 1972. The Origin of the Family, Private Property and the State. New York.

Field, Margaret. 1940. Social Organization of the Ga People. London.

Goody, Jack, and Joan Buckley. 1973. "Inheritance and Women's Labour in Africa," *Africa*, 43.

Gough, Kathleen. 1971. "The Origin of the Family," *Journal of Marriage and the Family.*

Hoffer, Carol P. 1972. "Mende and Sherbo Women in High Office," *Canadian Journal of African Studies,* 6.

———. 1974. "Madame Yoko: Ruler of the Kpa Mende Confederacy," in M. Z. Rosaldo and Louise Lamphere, eds., Woman, Culture, and Society. Stanford, Calif.

Kilson, Martin. 1958. "Nationalism and Social Classes in British West Africa," *Journal of Politics,* 20.

Leacock, Eleanor. 1972. "Introduction," in Frederick Engels, The Origin of the Family, Private Property and the State. New York.

Lebeuf, Annie. 1963. "The Role of Women in the Political Organization of African Societies," in D. Paulme, ed., Women of Tropical Africa. Berkeley, Calif.

Little, Kenneth. 1973. African Women in Towns. London.

Machel, Samora. 1973. Discourse to the Conference of Mozambique Women. Dar es Salaam, Tanzania.

———. 1975. "A libertação da Mulher é uma necessidade da Revolução," *O Tempo,* Apr. 6.

McCall, Daniel. 1961. "Trade and the Role of a Wife in a Modern West African Town," in Aiden Southall, ed., Social Change in Modern Africa. London.

Mills-Odoi, D. G. 1967. "The La Family and Social Change." M.A. thesis, Institute of African Studies, University of Ghana.

Mintz, Sidney. 1971. "Men, Women, and Trade," *Comparative Studies in Society and History,* 13.

O'Laughlin, Bridget. 1974. "Mediation of Contradiction: Why Mbum Women Do Not Eat Chicken," in M. Z. Rosaldo and Louise Lamphere, eds., Woman, Culture, and Society. Stanford, Calif.

Ottenberg, Phoebe. 1959. "The Changing Economic Position of Women Among the Afikpo Ibo," in W. R. Bascom and M. J. Herskovits, eds., Continuity and Change in African Cultures. Chicago.

Pelissier, René. 1975. "Economy," in Africa South of the Sahara. London.

Rodney, Walter. 1972. How Europe Underdeveloped Africa. Dar es Salaam, Tanzania.

Sacks, Karen. 1974. "Engels Revisited: Women, the Organization of Production, and Private Property," in M. Z. Rosaldo and Louise Lamphere, eds., Woman, Culture, and Society. Stanford, Calif.

Sanday, Peggy R. 1973. "Toward a Theory of the Status of Women," *American Anthropologist,* 75, no. 5.

Simons, H. J. 1968. African Women: Their Legal Status in South Africa. London.

Steward, Julian. 1972. "Causal Factors and Processes in the Evolution of Pre-Farming Societies," in R. Lee and I. DeVore, eds., Man the Hunter. Chicago.

Suret-Canale, Jean. 1971. French Colonialism in Tropical Africa, 1900–1945. New York.

Urdang, Stephanie. 1974. "Fighting the Other Colonialism: The Women's Struggle in Guinea-Bissau," *Africa/Southern Africa.*

Van Allen, Judith. 1972. " 'Sitting on a Man': Colonialism and the Lost Political Institutions of Igbo Women," *Canadian Journal of African Studies*, 6, no. 2.

Webster, Paula, and E. Newton. 1972. "Matriarchy: Puzzle and Paradigm." Paper presented at the 71st Annual Meeting of the American Anthropological Association, Toronto.

Wipper, Audrey. 1972. "The Roles of African Women: Past, Present and Future," *Canadian Journal of African Studies*, 6, no. 2.

Brain: Less Than Second-Class

Africa Digest, 20, no. 6 (Dec. 1973). London.

Beattie, John, 1964. Other Cultures. Evanston, Ill.

Brain, James L. 1966. "The Position of Women on Settlement Schemes in Tanzania." Paper presented at the Seminar on Rural Development, University of Dar es Salaam, Tanzania.

———. 1969. "Matrilineal Descent and Marital Stability: a Tanzanian Case," *Journal of Asian and African Studies*, 4, no. 2.

Burton, Sir R. F. 1860. The Lake Regions of Central Africa. London.

McCall, Daniel. 1961. "Trade and the Role of a Wife in a Modern West African Town," in Southall, ed.

Nyerere, Julius K. 1962. "Presidential Address to Parliament." Dar es Salaam, Tanzania.

———. 1967. Socialism and Rural Development. Dar es Salaam, Tanzania.

Richards, Audrey. 1969. The Multi-Cultural States of East Africa. Montreal.

Sjoberg, Gideon, 1960. The Preindustrial City: Past and Present. Glencoe, Ill.

Southall, Aidan, ed. 1961. Social Change in Modern Africa. London.

Young, Roland, and H. A. Fosbrooke. 1960. Land and Politics Among the Luguru of Tanganyika. London.

Index

Aba Riots, 46, 55, 59ff. *See also*
  Women's War of 1929
Abidjan market women, 7, 13, 135–56
Accra, Ghana, 17, 111–33
Adamson, Michel, 28–29
Adioukrou people, 150
adultery: and Creoles, 234. *See also*
  double standard of morality
Afigbo, A. E., 45, 47, 60n, 65n
Afikpo Igbo people, 65n–66n, 77n–78n
Africa: West, 4, 6, 9; precolonial,
  8–9, 10, 45–55, 157, 160n, 181; East,
  11, 14–15, 157–62 *passim*, 166, 170,
  173, 180, 181n; South, 166, 244, 248.
  See also by individual country name
Africa Digest, 281
African Methodist Episcopal Church,
  229n
African Party for the Independence
  of Guinea-Bissau and Cape Verde
  (PAIGC), 261–62
African Women in Towns, 2
Afro-Asian Association, 186
age-grade organizations: of Igbo, 54,
  65–66
Agni people, 150
agriculture, 5–6, 15f; and Luo, 5, 11,
  87, 90–109 *passim*; plow, 9; cash-
  cropping, 15, 79, 244n, 247f, 266,
  276; and Igbo, 53–54, 67, 79; and
  Ga, 116–18, 121–22, 250ff; hoe, 242;
  cooperatives, 260n, 261; tractor cul-
  tivation, 270f
Akan people, 136–37, 147
Albert, Ethel M., 160–61
Alur people, 166
Amazon armies, 4
ambulatory banker system, 13, 141–44,
  152
Amin, Samir, 245

anasi (senior Igbo wife), 53
ancestor worship, 219, 228, 266, 269
Anglican Church, 99–100, 104, 109;
  Church Missionary Society, 96–99,
  165, 217, 229; associations of, 222,
  225f
Angola, 256n
animal husbandry, 245. *See also* live-
  stock
animists, 136f
Ankole District, Uganda, 159n, 165
Annie Walsh Memorial School, 218
Anyango, Hilda, 109
Apamo, 90, 91n
Appollo people, 150
Aral Association, 186
Arab Girls' School, 198, 203
Arabs, 12; in Mombasa, 183, 185–86,
  190, 198–205, 210. *See also* Muslims
Arab Women's Cultural Association,
  200, 202–4. *See also* Muslim Wom-
  en's Cultural Association
Arab Women's Institute, 199–204. *See
  also* Muslim Women's Institute
armies: women in, 4, 7, 258
Arusha Declaration, 275, 281
Arwa, Joan, 100
ASA Review of Books, 2
Ashanti people, 9, 112, 136–37; queen
  mother, 246, 254n
associations, *see* women's associations
Ayawaso, Ghana, 112
Azikiwe, Nnamdi, 83
Azu, G. A. M., 117, 122

Bainouka "queens," 20
Baluchi people, 190
banking: ambulatory system of, 13,
  141–44, 152; and Ga women, 129.
  See also rotating credit associations

Bantu languages, 158n, 159
Banu Saada, 183n, 184, 187–97
Baoulé people, 150f
Baptists, 217
Barnes, John, 31
Barrett, D. B., 227n
Barth, Fredrik, 245
Basden, G. T., 46, 55
Bassir, Olumbe, 221
Bathurst settlement, 42–43
Baumann, H., 242
bazimu (lineage ghost cult), 178f
Beattie, John, 167, 172–73, 176, 272
Benakayange cult, 165, 178n
Benka-Coker, Hannah, 218
Berger, Iris, 11f, 14–15, 157–81
Bessell, M. J., 168–69
Bété people, 150
Biafra, 83–84
Biyago people, 43
birth association (*djigi moni*), 148, 152
Bissau, 43
Bi Uba, 201–2
Bösch, Fridolin, 167
Boserup, Ester, 15, 242, 247ff
Boufflers, Chevalier de, 32–33, 36
Brain, James L., 8, 17, 265–82
bridewealth, 3, 67, 93, 95, 246
Brooks, George E., Jr., 5, 6–7, 19–44
Brown, Beverly, 2
Brown, J. K., 245
Buckley, Joan, 242
Buganda, 158f, 164f, 174f
Buha, 158f, 161, 170ff
Buhaya, 159f
Bunyoro, 158ff, 167, 172–74, 178
Burundi, 157ff, 160n, 161, 167, 175, 181n
Busaidi dynasty, 185
business dealings, 6; moneylending, 6, 107, 124–25, 127f. *See also* capital
Busoga, 170
Bwakira Chini, Tanzania, 265, 268–72, 274–75, 279

Cacheu, 43
Calabar province, 59f, 73
Cape Verde Islands, 19, 38
capital: accumulation of, 6, 95, 107ff, 120–21, 132, 135, 148. *See also* ambulatory banker system; bridewealth; property, ownership of; rotating credit associations
capitalism, 218
Cariou, Dr., 30
cash, 101–2, 104f, 122, 140, 272–73
cash-cropping, 15, 79, 244n, 247f, 266, 276

cassava, 106, 247n, 249
Catholicism, 35, 222–24, 236
Caty Louette, 30
Chagga people, 272
childbirth, 242n
childcare, 245, 258, 260, 262
Christianity, 10–12, 15, 35; and Igbo, 56f, 75–77; and Ga, 112; and Luo, 96–97, 99–101; in Abidjan, 137; in Sierra Leone, 213–37
church associations, 11f, 213–37
Church Missionary Society, 96–99, 165, 217, 229
circumcision, 10
class stratification, 27, 159–60, 239–44 *passim*, 250–56, 263
Clignet, Remi, 1f
clitoridectomy, 10
cloth selling and trading, 116, 131–32, 143f, 146
Coast People's Party, 210
Colle, P., 168
colonialism, 2–4, 6, 12, 15–18, 246–48, 265; in Senegal, 21–34 *passim*, 41f, 44; and Igbo, 45f, 55–56, 58, 59–62, 70–82, 246–47; and Luo, 89f, 96–101; and spirit mediums, 164; in Mombasa, 183, 185f, 188n, 200; in Labadi, 250–56; in Tanzania, 268f. *See also* France; Great Britain; Portugal
commerce associations, 11, 148. *See also* rotating credit associations
common-law wives, 271, 274
competition: and *lelemama*, 194–97
concubinage, 232
conscription, 104–5
cooperatives, 56, 116, 144–45, 154, 260n, 261
Correia, Mae Aurelia, 43
cotton, 244n
Countess of Huntingdon's Connexion, 217, 217n
credit associations, *see* rotating credit associations
Creoles (in Freetown), 11f, 213–37
Cruickshank, Brodie, 114
Cummings-John, Constance, 218
Cwezi cults, 158, 162, 178

Dahomey, 7
dance associations, *see lelemama*
dancing, 24–25, 40, 54, 164
Daniell, W. F., 114
Dar es Salaam, University of, 281
de la Rivière, Poncet, 29n
Delcourt, André, 22f
Demanet, Abbé, 29–30
De Marees, Peter, 114

de Sabran, Mme., 33n
Devaulx, Governor (of Saint-Louis), 23
diaou moni (commerce association), 148
Dioula people, 136, 147–49, 151–55
District Women's Work Committee, 222, 225
divorce, 131, 207f, 210, 233, 266f, 271f
djigi moni (birth association), 148, 152
Dorcas Association, 222, 226
Dotson, Floyd, 215n, 235
double cropping, 105
double standard of morality, 225, 230–35, 237
Driever, Dorothy, 208n
dual-sex political system: of Igbo, 8, 13, 16, 45–58, 69–70, 84; of Ga, 14, 16
Dubellay, Governor (of Saint-Louis), 22
Duparel, Evrard, 30
Dutch, 21, 113

Ebrié people, 150
Ecstatic Religion, 157
economic associations, 11. *See also* rotating credit associations
economic factors, 5–16 *passim*, 239–64; and Igbo, 77–80, 84; and Luo, 89–102; and Ga, 116–33 *passim*. *See also* marketing; money economy; trading
Edel, May, 165, 179n
education, 6, 102, 106, 109, 248; of Igbo, 11, 76, 79f, 83; of Luo, 100; of Ga, 112, 122, 127–28, 131ff; in Mombasa, 198–99, 204–6, 209; in Freetown, 214, 218, 223; in Mozambique, 258–59
elite, 111; Luo, 102; and spirit medium cults, 159, 180–81; of Mombasa, 185, 192, 194, 197, 204; of Tanzania, 273f, 282
emandwa cults, 165, 173, 176, 179, 181n
Engels, Friedrich, 239ff, 242, 245
Ethiopia, 164
ethnic associations: in Abidjan, 13, 150–51
Europeans, 2, 3, 5, 15, 248; and *signares*, 7, 19–44; and Ga, 112, 114, 250. *See also* colonialism
Evangelical United Brethren Association, 222, 224f
Evans-Pritchard, E. E., 1, 3
extramarital liaisons: in Freetown, 232–34

Faber, Mary, 43
Facing Mount Kenya, 10
Fallers, Lloyd Ashton, 63
family planning, 111
famine, 103
farming, *see* agriculture
Fashole-Luke, Edward, 227n
Femmes d'Afrique noire, 3
Field, Margaret J., 127f, 254
Firth, Raymond, 161–62
fishing and fish selling: by Ga, 116–19, 121–22, 127, 131ff, 250f; in Abidjan, 138, 144
folgars (dances), 24–25, 40
food taboos, 91, 164, 244n
Forde, Daryll, 64, 68
France, 21–34 *passim*, 41f, 44, 136
Freetown, Sierra Leone, 11, 213–37
Frelimo, 257–60
funerals, 205, 229
Fyfe, Christopher, 229
furu moni (marriage association), 147, 152

Ga people, 6f, 14, 17, 111–33, 250–56
Gambia, 20, 25, 42–43
Ganda people, 120n, 159n, 180, 244
Geertz, Clifford, 140n
Ghana, 6, 14f, 250–56; Accra, 17, 111–33
Ghazali Muslim School, 198
Gluckman, Max, 172
Golberry, S. M. X., 33
Goldie, Sir George, 81
gold mining, 103–4
Goody, Jack, 242, 245
Gorée, Senegal, 21–22, 26–42 *passim*
Gough, Kathleen, 239–40, 241, 243
Gouro people, 137, 145–46, 150
Grain of Wheat, A, 9
Grant, James, 162
Gray, Sylvia, 198, 203
Great Britain, 16; and Senegal, 26f, 30–32, 41–43; Victorian values of, 46, 80–83, 246–47, 274; and Nigeria, 46, 55–56, 58, 59–62, 70–82; and Women's War of 1929, 59–62, 70–82; feminist movement in, 82; and Kenya, 87, 89–93, 96–97, 185f, 188, 200; and Ghana, 114, 123, 250; and Sierra Leone, 213–14, 217
Green, Margaret, 46
griots, 24–25, 27, 40
grumetes, 27–29
Guinea, Upper Coast, 20, 32, 41–43
Guinea-Bissau, 17–18, 20, 43, 256, 261–62, 264
Guismane, Deolinda, 259

302   *Index*

Hadhrami Arabs (in Mombasa), 185–
  86, 190, 203
Hajnal, J., 116
Harvest Committees, 222, 225–26
Hay, Margaret Jean, 5f, 16, 87–109
Henty, G. A., 114
Hima, 2, 160
hoe agriculture, 242
horticultural societies, 9, 239–40, 243
Horton, Robin, 172
Houphouët-Boigny, Félix, 144, 146
Hunde people, 158n, 171
hunting, 242, 245
hunting and gathering societies, 239–
  40, 242–43, 263
Huntingdon, Countess of, 217n
hut tax, 89f
Hut Tax War of 1898, 220n
Hutu class, 159, 171

Ibibio people, 60n
Ibinaal Watan, 183n, 184, 187–97
Igboland, 59n, 60, 70
Igbo people, 5, 7, 11, 13f, 59–85, 246–
  47, 249; dual-sex political system
  of, 8, 45–58; democratic village republics of, 14, 47, 65; and Women's
  War of 1929, 16, 46, 55, 59–62, 68,
  71–74, 81; constitutional village
  monarchy of, 47, 65n; Afikpo, 65n–
  66n, 77n–78n
ikporo ani (of Igbo), 51
illiteracy, 122f. *See also* education
ilogo (cabinet of *omu*), 48–52, 54, 56f
Imandwa, 158
income, 6, 230–31. *See also* cash
Indian population, 89n, 102, 186n,
  190, 201
Indian Women's Association, 201
inheritance, 3, 115, 160, 206–7, 230,
  278. *See also* lineage structure
interlacustrine region of East Africa,
  11, 14–15, 157–62 *passim*, 166, 170,
  180, 181n
invisibility of women, 59, 80–83, 85
Ivory Coast, 136, 142n; Abidjan, 7,
  13, 135–56
inyemedi (wives of the lineage), 14,
  51–53, 56f, 68–69
Iru class, 160
Islam, 10f, 136f, 148–49, 214. *See also*
  Muslims

Jones, G. I., 64, 68

Kalabari communities, 172
Kampala, 120n

Karp, Mark, 218n
Kenya, 16, 270; Luo in, 5f, 11, 87–109;
  Mombasa, 11f, 183–211
Kenyatta, Jomo, 10, 108, 206
Khalifa, Seyyid, 204
kibbutzim, 277, 280
Kiga people, 158n, 159, 165
Kilson, Marion, 133
Kilungu, 188, 189–90, 192, 194
Kimambo, I., 159n
Kingi, 188ff, 194
Kingsley, Mary, 81
Kingurungundwa settlement scheme,
  272, 279
kinship, 178–79, 219, 253–54. *See also*
  lineage structure
Kiranga cult, 158, 167f, 175
Kitara, 174
Knight-Baylac, Mme., 30
Kowe, Kenya, 11, 16, 87–109
Krio language, 219–20. *See also* Creoles
Krou people, 136f, 147
kubandwa cults, 166–67, 169, 180
!Kung people, 242
Kutu people, 265–78 *passim*

Labadi, Ghana, 250–56
labor, 239–42, 245, 246n; and Luo,
  97–99, 102–5, 109; division of, 105,
  239–40, 262–63; hiring of, 275
Ladies Working Band, 222, 226
Lagoon peoples, 136ff, 147
Lake Victoria, 175
land, control of, 6, 241, 247–48; and
  Igbo, 67; and Luo, 93; and Ga,
  126n, 127, 250–51, 254; communal,
  254, 260n, 261; in Tanzania, 266,
  272, 275, 278
language: political control of, 59–60;
  Bantu, 158n, 159; Swahili, 187f;
  Krio, 219–20; Mende, 220; Temne,
  220
Leacock, Eleanor, 239, 241, 242n
Lebeuf, Annie, 13, 46
Lebou peoples, 22f, 27, 36, 38
Lee, S. G., 166
Leiris, Michel, 164
Leith-Ross, Sylvia, 46
lelemama (dance associations), 12,
  183–203 *passim*, 211
Lemky, Fureya Barakat, 204
Lewis, Barbara, 6f, 12–13, 135–56
Lewis, I. M., 157, 165–70, 180
Lienhardt, Peter, 196
Lightburn, Isabella, 43
Lindsay, John, 26, 35
lineage ghosts, cult of, 178–80

lineage structure, 9; and Igbo, 45, 51–52, 64; and Luo, 88, 93; and Ga, 115, 250, 253–54; and spirit medium cults, 159, 178–80; and Creoles, 219; and settlement schemes, 265f, 278–80. *See also* matrilineality; patrilineality
Little, Kenneth, 2, 249
livestock, 90–93, 95, 101, 103, 245
loaning money, 6, 107, 124–25, 127f
Lourenço Marques, 259n, 260
Lovedu people, 14, 244
Loye Elizabeth, 101, 109
Luguru people, 265–78 *passim*
Luo people, 5f, 11, 87–109
Lyangombe, 165, 167

Machat, J., 30
Machel, Samora, 257–61
magic, 49–50, 228
male superiority, 1–9 *passim*; and spirit mediums, 157–73 *passim*. *See also* colonialism; patrilineality
Malinke oral traditions, 20
Man and Woman among the Azande, 1
mantse (Ga father of the town), 14, 250
manyei (Ga mother of the town), 14, 254–55
Many Wives, Many Powers, 1
Margaret, Princess, 200–202
marketing, 248–49; and women's groups, 7, 12–13, 82; in Abidjan, 7, 13, 135–56; and Igbo, 13f, 48–50, 56–57; in Kowe, 16, 102ff, 108; and Ga, 113, 115, 251–53. *See also* trading
"market queen," *see omu*
marriage, 6, 246, 253–54; polygyny, 1, 3f, 93, 95, 230, 254; patrilocal, 5, 45, 52, 93, 96; and *signares*, 24, 27, 34–38, 40–41; and Igbo, 53; and Luo, 93–95; and Ga, 116, 123, 125; Ordinance, 123; in Mombasa, 191f, 205, 207–8; in Freetown, 225, 230–35; in Tanzania, 267
marriage association, 147, 152
Marris, Peter, 218n, 230n
Martha Davies Confidential Benevolent Association, 222, 227
Marx, Karl, 239
matriarchies, 4, 9
matrilineality, 9, 137, 250, 265f
mbandwa cults, 167, 178–79
Mbuti people, 243
McEwen, Etta, 228
Mecca pilgrimages, 149, 223
Mende people, 14; language of, 220
menstrual taboos, 8f, 267

Methodists, 112; associations, 222, 224ff, 229
Mijikenda peoples, 186, 190
mikiri, 5, 12, 16, 69, 76
Mills-Odoi, D. G., 117, 254
mining, gold, 103–4
Mintz, Sidney W., 79, 248–49, 253
missionaries, 10f, 75–77. *See also* Christianity
mistresses, 233–34
Mbum people, 244n
Mohamed, Fatuma, 190n, 199n
Mombasa, Kenya, 11f, 183–211
Mombasa Times, 198, 202, 207–8, 209
Mondlane, Eduardo, 257
money association, 148, 152
money economy: income, 6, 230–31; loans, 6, 107, 124–25, 127f; and Ga, 15, 120–32 *passim*; cash-cropping, 15, 79, 244n, 247f, 266, 276; cash, 101–2, 104f, 122, 140, 272–73; and Luo, 101–6 *passim*. *See also* capital
Moor, Sir Ralph, 81
morality: double standard of, 11, 225, 230–35, 237; and spirit medium cults, 169–70
Mothers' Union, 222, 225, 230–34
Mozambique, 10, 17–18, 256–61, 264
Mozambique Liberation Front (Frelimo), 257–60
Mrs. Pinkney's Spiritualist Association, 222, 227
Muhashamy, Shamsa Mohamed, 199n, 202n, 204n
Muhumusa, 177–78
Mukakuanga, 175
Mullings, Leith, 6f, 14f, 17, 239–64; equality and symmetry, 10, 240, 244f, 256, 263
Muslims: in Mombasa, 10ff, 184–87, 190, 198–205, 210; in Freetown, 11, 214, 221, 223, 236; law of, 35, 206–7; and Igbo, 82, 84n; in Abidjan, 136f, 148–49
Muslim Women's Cultural Association (MWCA), 183n, 184, 193, 199–200, 205–11
Muslim Women's Institute (MWI), 183n, 184, 193, 199–200, 205–11
muvurati (rainmaker), 161
Mwaita, Fatma, 189–90, 192

Namaan, Ali bin, 207–8
National Council for Nigeria and the Cameroons (NCNC), 82–83
Ngoni people, 280
Ngugi, James, 9

nharas of Guinea-Bissau, 20, 43
Nigeria, 11, 13, 56–58, 172, 227n. *See also* Igbo people
Nkore, 158n, 159f, 173, 176
Northern People's Congress (NPC), 82
Nozolini, Caetano José, 43
Nuer people, 245n
Nyabingi, 15; cult of, 159n, 165, 168–69, 177ff, 180f
Nyakishenyi revolt of 1917, 178
Nyamwezi peoples, 157, 158n, 159, 161, 166, 170, 173, 180
Nyangaga, Chief, 99
Nyangweso, 103
Nyasa peoples, 192n
Nyemimei Akpee, 130
Nyerere, Julius K., 267–68, 271, 274, 277, 280–82
Nyika peoples, 186n
Nyoro people, 158n, 167–76 *passim*, 181
Nzinga, 4

Obamkpa, Nigeria, 49, 54–55
Obara, Yona, 99, 101
obi (male Igbo monarch), 13, 47, 55f
occupations, 6, 114–15, 118–19, 251, 253
ogbo (Igbo gathering), 68f, 76
Ogumbo, 90, 99, 101
Ogu Umunwanyi, see Women's War of 1929
Ogwashi-uku, 53n, 56
O'Hara, Charles, 31–32
Okonjo, Kamene, 8, 13, 45–58, 84
Olaka, Samili, 99
O'Laughlin, Bridget, 244n
Olsen, Mancur, 155n
Omani Arabs (in Mombasa), 185–86, 190
om na trit relationship, 232–33
omu (female Igbo monarch), 13–14, 47–57
onotu (cabinet of *obi*), 48, 56
Onwuteaka, J. C., 78
Oosthuizen, G. C., 230, 232
Organization of Mozambique Women (OMM), 259–60
Orondo, Rose, 100, 109
Ottenberg, Phoebe, 77n–78n
Ottenberg, Simon, 77n
otu inyemedi, 52–53, 56f
otu umuada, 52, 56f
Owerri province, 59f, 71, 73

PAIGC, 261–62
Pasha, Emin, 162–63
patrilineality, 9, 93, 115, 159, 179–80, 250, 278–80; and Igbo, 8, 45, 64

patrilocal marriage, 5, 45, 52, 93, 96
Paulme, Denise, 46
Pax Britannica, 77f
Pépin, Anne, 32, 36
Pépin, Nicholas, 36
political systems, 4f, 12–16, 159, 244, 254–55; of Igbo, 5, 12, 16, 47–56, 62–70, 76; dual-sex, 8, 13f, 16, 45–58, 69–70, 84; single-sex, 16, 45–58; and control of language, 59–60; and Muslims, 210
polygyny, 1, 3f, 93, 95, 230, 254
Pondo people, 244
Porter, Arthur T., 224
Portugal, 17, 19ff, 43, 185, 259n. *See also* Guinea-Bissau; Mozambique
prayer: and Creoles, 227–29
Preindustrial City, The, 273
Prélong (hospital director on Gorée), 34–36, 37n, 41
Proctor, Eliza, 43
professions, *see* occupations
property, ownership of, 6, 240, 243ff, 260, 263; and Ga, 123f, 126; and spirit mediums, 160, 173; in Freetown, 230. *See also* land, control of; livestock
prostitution, 233, 260
Protestant women's associations, 11f, 213–37
Pruneau de Pommegorge, Antoine Edmé, 23–25
purdah, 205, 209

queens, 4, 9; Igbo *omu*, 13–14, 47–57; Lovedu, 14; Bainouka, 20; Ashanti, 246, 254n

Rading' Obura, Patricia, 94–95
Rahman, Hajah Iyesha, 223
Ranger, T. O., 159n
Rattray, R. S., 9
real estate investment, 126n, 127. *See also* land, control of
religion, 5, 10–11, 112, 150, 207–8. *See also* Christianity; Muslims; spirit mediums
residence system, 45, 178–79; of Luo, 5, 93, 96; of Igbo, 45, 51–53; of Ga, 115–16, 125, 250f, 254. *See also* matrilineality, patrilineality
"Revivalist" women's associations, 222, 227
Rhodesia, 248
rinderpest epidemic, 90, 91n
rites of passage, 8–10, 219, 267
Robertson, Claire, 6f, 15f, 111–13
Robins, Catherine, 179n
Rodegem, F. M., 167

role differentiation, *see* sex-role differentiation
Rosaldo, Michelle, 5
rotating credit associations, 11; in Abidjan, 13, 140–41, 143–44, 151f, 154; and Ga women, 129–30
Rukiga, 178, 181n
Rundi, 158n, 168, 170, 173, 175
Rutajirakijuna, 177
Ruvuma Development Association, 280
Rwanda peoples, 157ff, 160n, 165, 169–80 *passim*, 181n
Ryangombe, 158

Sacks, Karen, 243–44
sacrifices: among Igbo, 49, 56
safina moni (soap association), 148
Sai, F. A., 126
Saidi, Fatma, 188n, 190n
Saint-Louis, Senegal, 21–42 *passim*
Sanday, Peggy R., 77n–78n, 243, 245n–46n
savings associations: of Ga, 127, 129–30; in Abidjan, 140–42. *See also* ambulatory banker system; rotating credit associations
Scotchi, 188f
secret societies, 9. *See also* spirit mediums
seed distribution, 5, 95–96
Seme lineage (Luo), 88f, 93, 102
Senegal, 5, 19–44, 249
Senegal Company, 22–23, 28–29, 37
Senegambia region, 7, 20, 31f, 41–43
senoras in the Gambia, 20
Sese Islands, 159
settlement schemes (Tanzania), 17, 265–82
sex-role differentiation, 7, 10, 13, 105, 133, 239–64, 273–74. *See also* male superiority
sexuality, 2, 10, 232–34
Shi people, 158n, 168, 178n
Sierra Leone, 11f, 14, 213–37
signares, 7, 19–44
Simbine, Graça, 260
Sjoberg, Gideon, 273
slaves: ancestry from, 12, 186, 188, 192, 197; and *signares*, 25–26, 28–30, 34, 38–39; trading of, 78, 246; in Mombasa, 186
Slessor, Mary, 77
smallpox, 174
soap association, 148
socialism, 17; Nyerere on, 277, 281
Socialism and Rural Development, 281
Soga people, 158n

soldiers: women as, 4, 7, 258
Somali people, 245n–46n
Somerset, Anthony, 218n
songs: in Swahili society, 193, 197
South Africa, 166, 244, 248
Southall, Aidan, 166
Speke, John, 164–65
spirit mediums, 10ff, 14–15, 157–81, 255n
spirit-possession, 11f, 161–62, 165–66
status, 8, 16–17, 243, 246; and Igbo, 8, 67–68; and colonialism, 9, 16–17; and spirit mediums, 157, 160, 170, 172–73, 176–77, 180–81; and *lele-mama*, 191–92; and Ga, 255–62
Steady, Filomina Chioma, 11, 213–37
sterility, 167
Strobel, Margaret, 11f, 183–211
suffrage: in Mombasa, 183–84, 210
Sumbwa people, 158n, 167, 176
Sunni Muslims, 186–87
susu, 129–30
Swahili, 184, 186, 190f; language, 187f; songs, 193, 197
Swezi society, 159, 165, 167, 177n, 181

Tanzania, 8, 17, 157f, 164, 167, 265–82
Tanzania African National Union (TANU), 271, 280
taxes, 71–72, 103
Temne language, 220
Teshie, Ghana, 122
Thenashara Taifa, 185
Thomas, W. Northcote, 46
title-taking: among Igbo, 8, 50–51, 54–57, 67
Toro people, 158n, 176, 178
Transvaal, 14
trading, 6–7, 179, 248–49; and *signares*, 7, 19–44; by Ga, 15, 17, 112, 114–15, 127, 131–32, 251, 253; in Kowe, 16, 87, 92, 102–5, 108f; and Igbo, 67, 77–79; and Dioula, 136; in Freetown, 214, 223, 230–31, 237
Turner, Victor W., 163
Tutsi class, 159, 171
Twelve Tribes of Mombasa, 185–86, 190

Uganda, 2, 157ff, 165f, 168f, 175, 177, 179, 244
Ujamaa, 268; villages, 17, 281–82
Ukutu (Tanzania), 265–67, 271, 273, 275
Uluguru (Tanzania), 265–67, 271, 273, 275
umuada (daughters of the lineage), 14, 51–52, 56f, 68
Umuganzaruguru cult, 168

United Church Women, 222, 235–37
United States of America, 8, 224, 227
Unyamwezi, 158f, 167, 176, 178–81
Urdang, Stephanie, 262
Ussher Town, Ghana, 111, 113, 115, 117
Usukuma, 158f, 176f
Usumbwa, 159

Van Allen, Judith, 5, 7f, 12, 14, 46, 246–47; on Women's War of 1929, 16, 59–85
Van der Burgt, J. M. M., 175
Vaz, Bibiana, 20n
Victoria, Queen, 188n
Victorianism, 46, 80–83, 246–47, 274
Village Settlement Agency, 268, 272
village communities, 64–66, 241f, 244, 246n, 251, 255, 263; and settlement schemes, 17, 265–82
Villeneuve, Geoffroy de, 34, 38
virginity, 234; and bed sheet display, 34f, 205–6

wari moni (money association), 148, 152
wealth, 93–94, 107, 117, 122. *See also* money economy; property, ownership of
Weber, Max, 63, 219
Webster, Paula, 239
weddings, 34f, 191f, 205, 207–8, 235

Wesleyans, 217, 227n
Whisson, Michael, 93
widows: Igbo, 49f
Williams, D. K., 103
Wilson, Peter J., 171
Wipper, Audrey, 247
Wolin, Sheldon, 156
Wolof peoples, 20n, 22f, 25–27, 29n, 33, 35, 42
Woman's Role in Economic Development, 15
Women of Tropical Africa, 3–4, 46
women's associations, 4f, 10–12; spirit medium cults, 10ff, 14–15, 157–81; Protestant, 11, 213–37; rotating credit, 11, 13, 129–30, 140–41, 143–44, 151f, 154; of Creoles, 11f, 213–37; of Igbo, 11f, 16, 52–53, 56f, 68–70, 76, 84; Muslim, 11f, 183n, 184–211 *passim*; in Abidjan, 12–13, 140–41, 143–44, 151f, 154; *lelemama*, 12, 183–203 *passim*, 211
Women's War of 1929, 16, 46, 55, 59–62, 68, 71–74, 81
World War II, 104–5

Yoruba people, 235

Zaire, 158n, 165, 171, 243f
Zanzibar, 185, 187, 210
Zinza, 158n
Zoukou, Solange N'Guessan, 139n
Zulu people, 116, 172

The authorized representative in the EU for product safety and compliance is:
Mare Nostrum Group
B.V Doelen 72
4831 GR Breda
The Netherlands